T

MODIGLIANI

ALSO BY JEFFREY MEYERS

BIOGRAPHY

A Fever at the Core: The Idealist
in Politics

Married to Genius

Katherine Mansfield

The Enemy: A Biography
of Wyndham Lewis

Hemingway

Manic Power: Robert Lowell
and His Circle

D. H. Lawrence

Joseph Conrad

Edgar Allen Poe: His Life and Legacy

Scott Fitzgerald

Edmund Wilson

Robert Frost

Bogart: A Life in Hollywood

Gary Cooper: American Hero

Privileged Moments: Encounters
with Writers

Orwell: Wintry Conscience of
a Generation

Inherited Risk: Errol and Sean Flynn
in Hollywood and Vietnam

Somerset Maugham

Impressionist Quartet: The Intimate
Genius of Manet and Morisot,
Degas and Cassatt

CRITICISM

Fiction and the Colonial Experience

The Wounded Spirit: A Study of
T. E. Lawrence's *Seven Pillars of
Wisdom*

A Reader's Guide to George Orwell

Painting and the Novel

Homosexuality and Literature

D. H. Lawrence and the Experience
of Italy

Disease and the Novel

The Spirit of Biography

Hemingway: Life into Art

BIBLIOGRAPHY

T. E. Lawrence: A Bibliography

Catalogue of the Library of the Late
Siegfried Sassoon

George Orwell: An Annotated
Bibliography of Criticism

EDITED COLLECTIONS

George Orwell: The Critical Heritage

Hemingway: The Critical Heritage

Robert Lowell: Interviews and
Memoirs

The Sir Arthur Conan Doyle Reader

The W. Somerset Maugham Reader

EDITED ORIGINAL ESSAYS

Wyndham Lewis: A Revaluation

Wyndham Lewis *by Roy Campbell*

D. H. Lawrence and Tradition

The Legacy of D. H. Lawrence

The Craft of Literary Biography

The Biographer's Art

T. E. Lawrence: Soldier, Writer,
Legend

Graham Greene: A Revaluation

MODIGLIANI

⚜ *A Life* ⚜

JEFFREY MEYERS

HARCOURT, INC.

Orlando Austin New York San Diego Toronto London

www.HarcourtBooks.com

Library of Congress Cataloging-in-Publication Data
Meyers, Jeffrey.
Modigliani: a life/Jeffrey Meyers.—1st ed.
p.   cm.
Includes bibliographical references and index.
1. Modigliani, Amedeo, 1884–1920.
2. Painters—Italy—Biography.   I. Title.
ND623.M67M49   2006
759.5—dc22   2005026180
ISBN-13: 978-0-15-101178-0   ISBN-10: 0-15-101178-8

Text set in Garamond MT
Designed by Liz Demeter

Printed in the United States of America

First edition
K J I H G F E D C B A

For Marvin Eisenberg

Contents

1. Eugenia Modigliani, mother—Klüver/Martin Archive
2. Emanuele Modigliani, brother, 1908—Archivio Centrale dello Stato, Rome
3. Modi with nursemaid, c.1886—Klüver/Martin Archive
4. Modi with slight beard, 1901—Klüver/Martin Archive
5. Modi with long cravat, c.1908—Klüver/Martin Archive
6. Anna Akhmatova, 1920s—Anna Akhmatova Museum, St. Petersburg
7. Modi seated in his studio, 1915—Klüver/Martin Archive
8. Beatrice Hastings, 1922, photo by Man Ray—Artists Rights Society, New York
9. Modi, Max Jacob, André Salmon and Ortiz de Zarate, Paris, August 12, 1916, photo by Jean Cocteau—Artists Rights Society, New York
10. Modi with hands on hips, 1917—Klüver/Martin Archive
11. Jeanne Hébuterne, 1919—Klüver/Martin Archive
12. Modi in his studio with foot on bench, 1918—Klüver/Martin Archive
13. Modi in profile, seated in front of Japanese screen, 1919—Klüver/Martin Archive
14. *Paul Alexandre,* 1909—Collection of Yamazaki Mazek Corporation, Japan
15. Baulé statue, Ivory Coast—Jeffrey Meyers Collection, Berkeley, California
16. *Head,* 1911–13—Solomon Guggenheim Museum, New York
17. *The Amazon,* 1909—Mrs. Alexander Lewyt

⊰ I AM PLEASED to acknowledge the help I received from friends, colleagues, museums and libraries while writing this book. I am grateful to Robert Alter, Dr. Michael Aminoff, Elena Balashova, Miriam Cendrars, Alex Colville, Nora Crook, Joseph Frank, Stephen Gray, Mason Klein, Christian Kopff, Julie Martin, Serena Modigliani, Philip Pearlstein, Mark Polizzotti, Bin Ramke, Renée Sichel Wagenseil and especially Kenneth Wayne.

I had useful information on Modigliani from Art Resource (Jennifer Belt), the Centre d'Etudes Blaise Cendrars (Berne), the Fattori Museum in Livorno, the Courtauld Institute of Art and the Tate Gallery (Sue Breakell) in London, the Museum of Modern Art in New York; the libraries at the University of California, Berkeley, and Stanford University; on Beatrice Hastings from the National Library of South Africa in Cape Town, the National English Literary Museum in Grahamstown, the Port Elizabeth Public Library and the University of Port Elizabeth; and on Simone Thiroux from Carolyn Hillman, Ann Kitz, Marian Smith, the Art Gallery of Ontario, Laval University and the University of Montreal.

I have used English translations of Latin, Italian, French, Spanish and German sources when available; otherwise the translations are mine.

As always, my wife, Valerie Meyers, helped with the research, read and improved each chapter, and compiled the index.

⊰ MODIGLIANI: A LIFE moves from the *bande à Manet,* the subject of my previous book, *Impressionist Quartet: The Intimate Genius of Manet and Morisot, Degas and Cassatt,* to the *bande à Picasso;* from the story of four Parisian painters born in the 1830s and 1840s, to one born in Livorno, Italy, in 1884. Modigliani settled permanently in Paris in 1906 and died there, tragically, at the age of thirty-five. He remained outside the art movements of the early twentieth century—Cubism, Fauvism, Futurism—and became the greatest Italian painter since Tiepolo. A commercial and critical failure in his lifetime, his work seems now the most accessible and appealing of the modern era. There have been three major exhibitions of his art in the last few years. The public's appetite for his original and distinctive work has continued to grow, but the details of his dramatic life and tormented character remain largely unknown.

This book illuminates Modigliani's Jewish-Italian background and temperament; his intellectual influences: Rimbaud, Lautréamont, Nietzsche and D'Annunzio; his artistic heritage: the classical tradition of the nude from Botticelli to Manet; his intense friendships with the writers and painters who came from all over Europe to create the most stimulating artistic milieu of the twentieth century; his relations with the most important women in his life: the Russian poet Anna Akhmatova, the South African feminist Beatrice Hastings, the French-Canadian Simone Thiroux and the self-sacrificial young Parisian Jeanne Hébuterne; his addiction to drink and drugs: to absinthe, ether and hashish; the reasons for his self-destructive impulse; the lifelong tuberculosis that finally killed him; the meaning of his poetry; the significance of his innovative sculpture, portraits and nudes; and his posthumous legend.

I have tried to bring Modigliani's friends to life by describing the background, appearance, character and art of the impressive cast of artists and writers that surrounded him: Max Jacob, Pablo Picasso, Maurice Utrillo, Constantin Brancusi, Jacob Epstein, Jacques Lipchitz, Jules Pascin, Moïse Kisling, Chaim Soutine, Diego Rivera, Jean Cocteau and Blaise Cendrars. I also explain the nature of their friendships with Modigliani, and show how he expressed his feelings about them, and revealed their characters, in his portraits.

Modigliani's life was marked by sudden and quite radical changes: from health to sickness, Italy to France, bourgeois to Bohemian, sober and clear-minded to drunk and drugged, sculpture to portraits and nudes. In Paris he moved from one squalid tenement to another; frequently changed patrons, shifting from Paul Alexandre to Paul Guillaume to Léopold Zborowski; and moved restlessly, often violently, from Anna and Beatrice to Simone and Jeanne. This biography aims to capture the protean artist, and show how his alluring and strangely tranquil art grew, paradoxically, out of a reckless and convulsive life.

There is no excellent beauty that hath
not some strangeness in the proportion.

—Francis Bacon, "Of Beauty" (1597)

One

Livorno Childhood, 1884–1899

I

⊰ Amedeo Modigliani, full of talent and ambition, arrived in France from his native Italy in his early twenties. Stimulated by the artistic ferment of Paris, he spent the rest of his short life there. But his mind and character were rooted in his Jewish and Italian heritage, and whenever he was at a low point he dreamed of going home. As he lay dying in a charity hospital, his last thoughts were of Italy.

Modigliani came from the city of Livorno, the Tuscan port between Genoa and Rome, which had a unique place in the history of Italy. The Duchy of Florence bought the original fortress from Genoa in 1421 after the silting up of the Arno and consequent decay of the port of Pisa, and during the next century Livorno prospered under the rule of the Medicis. In the twenty-two-year reign of Ferdinando I, who became Duke of Tuscany in 1587, Livorno was rapidly transformed from an insignificant fishing village into a great international port. Ferdinando was the son of Eleanora di Toledo (the subject of a Bronzino portrait). Though he never took holy orders, he became a nominal cardinal at the age of fourteen. A powerful leader, he strengthened the Tuscan navy, defeated the Barbary pirates off the coast of North Africa, crushed the Turks and took lavish spoils. In Livorno, the colossal statue *Monumento dei Quattro Mori* celebrates Ferdinando's victories over the infidels and portrays him with four huge Moorish slaves supine at his feet.

Ferdinando also built the famous Villa Medici in Rome (later the home of the French Academy and of the Prix de Rome) and bought many priceless paintings and statues. He was a munificent patron of the arts, and created one of the most decorative and artistically vibrant courts in Europe. An English historian praised Ferdinando's achievements and wrote that "though extravagant and ostentatious, he immediately displayed a sincere concern for the well-being of Florence." His benign, efficient rule reduced corruption, stabilized the economy, encouraged farming, revived trade and strengthened the fleet. He developed Livorno, "the masterpiece of the Medicean dynasty," and filled it with new citizens from all over Europe.

Ferdinando was a commercially shrewd as well as an exceptionally enlightened and progressive ruler. By the charter of July 10, 1593, he declared Livorno a free port, exempt from all financial restrictions and beyond the customs frontier of the dukedom. He also created a refuge for all the oppressed people of Europe: Armenians and Orthodox Greeks from Turkey, "Catholics from England, Huguenots from France, Mahometan Moors from Christian Spain, Christian Moors from Mahometan Barbary, Corsicans loathing the Genoese yoke, Flemings fleeing before [the Spanish Duke of] Alva, and — above all — Jews."

Only twenty years after Ferdinando's charter, Livorno, with its thriving communities of English and Dutch merchants, had become one of the great centers of Mediterranean trade and, rivaled only by Amsterdam, of Jewish culture. Cecil Roth, the historian of the Jews, using the English name for Livorno, emphasized its extraordinary freedom and wrote: "The only place in Italy where Jewish intellectual life was completely untrammelled was Leghorn. Here, in accordance with the Charter of 1593, there was no interference with Hebrew literature; and in consequence the city became a great center of learning, ultimately outstripping the older seats of culture in the Mediterranean." The great synagogue, begun in 1602 and enlarged in

1789, was one of the major sights of the town, and was often visited by royalty and even by Napoleon himself during his triumphant campaign in northern Italy.[1]

Livorno attracted distinguished visitors as well as persecuted
minorities. The English novelist Tobias Smollett lived a few
miles outside Livorno for the last two years of his life, finished
Humphrey Clinker there and in 1771, the year of its publication,
was buried in the English cemetery. Writing from Monte Nero
in May 1770, he told a friend that "I am at present rusticated on
the slope of a Mountain that overlooks the sea, in the neighbour-
hood of Leghorne, a most romantic and salutary situation."
Percy Shelley, comparing Livorno to the bustling port on the
Thames, called it the "Wapping of Italy" and "the most unattractive of cities." His wife, Mary, condemned it as a "stupid town."
But when they settled next to a farm in August 1819, she soft-
ened her judgment and rhapsodized about the pleasures of rural
life: "We live in a little country house at the end of a green lane
surrounded by a *podere*. . . . It is filled with olive, fig and peachtrees
and the hedges are of myrtle. . . . The people are always busy. . . .
They sing not very melodiously but very loud—Rossini's
music."[2] Shelley wrote *The Cenci* and *The Mask of Anarchy* near
Livorno, and in its port took delivery of his schooner, the *Ariel,*
in which he later drowned. Modigliani identified with the flamboyant and rebellious Shelley and agreed with his exalted assertion in *A Defence of Poetry* that artists and "poets are the
unacknowledged legislators of the world."

At the beginning of the nineteenth century, Livorno's hu-
mane tolerance of Jews was strikingly different from the harsh
conditions they endured in the rest of Italy. Napoleon's rule and
influence were enlightened, but when his armies left the local
rulers became unmistakably reactionary. "In the States of the
Church it was unbending: under the reinstated Pope Pius VII
[1800–23] the gates of the Roman ghetto were firmly shut upon
its Jewish community once more. In Ferrara the ghetto chains

were put back." Cecil Roth observed that Livorno "was thus, with Pisa, virtually the only place in Italy where the repressive policy of Catholic reaction [against the Jews] made no headway. The Ghetto, with all the degradation which it implied, was never introduced; there was barely any restriction on economic life."

Jewish culture prospered throughout the nineteenth century and the city remained an important center of Hebrew printing. Livorno suffered a decline when it ceased to be a free port in 1868. Though the Jewish population (in a city which then had 100,000 people) decreased in the late nineteenth century from 5,000 to only 1,700, there is still today a higher proportion of Jews in Livorno than in any other Italian city. A cultural historian explained how families like the Modiglianis practiced a less orthodox form of Judaism during Amedeo's lifetime, and how well educated and politically active Jews like his brother Emanuele began to influence society. Until the start of the Great War, Italian Jews usually observed the important ceremonies and holidays, rarely entered mixed marriages and confined their social life to the family. "Italian Jews were brought into society primarily through their entry into civil administration and university positions, professional activities that had a political impact." Arnoldo Momigliano, an eminent Italian historian, concluded that Livorno "remained the easiest Italian town to live in during at least two centuries and developed that Jewish style of its own which is preserved in the books of [Rabbi Elia] Benamozegh and of which perhaps the paintings of Amedeo Modigliani show traces."[3]

Modigliani's Livorno was the ugliest place in the most beautiful province of Italy. Karl Baedeker's guidebook reported that it "contains little to detain the traveler" and the English writer Augustus Hare asserted: "There is nothing whatever worth seeing in Leghorn." In *Italian Hours*, Henry James magisterially declared: "It has neither a church worth one's attention, nor a municipal palace, nor a museum, and it may claim the distinction, unique in Italy, of being a city of no pictures." After that harsh judgment, James (like Mary Shelley) relented a little and confessed: "[But] as I sat in the garden and, looking up from my book, saw through a gap in the shrubbery the red house-tiles against the deep blue sky and the grey underside of the ilex-leaves turned up by the Mediterranean breeze, it was all still quite Tuscany, if Tuscany in the minor key." Though Livorno itself was culturally limited, it was close to the Tuscan masterpieces in Florence and Siena. Pisa, only twelve miles up the Arno, had the famous Leaning Tower, a cemetery and a cathedral with mosaics by Cimabue, paintings by Andrea del Sarto and a pulpit carved by Giovanni Pisano.

Livorno was the birthplace, a generation before Modigliani, of Pietro Mascagni, composer of the popular opera *Cavalleria Rusticana* (1890). His biographer explained that the city was gradually transformed, while Modigliani was still living there, from a thriving port and site of a naval academy to a town of ship-building and heavy industry. Livorno became the trading center of the Mediterranean. It imported goods from northern Europe and sold them in Italy and the Levant; imported cotton from Egypt and sold it in northern Europe. It processed cowhides, turned coral into jewelry and bartered it for diamonds. "During the nineteenth century…it was a city of foundries, steel mills and shipyards.…It was a gritty city, but a city of waterfront esplanades, set off by green hills as well as a city of grimy docks and warehouses.…For all its prosperity, it was an overcrowded city in which much of the population was packed into unsanitary tenements."

A modern guidebook describes Livorno as "full of sailors and African pedlars, blissfully unafflicted with architecture and art, as picturesque and romantic as Buffalo, New York.…Instead of rusticated *palazzi* and marble temples, it has canals, docks and a very lively citizenry famous for free thinking and tolerance. Instead of winding country lanes, there are big white

ferries to carry you off to…Corsica or Sardinia." Though
Modigliani grew up in a busy port, he felt no passion for ships
and the sea, no Gauguinesque longing for exotic travel, no response to Baudelaire's "Invitation to the Voyage":

> See, sheltered from the swells
> There in the still canals
> Those drowsy ships that dream of sailing forth;
> It is to satisfy
> Your least desire, they ply
> Hither through all the waters of the earth.[4]

II

THE MODIGLIANIS and the Garsins, the maternal side of the
family, were Sephardic Jews. Expelled from Spain by the Inqui-
sition at the end of the fifteenth century, they moved eastward
to France and to Italy. The Modiglianis, who took their name
from a town between Florence and Forlì in central Italy, came to
Livorno from Rome in the mid-nineteenth century. A grandfather, after lending money to a Roman cardinal, foolishly believed he was exempt from papal law. As Modigliani told the
Russian writer Ilya Ehrenburg, the grandfather "had wanted to
grow vines, and had bought a small plot; but the law prohibited
Jews from owning land. Enraged, [he] had moved to Leghorn,
where many Jewish families had lived from time immemorial."
A Garsin ancestor, a notorious Don Juan, was surprised by a
jealous husband whose wife he had bedded and managed to escape in his nightshirt, but caught pneumonia and died young.

Modigliani's great-grandfather, Giuseppe Garsin, the son of
Solomon and Regina Spinoza Garsin, was born in Livorno in
1793 and moved to Marseilles, France, in 1835. His son Isaaco,
the most interesting member of that cosmopolitan family, lived
briefly in Algeria, where he married his cousin, and returned to
Marseilles in 1852. Four generations of the family then lived in

the large house at 21 rue Bonaparte. The handsome, brilliant and well read Isaaco—fluent in French, Italian, Spanish, English, Arabic and Greek—had a severe nervous breakdown in 1873 when the London and Tunis branches of his business failed. As an old man he was ruined, neurotic and embittered, suffered from persecution mania and became mentally unbalanced, even insane. Isaaco moved to Livorno to live with his daughter in 1886, when Modigliani was two years old. The old man and the child spent a great deal of time together, walking through the streets of the town and along the waterfront, and Isaaco introduced the boy to art and philosophy. Until his death in 1894, Isaaco was a powerful influence on his favorite grandson.

The Garsins proudly claimed as their ancestor the seventeenth-century Jewish-Dutch philosopher Baruch (or Benedict) Spinoza. He had no children, but the line continued through his younger brother Gabriel. Spinoza's *Ethics* (1677) was Isaaco's Bible. The philosopher taught that the emotions, which lead men to live by impulse instead of allowing them to see things under "the aspect of eternity," must be subjected to rational control. He wrote that "Man's lack of power to moderate and restrain the affects I call bondage"; the control of the emotions he called freedom. Spinoza argued, as Isaaco taught the young Amedeo, that men are subjected to bondage when they allow the passions to operate in egoistical blindness, and can achieve true freedom only in the "intellectual love of God."

Isaaco's mental illness affected two of his daughters. Modigliani's aunt Laura Garsin suffered from sexual fears and persecution mania, cut herself off from human contact and had to be committed to an insane asylum. Writing his most substantial letter, from Paris in November 1915, Modigliani expressed compassion for the deeply troubled Laura and tried to comfort his mother, who had to take care of her: "if she retains her intelligence—her marvelous intelligence—it is a great deal. I am very moved that she remembers and takes an interest in me even in the state of forgetfulness of human things in which she finds herself. It seems to me impossible that such a person can't be led back to life, to a normal life." That same year in Marseilles, aunt Gabriella Garsin, who'd lived with the family when Modigliani was a child, committed suicide by throwing herself down a steep flight of steps.

Like most twentieth-century artists and writers, Modigliani had a strong mother and weak father. His trilingual mother, Eugenia (Isaaco's daughter), was born in Marseilles on January 28, 1855, and educated by an English Protestant governess and at a French Catholic school. A late photograph portrayed a formidable, heavyset woman with white hair, strong nose, wide mouth and square chin. His father, born in Rome in 1840 and given the Roman name of Flaminio, was a mild-looking man with bald head and full beard. The marriage, arranged by the families, who had business connections, took place in Livorno in 1872. Four children were born in the next twelve years: Giuseppe Emanuele, the future Socialist deputy, in 1872; Margherita, who never left home, in 1874; Umberto Isaaco, who studied electrical engineering in Belgium, in 1878; and the youngest, Amedeo Clemente, on July 12, 1884. He was named after Eugenia's brother Amedeo Garsin (later his patron and benefactor) and her sister Clementina; and was called Dedo by his family and Modi by his friends in France. The prosperous Uncle Amedeo, trading from Marseilles, founded the Company for the Development of Madagascar. After a severe attack of typhoid fever, he suffered lesions in his lungs and died of tuberculosis at the age of forty-five, in 1905.

In 1884, when Dedo was born, the most dramatic news came from Africa. At the Berlin Conference the European powers carved up the continent and began to exploit their colonies; the Mahdi captured Omdurman and would soon cut off the head of General Gordon; prospectors discovered gold in the Transvaal. Italy, eager for its share of the spoils, also ventured into Africa. In Modigliani's lifetime, Italy was defeated by the Ethiopians at

Adowa in 1895, and invaded Libya in 1911. In 1884 Seurat painted his *pointilliste Bathers at Asnières,* and Rodin, whose massive work Modi would later reject, carved the ponderous *Burghers of Calais.* Ibsen published *The Wild Duck,* a devastating analysis of misguided illusions, and D'Annunzio, a major influence on Modi's life and thought, brought out his novel, *The Book of the Virgins.*

Despite the strain of insanity, Modigliani's Spanish-Italian-French-Jewish family enjoyed the comfortable, even lavish life of upper-middle-class Tuscan intellectuals. They lived at 33 via Roma (which runs south from the center of the city) in a three-story house. Attached to buildings on both sides, it had an oval doorway and green shutters on the upper floors. According to the diary Eugenia kept during Dedo's childhood, their hospitality was bountiful: "the house in via Roma [was] huge and full of servants, the meals fit for a Pantagruel, with the table always set for an endless number of relatives and friends, great receptions in a series of vast drawing rooms on the second floor or in the ground-floor hall that opened into the big and still well-tended garden."[5]

Eugenia, well read, refined and cosmopolitan, found the Modiglianis uncultivated, domineering and oppressive. Flaminio, a weak man, was often absent on business and played an insignificant role in the life of the family. His "fortune, rather conspicuous in origin, was founded on the sale of lumber and coal, and especially on the mines in Sardinia, where for decades the saying ran: 'rich as a Modigliani.'" When Flaminio's mismanagement coincided with an economic depression, "the complex patrimony of the Modigliani family [like that of the Garsins in the previous generation] was almost entirely liquidated between 1884 and 1886." After the financial catastrophe, Flaminio was reduced to running a small agency in Livorno and earned commissions by selling coal, wool and hides.

According to the rather melodramatic family history, the bankrupt Modiglianis were protected by a law that prevented creditors from seizing the bed of a pregnant woman or mother with a newborn child. The villainous bailiffs entered the house just as Eugenia went into labor with Dedo, and the family protected their most valuable possessions by piling them on top of the woman in childbirth. After their financial ruin, the family moved from the house of rich feasts and grand receptions to a more exiguous existence in a modest dwelling at 4 via della Ville. A photo of the two-year-old Dedo shows him, with hair cropped short and a slightly startled look, wearing only an undershirt and displaying his manly parts. He's firmly held by an unusually pretty, full-breasted nursemaid, with dark hair parted in the middle and long white scarf around her striped dress, exactly the sort of compliant domestic he would later seduce. Analyzing the character of her beloved son, Eugenia called him "a little spoiled, a little capricious, but as pretty as a picture." Though his parents were not particularly attractive, Dedo was very good-looking indeed, and from boyhood on was irresistible to women.

After bearing four children, and still in her twenties, the capable and industrious Eugenia assumed the dominant role and soon became the main support of the family. She wrote, with frustrating vagueness, that "I am doing a translation of D'Annunzio's poetry, and last summer a publisher brought out a short story of mine, so I hope to write a whole novel. At any rate, writing amuses me." Soon afterwards, her granddaughter noted, "she became the ghost-writer for an American, for whom over the years she composed a series of studies on Italian literature."[6] No trace of her literary work has survived.

Eugenia also began to give lessons to the local children and started a private coeducational school in her house. Dedo became one of her pupils and was taught at home until he entered elementary school at the age of ten. Three lively photos, taken between 1894 and 1897, portray his progress through school. In 1894, his first year of formal education, he's angelically handsome. Seated in the front row, he has long wavy hair (unlike the other boys, whose hair is cut short) and wears a wide Eton collar, tie, dark jacket, light trousers and brown boots. The following year, in another school photo, he appears with seven other boys and their elderly, bespectacled teacher. Standing stiffly in the front row, with arms rigidly at his side and curly hair over his ears, he's dressed in a military tunic with two rows of brass buttons and a wide belt with two clasps. He's smaller, and looks more sensitive and delicate, than his rougher classmates. In 1897 the thirteen-year-old Dedo appeared in an end-of-term theatrical performance at his mother's school. Partly hidden, he wears a top hat and an engaging smile. The other children (four boys and eleven girls) are decked out in peasant costumes or fancy dress. In all these photos Dedo is as charming and appealing as a little prince.

In 1897 Dedo had his bar mitzvah in the great synagogue of Livorno. Like many Jewish adolescents, he dutifully recited the unintelligible prayers that meant very little to him. Franz Kafka, a close contemporary who also died of tuberculosis, dryly described his own bar mitzvah the previous year: "The 13th birthday is a special occasion. Up near the altar in the temple I had to recite a piece learned by heart with great difficulty, then at home I had to make a brief speech (also learned by heart). I also received many presents."

Dedo's maturity, seriousness and precocious intelligence, nurtured by Grandfather Isaaco, earned him the nickname of "the professor." When he started art school his father called him "Botticelli." A schoolmate, noting his dominant characteristic, mentioned "a strange sense of superiority. He did not find people of his category in Livorno, but he was right." Distracted by his determination to be an artist, he was not a good student, and left school at fourteen. In July 1898, Eugenia, disappointed yet resigned, recorded that "Dedo did not do brilliantly in his examinations, which did not surprise me much, because he has not studied well all year. At the beginning of August he starts drawing lessons, which he has wanted to do for some time. He already sees himself as a painter."[7]

Young Dedo's first teacher, Guglielmo Micheli, was a pupil of Giovanni Fattori, the leader of the Italian Macchiaioli group. They painted light and shade with tiny brushstrokes of contrasting spots, or *macchie*, and portrayed charming scenes of rural life and labor, sunny landscapes and military maneuvers. Like the French Impressionists, whom they imitated, they believed in painting out of doors and in "the scrupulous study of nature and of contemporary life." In April 1899 Eugenia, pleased by his zealous commitment and gratified by his rapid progress, wrote: "Dedo has completely given up his studies and does nothing but paint, but he does it all day and every day with an unflagging ardor that amazes and enchants me. If he does not succeed in this way, there is nothing more to be done. His teacher is very pleased with him, and although I know nothing about it, it seems that for someone who has studied for only three or four months, he does not paint too badly and draws very well indeed."

A fellow student described their idiosyncratic method: "Dedo was doing a charcoal drawing…a still-life with drapery behind it; the technique of these drawings consisted in partly burning the paper and using the smoked parts as half-tints. Fattori saw the drawing and was very pleased with it." Dedo soon rejected Micheli's old-fashioned tuition and struck out on his own. He was once mistaken for an itinerant peddler: "On Sundays they all used to meet at [Gino] Romiti's studio to draw from the nude, and little by little they stopped working with Micheli to go off on their own and paint in the country.…When two of them were going cross-country with their paint-boxes slung on their shoulders, a farm wife asked them whether they had any combs for sale."

Dedo's earliest surviving work, an accomplished charcoal *Self-Portrait* of 1898, shows him in bust length and three-quarter view, with the right side of his face heavily shaded. He has short black hair, deep dark eyes and a characteristically serious expression. In his blurry and rather mournful *Tuscan Landscape* of 1898, painted in the spotted Macchiaioli style, a road, forming a broad gray pyramid, cuts through two triangular autumnal fields to create a deep perspective. There is an isolated tiled-roof farmhouse on the right, a tall leafy tree on the left and a few tiny scattered houses at the far end of the road. In the distance, mountains curve and bend under a thick cloudy sky. Georg Trakl, the Austrian poet and contemporary of Modi, described a similarly gloomy scene in "De Profundis":

> There is a stubble field on which a black rain falls.
> There is a tree which, brown, stands lonely here.
> There is a hissing wind which haunts deserted huts—
> How sad this evening.

Another contemporary, the Austrian Expressionist painter Egon Schiele, expressed the same fin de siècle sadness, and wrote: "One experiences an autumnal tree in summer most profoundly, with one's entire heart. This melancholy I want to paint."[8]

At the turn of the century Italy, which had not become a unified and independent country until 1861, had declined from its former greatness and was weakened by grave social and economic problems. It was mainly an agricultural society, with widespread illiteracy and a high mortality rate. Its backwardness and poverty provided a striking contrast to the great civilizations of ancient Rome and the Renaissance. Its constitutional monarchy, created by unification, was "the least liberal and most corrupt in Western Europe; it had, in the eyes of the young, failed to carry on the work of the Risorgimento"—which had freed Italy from the reactionary Bourbon kings. In 1897 anarchists tried to assassinate the unpopular King Umberto, and finally succeeded in 1900.

In 1898, the year Dedo left school to study art, another disaster struck the family. Dedo's idealistic, combative brother,

Emanuele, had entered politics. He had "a warm humanity, a quick and lucid intellect, an easy-going and forceful way of speaking, an acute sense of irony, an imposing and considerable presence." After earning a law degree from the University of Pisa, Emanuele had been elected to the Livorno City Council and become active in the Socialist movement. On May 4, 1898, in Piacenza (southeast of Milan), after secretly attending meetings that opposed the harsh new tax on bread, he took part in a political demonstration that the government considered subversive. As poor, starving peasants rioted in the streets, martial law was imposed and Emanuele was arrested. He was accused of "having instigated and convened a meeting to rebel against authority and inciting the hatred of various social classes in a way that endangered public safety."9

On July 14 the Military Tribunal of Florence convicted Emanuele of two offenses, fined him 750 lire and sentenced him to two-and-a-half years in jail. He actually served eight months in the Domenicani prison in Livorno. Though Eugenia was proud of Emanuele's defense of the poor and his political idealism (he became a deputy in the Italian parliament in 1913), she was publicly disgraced by having a son in prison. Emanuele's misfortune apparently warned Dedo off politics for life. Intent on his art and his personal problems, he remained largely indifferent to the cataclysmic events of his lifetime.

Modigliani's Livorno childhood made him proud of his learned Mediterranean ancestry, of the equality and religious freedom granted to the Jews, of the artistic and intellectual heritage of Tuscany. But he was humiliated by the Garsins' and the Modiglianis' economic decline, and by his father's failure, disgrace and relative poverty. His father was distant and authoritarian, but Dedo formed an intense bond with his sensitive and cultured mother. Eugenia encouraged his artistic ambitions and, after he'd left home, gave him emotional and financial support. In Paris he became accustomed to hardship, but always felt entitled to middle-class comfort and to more money than he actually had.

As the youngest child, with an absent father and two older brothers away at the university, Dedo was brought up, after the death of his mentally unbalanced grandfather, with two crazy aunts. He did not enter school until he was ten and had only four years of formal education. From his ancestors he inherited physical beauty, an ability to charm and seduce the ladies and a streak of compulsive Don Juanism, as well as weak lungs, a susceptibility to tuberculosis and a strain of mental illness. Though taught to revere Baruch Spinoza, his own chaotic and self-destructive life would be dominated by emotion rather than by reason.

Two

ITALIAN JOURNEY,
1900–1905

I

⌐ DEDO WAS always a delicate child, and in his boyhood and teens was ravaged by three diseases that almost killed him. In the summer of 1895, when he was eleven years old, he developed chills, fever and a dry cough, which led to pleurisy—an inflammation of the lining of the lungs. Eugenia, though naturally alarmed by his illness, observed that her beloved youngest son enjoyed being coddled: "Dedo had a bad case of pleurisy and I still have not recovered from the terrible fright that it gave me. The child's character is still so unformed that I cannot say what I think of it. He behaves like a spoiled child, but he does not lack intelligence. We shall have to wait and see what lies inside this chrysalis. Perhaps an artist?"

Three years later (when Emanuele was sent to prison) Dedo contracted typhoid, an infectious disease that caused severe headaches and high fever. In the days before antibiotics, he became delirious, wavered between life and death for several weeks, and took a long time to recover. These illnesses undermined his chronic poor health. In September 1900, when he was sixteen, he suffered a violent hemorrhage from lesions in his lungs, which must have been a terrifying experience. D.H. Lawrence's wife, Frieda, who witnessed a similar episode in Italy in 1926, wrote that Lawrence suddenly "called from his room in a strange, gurgling voice; I ran and found him lying on his bed; he looked at me with shocked eyes while a slow stream of blood came from his mouth. 'Be quiet, be still,' I said. I held his head, but slowly and terribly the blood flowed." Dedo's doctor thought he would die; but his mother once again nursed him back to health and promised a long, recuperative journey when he was well enough to travel. Though he seemed to recover, he was in fact infected with tuberculosis, an incurable lung disease that blighted his young life. Temperamentally reckless, he was unable to look after himself and always needed—but rarely found—someone to take care of him. From this point on, he felt he was doomed and believed he would die young.

Instead of taking her son to a sanatorium in the dry air of the Italian Alps, in November 1900 Eugenia took him south, beyond the confines of Tuscany. He spent the winter studying art while living in Naples and just outside that city in the village of Torre del Greco. Forty years earlier the young Edgar Degas, who had many relatives in Naples, also went south to study in the Museo Nazionale and had the same experience as Dedo: " 'Let me get it well into my head,' he wrote in his notebook, 'that I know nothing at all. That's the only way to advance.' In the museum Degas sketched the ancient statues and copied, among other things, Titian's portrait of Pope Paul III and several of the mural paintings that had been removed from the [Roman] ruins of Pompeii, Herculaneum, and Stabiae; he took note of 'the most beautiful Claude Lorrain one can see. The sky is like silver, and the shadows speak to you.' Some time during the summer he went down the coast to Sorrento, celebrated for its sumptuous sunsets."

In March 1901 Eugenia and Dedo moved to Capri, a legendary island in the Bay of Naples. "The depravity of Tiberius, or the salacity of Suetonius," wrote Anthony Burgess, "had left its mark on an island all sodomy, lesbianism, scandal, and cosmopolitan artiness." The island's natural beauty—as well as its tolerance for unnatural behavior—had attracted many writers. In the nineteenth and early twentieth centuries Ivan Turgenev and Maxim Gorky, Gerhart Hauptmann and Rainer Maria Rilke,

Norman Douglas and Somerset Maugham had visited and ex-
tolled the island. Joseph Conrad, who came to Capri in 1905,
complained of the hot winds, violent contrasts and sexual scandals: "This place here, this climate, this sirocco, this transmon-
tana, these flat roofs, these sheer rocks, this blue sea—are
impossible....The scandals of Capri—atrocious, unspeakable,
amusing, scandals international, cosmopolitan and biblical."[1]

The precocious and sophisticated Dedo found the island exciting. Alluding to its decadent atmosphere, he told a friend that
the very name of Capri was "enough to arouse a tumult of beautiful images and ancient voluptuousness in my spirit....[There is]
a vague feeling of sensuality always present in the classic beauty
of the countryside." He took advantage of the permissive milieu,
and boasted of a romantic interlude with an unchaperoned and
apparently all-too-eager young tourist: "I went off alone for a
country walk in the moonlight with a Norwegian girl...really a
very erotic type, but very lovely too."

Dedo's confidant and close friend was Oscar Ghiglia, five
years his senior, whom he'd met at art school in Livorno in 1899.
Ghiglia had a dashing appearance, with a high forehead, dark
hair, thick curving mustache and brooding expression. He'd led
an adventurous life and been a peddler, tinker, blacksmith's ap-
prentice, pork butcher and paint grinder before deciding to
study art. In March and April 1901 the sixteen-year-old Dedo—
while traveling in Capri, Rome and Venice, wrote five serious,
thoughtful and precocious letters to Ghiglia—quite different
from the hasty factual notes he dashed off during the rest of
his life.

Showing the same passionate commitment to art that had
surprised and impressed Eugenia, Dedo dismissed his mediocre
teacher in Livorno: "Micheli? My God, how many of them there
are in Capri...regiments!" He also swore to extract the fullest
possible meaning from all the new sensations: "[I plan] to dedi-
cate myself faithfully (body and soul) to the *organization* and *de-*

velopment of every impression, of every germ of an idea that I have collected in this place as if in a mystic garden." Travel— with all the excitement and pleasure in his own sensations and ideas—gave him a new perspective and strengthened his belief that he would become an artist. Eugenia, fearing that her son might be corrupted by the vicious atmosphere of Capri, took him away. They briefly visited Amalfi, on the exquisite peninsula south of Naples, and spent the winter in Rome.

From Rome, Dedo wrote Ghiglia a rather pedantic letter that suggested he was following a rigid program of self-improvement, absorbing the atmosphere of the ancient capital and trying to concentrate on what would stimulate his own art: "Rome is the orchestration with which I surround myself, the limited area in which I isolate myself and concentrate all my thoughts. Its fever-ish delights, its tragic landscape, its beautiful and harmonious forms—all these things are *mine* through my thought and my work." He tried to discover the inspiration and meaning of art, saw himself as a serious student—in contrast to the vulgar horde of tourists—and self-consciously defined his own charac-ter and destiny: "I am trying to formulate as clearly as possible the truths of art and life that I have discovered scattered among the beauties of Rome....One should consider all great works of art just as one does the works of nature. First in its aesthetic re-ality, then outside of the development and mysteries involved in its creation, the very thing which excited and moved its cre-ator....[But] the barbarism of tourists and vacationers makes it impossible for me to concentrate just when I need to."[2]

In May 1901, stimulated and enlightened by his Grand Tour of Italy, Dedo shared a studio with Oscar Ghiglia in Florence and became the pupil of his teacher's teacher, Giovanni Fattori, then in his late seventies. The vigorous but taciturn son of working-class people, Fattori had very little education and "was a man of limited culture, without intellectual pretensions, who rarely left his Tuscan home." But he was the most productive painter and "strongest artistic personality" among the Italians of the late nineteenth century. He married his third wife when he was eighty-two.

Dedo's attitudes toward Livorno, national politics and the Italian artistic tradition were similar to Fattori's. In his autobiography Fattori expressed fondness, even longing, for his native city and wrote: "The people of Livorno had always been good Italians and always open to generous undertakings, and despite their faults, I love them and always have, and am proud of being a Livornese." He also expressed extreme disgust for and distance from the corruption of contemporary politics—a view that Modi would later echo in conversations with Ilya Ehrenburg: "I live in a century of unparalleled depravity, falsehood, dishonesty, swept into the abyss with the other few victims of honesty, love and work; I and they will be dragged into the mud that will drown us." Finally, he emphasized that contemporary Italian painters could still be nourished and inspired by, without slavishly following, the great masters of the fifteenth and fourteenth centuries: "The artists of the past, the *quattrocentisti* and *trecentisti* and Raphael and Leonardo and Donatello and Michelangelo and the others are always to be looked at and adored, but never imitated."[3]

In contrast to the rigidly conservative teachers at the moribund art academies, Fattori offered his students greater freedom and a more relaxed atmosphere. He helped inspire original talents rather than skilled imitators and encouraged them to draw spontaneously without subjecting them to harsh criticism. The students attending the school where he taught, the Scuola Libera di Nudo (Free School for Nude Studies), followed the traditional curriculum. They began by copying antique casts and classical statues, did drawings from Old Masters in museums and from models in the studio, studied the basic techniques of painting, took lessons in perspective and learned anatomy from dissected corpses. Gino Severini, born in Tuscany the year before

Dedo, enrolled in a similar art school in Rome and also signed up for an anatomy course. "But after the first lesson spent drawing a dead man's head, half of which was skinless," he recalled, "I was overcome with such disgust that I never wanted to go back."

Fattori had met the young Edgar Degas in 1859 at the Caffè Michelangiolo on the via Larga, and it was still a traditional meeting place for Florentine artists. Dedo frequented the crowded room that was reserved for local painters, who covered its walls with their works, and took part in the intense conversations about art and politics. Roy McMullen observed that though the Macchiaioli were violently opposed to the Italian art establishment, still turning out mythological and historical pictures, and insisted "on the need to be realistic, contemporary and unpretentious…they tended, like provincial painters everywhere, to be one revolution behind" the avant-garde. After a few months in Florence, Dedo grew restless and felt he had nothing more to learn from Fattori. He quarreled about this with Ghiglia—who remained loyal to the master and published a book about him, *L'Opera di Giovanni Fattori,* in 1913.

In one of his typically sudden shifts in direction, Dedo unexpectedly announced his desire to be a sculptor, and spent the summer of 1902 in Pietrasanta, the most famous quarry in Italy, a few miles below Carrara and thirty-five miles north of Livorno. Here Michelangelo had found the marble for his statues. A local stone mason taught Dedo how to use a hammer and chisel, and he carved two heads and a torso. He sent photos of his work to a friend in Livorno, asking him to make enlargements and copies, but had to abandon his first statues. He may have been dissatisfied with his amateurish efforts or simply found them too heavy to carry home. Still weak from his recent illnesses and exhausted by the effort of carving in stone, he was forced to leave Pietrasanta. At the very outset of his career poor health checked his progress as an artist.

Dedo spent the winter copying paintings in Rome. He went
to Venice in May 1903, the year after the Campanile unexpectedly collapsed, and enrolled in another Scuola Libera at the
Institute of Fine Arts. In *Death in Venice* (1912), Thomas Mann
described the expansive lagoons and serpentine canals, and the
breathtaking first sight of the main square in that "most improb-
able of cities." Mann's hero saw that "group of incredible struc-
tures the Republic set up to meet the awe-struck eye of the
approaching seafarer: the airy splendour of the [Doge's] palace
and Bridge of Sighs, the columns of lion and saint on the shore,
the glory of the projecting flank of the fairy temple [St. Mark's],
the vista of gateway and clock."[4] Dedo's modest means and
loosely structured art studies left him free to absorb the tremendous aesthetic experience of traveling around Italy. He took possession of Italian culture and chose what he needed to create his
own art.

Dedo lived in the San Barnaba quarter, near the Ca' Rezzon-
ico and the Grand Canal. He soon met Ardengo Soffici, born
near Florence and a few years older than himself. Like Severini,
he was a future Futurist. Soffici — remembering Dedo as an unusually cultured young man, interested in philosophy, knowl-
edgeable about poetry and a frequent visitor to the Accademia
and other museums — called him "an adolescent from a good
family, well dressed, well behaved, refined and delicate in appearance, who while in Venice enjoyed studying Bellini, Carpaccio,
[Titian, Veronese] and several of the Sienese painters." One of
his favorite paintings, which John Ruskin called "the best picture
in the world," was Carpaccio's *Two Courtesans* (1510), a resplen-
dent portrait of two lavishly dressed women observing the passing world from a Venetian balcony. In his own work Modigliani
chose to deny his subjects such gorgeous colors, rich fabrics and
exotic accessories, and reduced them to the bare essentials.

In Venice the eighteen-year-old Dedo ceased to be the conventional young man. He slacked off from his studies, cut his

classes, and did most of his drawings in cafés and brothels. Inspired by Rimbaud, he attended séances, began to drink heavily
and experimented with hashish. He also spent a great deal of
time in stimulating talks with his friends. His most important
Venetian companion was the Chilean painter Manuel Ortiz de
Zarate, who remained close to him until the very end of his life.
Born in Como, Italy, in 1887, when his father was touring Europe as a concert pianist, he was taken to Santiago at the age of
four. His parents wanted him to study engineering, but at seven-
teen he rebelled and left home to become an artist in Paris. His
father then relented and helped him get a study grant from the
Chilean government. The poet Guillaume Apollinaire called
Zarate, with some exaggeration, "the only Patagonian in Paris."

Zarate was a hulking, muscular man of great strength and
mild temperament. He had a leonine head, thick curly hair,
swarthy complexion, deep brooding eyes and sensual lips, and
liked to wear a small derby hat. A friend called him "a good madman, sweet and gentle," and Dedo loved his wit, warmth and vitality. Zarate, who today rates only a few lines in a whole book
on Chilean painting, began as a follower of Cézanne and the
Fauves, and did striking self-portraits and pictures with "violent
contrasts of light and shadow." He adored Paris, and urged Dedo
to leave provincial Italy and move to the art capital of the world.

Most of the art from the beginning of Modigliani's career has
been lost or destroyed. He'd studied art in Livorno, Florence and
Venice, but of all the paintings he did from 1901 to 1907 only
eight undistinguished works, seven of them portraits of women,
have survived. The most interesting picture is the *Small Portrait
of a Girl* (1904–05), executed with Macchiaioli technique and in a
realistic style. The girl is seated in a straight chair, in front of a
flowery background, and wears a dark skirt and spotted white
blouse with puffed sleeves. Her hands are folded in her lap, her
long hair is wrapped around her head. She looks off to the left
with rather sad, widely spaced eyes, and a subtle, enigmatic smile.

It's worth noting that, apart from Fattori, Dedo did not seek out any established painter working in Italy in the early years of the twentieth century. During and after his formal art training he rejected the realistic style that had oppressed Italian painting for more than a century. In this respect, he followed the conventional pattern of art pupils: study, revolt, struggle, success — except that he did not live long enough for the last stage. His younger contemporary Giorgio De Chirico, born in Greece of Sicilian parents, explained why all the bolder, more innovative painters left for Paris: "There are no modern art movements in Italy. No dealers, no galleries. Modern painting does not exist. There is only Modigliani and [me]; but we are almost French."[5]

II

MODIGLIANI'S FORMAL education was limited. He had left school at fourteen, but discussed literature with his grandfather, mother and aunt, and read widely during his long periods of convalescence. When the twenty-two-year-old Dedo arrived in Paris in 1906, he had not only spent years painting, drawing and studying art in Italy, but had also acquired (as many friends observed) an impressive knowledge of poetry. No modern painter had a greater appreciation of poetry or was more profoundly influenced by philosophy. In addition to Spinoza, the family god, he was familiar with works in English, Italian and French. He read Shelley, Wilde and Whistler; fluently recited Dante's *Inferno* and *La Vita Nuova,* Petrarch's love sonnets, Ariosto's epic *Orlando Furioso,* Leopardi's lyrical *Canti* and Carducci's patriotic declamations in the *Odi Barbare.* He knew the poems of Villon, Ronsard, Baudelaire, Mallarmé and Verlaine as well as the dynamic philosophy of Henri Bergson. The art critic Adolphe Basler wrote: "In his studio in the Cité Falguière I saw books in every corner.... Talking to him was a real pleasure." Ilya Ehrenburg "was astonished by the scope of his reading. I don't think I have ever met another painter who loved poetry so deeply."

Modigliani's French listeners missed the meaning of the words when he declaimed long passages of Italian poetry, but they understood his need to express himself, make an impression and assert his Italian identity. Later on, the poignant lines from the *Inferno* that he loved to quote seemed to reflect the tragedy of his own sharp decline. They expressed his intellectual confusion:

> In the middle of the journey of our life I came to myself within a dark wood where the straight way was lost (I.1);

his disappointments and failures:

> Without hope we live in desire (IV.42);

his sense of hopelessness and depression:

> What sweet thoughts, what longing led them to the woeful pass (V.113);

the contrast between his great expectations and abject wretchedness:

> There is no greater sorrow than to remember happy times in misery (V.121);

and his descent into poverty, alcoholism and drug addiction:

> Consider your origin: you were not born to live like brutes, but to follow virtue and knowledge (XXVI.118).[6]

These famous and familiar lines, schoolboy knowledge for most Italians, contained bitter truths for Modigliani.

Dedo was fascinated by three dandies of the 1890s—Whistler, Wilde and D'Annunzio—and praised their lavish way of life and rebellious works. They all proclaimed the superiority of the artist and encouraged his freedom from conventional

rules of behavior. He owned copies of Mrs. Arthur Bell's book
on Whistler (London, 1904), D'Annunzio's poems *Canto Novo*
(1882) and Nietzsche's *Thus Spake Zarathustra* (1883–92), first published the year before he was born.

His mother gave him Wilde's "The Ballad of Reading Gaol"
(1896) when he left for Paris. He would have been struck by
Wilde's observation: "all men kill the thing they love"—an idea
which had tragic implications for the women he became involved with at the end of his life. Wilde, the quintessential fin de
siècle aesthete, made a sharp distinction between the exaltation
of art and the banality of ordinary life, and declared: "It is
through art, and through art only, that we can realize our perfection; through art, and through art only, that we can shield our-
selves from the sordid perils of actual existence." This credo of
art for art's sake had a strong appeal for Modigliani, encouraging him to despise the ordinary claims of life and to neglect his
own health. He also identified with Baudelaire's albatross which,
like the outcast artist or poet, soars above the ignorant multitude
but is shot down, crippled and mocked: "The Poet shares the
fate of this prince of the clouds, / who rejoices in the tempest,
mocking the archer below; / exiled on earth, an object of scorn,
/ his giant wings impede him as he walks."

Modigliani was only too eager to embrace extreme ideas that
would explain and exalt his role as an artist. The poet Arthur
Rimbaud provided the aesthetic justification for what Baudelaire
called the "artificial paradise" of hashish. Rimbaud had demanded an artificially induced, self-destructive, deliberate derangement of all the senses that would enable the tormented,
sacrificial, even insane artist to become "the great invalid, the
great criminal, the great accursed" and to plunge into unknown,
unheard of, unnamable spiritual visions. In a letter of 1901 to
Oscar Ghiglia, Dedo, under the malign influence of Rimbaud's
revolutionary ideas and intense hostility to bourgeois morality,
told his older friend: "You must have that holy cult, the cult of
everything that can exalt and excite the intelligence! Try to pro-

voke and perpetuate these fertile stimulants, for they alone can lift the intelligence up to the highest creative levels. It is for them that we must fight. Can we allow them to be shut away from us behind a hedge of narrow-minded moralizing?"[7]

Dedo usually carried a copy of Lautréamont's *Les Chants de Maldoror* in his pocket—sometimes torn into sections for portability. He would spontaneously erupt with passages of his favorite author, whether or not his companions wanted to hear his ranting. Isidore Ducasse, the self-styled Comte de Lautréamont, was born in Montevideo, Uruguay, of French parents in 1847. He came to France in 1860 and died there at the age of twenty-three. The first part of his prose poem appeared in 1868, the second was published posthumously in 1890. Like Modigliani, he led a wretched existence, died miserably and achieved posthumous fame.

Lautréamont's rapturous, hallucinatory, satanic monologue, which shares the cruelty and black humor of the Marquis de Sade and Antonin Artaud, resembles the musings of a maniac. Maldoror, the defiant and unconstrained antihero, a rapist and murderer, absolutely revels in the most disgusting and self-destructive behavior. He rejoices in the violation of virginal innocence and the infliction of suffering and degradation, and uses morbid imagery and sadistic fanaticism to exalt the principle of evil.

This almost unreadable book fascinated Modigliani and his contemporaries. André Gide, writing in 1905, described its extraordinary emotional impact: "Here is something that excites me to the point of delirium. He leaps from the detestable to the excellent." It is hard to imagine how this repellent fantasy attracted readers as sensitive and intelligent as Modigliani and Gide. On the positive side, Lautréamont gave savage voice to the deep impulse of writers and artists to reject normal life and fulfill their own creative destiny. Yet Maldoror's scorn for humanity is so great that he no longer cares what anyone else thinks or feels, an illogical and preposterous position for an artist. Ultimately, the book celebrates cruelty and absolute power.

Two literary historians give some idea of its bizarre tone and shocking content. The perverse hero has strange tastes, expressed in disturbing shifts of style and mood: "Maldoror, a demonic figure, expresses his hatred of mankind and of God, and his love of the Ocean (a famous passage), blood, octopuses, toads, etc. There are nightmarish encounters with vampires and with mysterious beings on the seashore. The work is an amazing profusion of apostrophe and imagery, at once delirious, erotic, blasphemous, grandiose and horrific." In the 1920s, Lautréamont's deliberate cruelty appealed to the Surrealists and Dadaists. The prose poems "express his loathing of humanity through a Byronesque figure called Maldoror. His sadism, his voluntary self-abandonment to fantasies from the depths of his mind, his adoration of the sea as the cradle of thoughtless cruelty, led to his being acclaimed later by the surrealists as a forerunner. In a famous passage, Maldoror watches shipwrecked sailors torn to pieces by sharks and then mates with the most dreadful shark of all."[8] Describing this sexual encounter, Lautréamont exclaims that "their throats and breasts soon fuse into one glaucous mass exhaling the odors of sea-wrack." Maldoror gleefully boils kittens in a tub full of alcohol, and convulsively confesses: "I am filthy. Lice gnaw me. Swine, when they gaze upon me, vomit. Scabs and scars of leprosy have scaled off my skin, which exudes a yellowish pus."

Modigliani's friend Beatrice Hastings, in a clear-eyed judgment that opposed his own, called Lautréamont "a poor, self-tormented creature for whom, had he lived, no earthly refuge was possible but an asylum." Modigliani, who could never quite tear himself away from this book, frankly admitted it "had ruined...his life." He may have been particularly thinking of a bombastic, suicidal passage in which Maldoror defiantly confronts the world with no more than the strength of his artistic genius: "Whether I gain a disastrous victory or whether I succumb, the battle will be good: I alone, against humanity. I shall not employ weapons made of wood or iron; I shall kick aside the strata of minerals extracted from the earth: the powerful and seraphic sonority of the harp will become beneath my fingers a formidable talisman."[9] Lautréamont, like Nietzsche, believed the defiant law breakers were the real creators.

Dedo first read Nietzsche's *Thus Spake Zarathustra* as an art student in Italy, when, as his friend Severini observed, "Nietzsche's poetic madness found its way into our souls." Nietzsche, who actually became insane in 1890, also believed that art was sacred, that every pleasure in life had to be sacrificed to creativity and that the true artist appealed only to those rare individuals capable of understanding his exalted ideas. He felt that disease could bring a new awareness to the artist who was able to survive its grave assaults. The damage could be valuable if physical pain was transformed into intellectual achievement: "Sickness itself can be a stimulant to life.... We seek life raised to a higher power, life lived in danger.... What does not destroy us makes us stronger." Nietzsche, who — like Rimbaud and Lautréamont — believed the artist's derangement gave him the power to see and tell the truth, exclaimed: "One has to pay dearly for immortality: one has to die several times while still alive."[10] Modigliani was drawn to these subversive ideas which, taken literally, reinforced the denial of his own disease and refusal to seek a cure.

Several penetrating, even agonizing aphoristic passages from *Zarathustra,* which Dedo had studied with deadly seriousness, seem to mark the *via dolorosa* of his life. Modigliani shared Nietzsche's defiant, iconoclastic attitude:

> Brave, unconcerned, mocking, violent — thus wisdom wants us.... The man who breaks their table of values, the breaker, the lawbreaker; yet he is the creator,

and his belief in the regenerative power of sex:

> Sex... for the lion-willed [is] the great invigoration of the heart.

Nietzsche taught him that suffering transfigured the artist and that art redeemed the sufferer:

> That brief madness of bliss is experienced only by those who suffer most deeply....Spirit is the life that itself cuts into life: with its own agony it increases its own knowledge.

He also learned that creativity depended on cultivating disorder and submitting oneself to a chaotic, even self-immolating life:

> I love those who do not want to preserve themselves....One must still have chaos in oneself to be able to give birth to a dancing star....With my own blood I increased my own knowledge.[11]

Dedo's most important letter to Ghiglia, written from Venice in April 1901, when his friend in Livorno was going through a personal crisis and had become severely depressed, is suffused with the Nietzschean ether. He adopted Nietzsche's concepts of self-overcoming and the will to power, and portrayed the artist as a tragic genius and sacrificial agent of cultural regeneration: "People like us (if you'll excuse the plural) have different rights, different values than do normal, ordinary people because we have different needs which put us—it has to be said and you must believe it—above their moral standards. Your duty is never to waste yourself in sacrifice. Your *real* duty is to save your dream. Beauty herself makes painful demands; but these nevertheless bring forth the most supreme efforts of the soul. Every obstacle we overcome means an increase in will-power and provides the vital and progressive renewal of our inspiration."

Dedo's mother had translated into French works by the poet, playwright and novelist Gabriele D'Annunzio (1863–1938), the most famous Italian author of his time. At the turn of the century D'Annunzio was notorious for his heated rhetoric, his luxurious way of life and his flamboyant love affairs. During the Great War he became an outstanding hero in all three military services. After the war, he ruled the independent city of Fiume for a year before being blasted out by the Italian government. (For Dedo, Nietzsche's ideas were filtered through and reinforced by D'Annunzio.) Denis Mack Smith, the historian of modern Italy, defined the quintessential qualities that so strongly appealed to the young and impressionable Dedo: "Perpetually lonely and unsatisfied, [D'Annunzio] took everything to excess, seeking always for new experiences and indulgences, for greater speed, greater passion, a more shocking private life, a more violent assault on convention than anyone else.... He preached that everything should be forgiven the artist, who was a superman above ordinary morals, just as he should also be above the payment of debts."

D'Annunzio penned a characteristically Nietzschean passage — mocking conventional morality, emphasizing self-overcoming, transcending good and evil — in *Il Trionfo della morte* (*The Triumph of Death,* 1894): "Where lives the strong, tyrannical dominator, free from the yoke of any false morality, sure in the feeling of his own power, convinced that the essence of his person overcomes in value all accessory attributes, determined to raise himself above Good and Evil by the pure energy of his will, capable of forcing life to maintain its promises to him?"[12] Dedo, unlike D'Annunzio, was never able to force life to reward his genius.

Dedo was also drawn to the D'Annunzian connection between sexuality and creativity, between spilling sperm and spreading paint. In his autobiographical *Le Faville del maglio* (*Sparks from the Hammer,* 1924–28), D'Annunzio, using a sculptural metaphor in his title, confessed that this concept had dominated his life: "Always something fleshly, something resembling a carnal violence, a mixture of atrocity and inebriation, accompanies the begetting of my brain." In a similar fashion Modigliani — alluding to D'Annunzio's novel *Il Fuoco* (*The Flame of Life,* 1900) — exclaimed: "I need a flame in order to paint, in order to be consumed by fire."

Modigliani's fiery inscription, combining spirituality and sensuality, on his drawing *Portrait of a Woman with a Hat* (c.1917–18), is, like his model, unidentified. But it sounds very much like D'Annunzio: "By chance the woman of great soul and beauty would also burn with an immeasurable fire of insane desires." Another aphoristic inscription, on his drawing of Lunia Czechowska (c.1919), quotes a passage from D'Annunzio's expensively produced journal *Il Convito (The Banquet,* 1895) that exalted the godlike power of the artist: "Life is a gift from the few to the many, from those who know and have to those who don't know and don't have."[13]

Dedo must have been struck by Nietzsche's assertion in *Ecce Homo* (1888): "As an *artist* one has no home in Europe, except in Paris." His uncle Amedeo, who'd paid his expenses in Venice, died in 1905; but the always encouraging Eugenia promised to support him, and in January 1906 he left for Paris. Though Dedo thought of himself as unique, he was part of the wave of Italian emigration that had begun in the late nineteenth century. As Denis Mack Smith wrote: "By 1876 a hundred thousand people were leaving Italy a year, by 1901 half a million, and in a single year of 1913, 872,000 people left the country, that is to say one person in every forty. By 1914 there were thus five to six million Italians living abroad as compared with thirty-five million inside Italy."[14]

Unlike his compatriots, however, Dedo was not going to an entirely foreign country. Eugenia's family had lived in Marseilles since 1835. She was French, not Italian; and Dedo, fluent in his mother's tongue, was returning to her homeland. As he left, Eugenia urged him yet again to be a good son, to write often and come home regularly, to follow the doctor's orders and take care of himself. But he had already absorbed the potentially explosive cocktail of Rimbaud and Lautréamont, Nietzsche and D'Annunzio, into his bloodstream. Paris transformed the *figlio di mamma,* stimulated by the dangerous influences that granted him absolute freedom, and set him on the path to self-destruction.

Three

Down and Out in Paris,
1906–1908

I

◁ Modigliani, his friends agreed, had a "very lively and profound knowledge of the French language" and "spoke very pure French, with neither a Parisian nor an Italian accent." When Picasso first came to Paris he knew nothing of the language, and Max Jacob had to communicate with him in broken French and with broad gestures. Modi's perfect command of the language made him much less of an outsider. Able to make personal contact with Parisians, he felt immediately at ease and ready to enjoy the cultural life of the city. He disliked his first name, Amedeo, and in Paris was known as "Modi," which sounded, all too appropriately, like *maudit,* or cursed, the word used to describe the doomed Romantic artist.

Many nineteenth and twentieth century artists and writers were adventurous travelers. Lautréamont was born in Uruguay and sailed to France in his youth. Baudelaire went to Mauritius, Manet to Brazil, Degas to Louisiana, Gauguin to Tahiti, Rimbaud to Abyssinia. Modi's friend Ossip Zadkine roamed from Russia to Scotland, Blaise Cendrars wandered from St. Petersburg to Panama. Despite his Mediterranean heritage, Modi remained narrowly confined to Italy and France, and never ventured south of Naples or north of Normandy. He had neither the money nor the desire to spend weekends in the country and summers painting on the Channel coast or in the Pyrenees. He was anchored in Paris, where he lived the Bohemian life. He read at the Bibliothèque Sainte-Geneviève; visited museums, galleries and the latest exhibitions; and, most of all, talked to other artists and saw their latest work.

Modi first arrived during the peaceful years of the belle époque, when trade and colonialism had made Paris wealthy. Industrialization had brought material comforts as well as the encroaching factories whose smoke curled menacingly from the chimneys in Impressionist paintings. Absorbed in his art, he was strangely uninterested in the modern inventions that were changing the world at the beginning of the twentieth century. He lived in the crumbling, lamplit buildings of the previous era, and could never afford rooms with electric light. He ignored the typewriter, automobile and airplane, photography and the cinema. He was also indifferent to the crucial political issues of 1906: the heated debates about the separation of church and state and the continuing anarchist threats that had helped send his brother to prison.

It was also a period of ferment in the center of the art world. Lautrec had died in 1901, Gauguin in 1903, Cézanne in 1906, and new talents were arriving on the scene. In 1906 the Fauves, led by Matisse and exalting pure color, held a major exhibition; and Picasso, influenced by African art, began to paint the innovative and shocking *Demoiselles d'Avignon.* The young, often isolated painters, faced with hostile critics and an uncomprehending public that was slow to buy their work, sought out and encouraged each other to make it new. As Modi continued to learn his craft, he joined this distinct and largely down-and-out community. Though his life in Paris was exciting and intensely creative, it could also be lonely and squalid.

Like most of the struggling young artists from every country in Europe, Modi soon gravitated to Montmartre, the center, until 1914, of avant-garde art and left-wing politics. Perched on a butte, about five hundred feet above the northern outskirts of Paris, it was not incorporated into the city until 1860. In 1906 it still seemed like a village, with windmills, empty fields and herds of animals being driven through the quaint cobblestoned streets and steep narrow alleys. Montmartre offered cheap wine and entertainment in bars, cafés-concerts and dance halls like the Moulin de la Galette and the Moulin Rouge. The artists—crowded in among ordinary workers, circus performers, tramps and petty criminals—lived in decrepit tenements and in rough studios made of wood and corrugated iron. There was no running water or electricity; one primitive toilet served for an entire building. Rooms were heated with old stoves, expensive to run, which puffed out smoke. The church of the Sacré Coeur, a marble monstrosity under interminable construction, towered above the quarter that would soon be idealized in the quaint cityscapes of Maurice Utrillo.

Modi did not copy paintings in the Louvre (he'd done enough of that in Italian museums). He preferred to do quick sketches of nude models during their fifteen-minute poses at the Académie Colarossi, across the river in Montparnasse, on the rue de la Grande Chaumière. The biographer of Gauguin, a former pupil at Colarossi, described its unconstrained atmosphere and unusual method of recruiting models:

> The Académie Colarossi [was] a ramshackle set of studios where artists and students could pay to use the models and receive a little tutoring if they wished. The Colarossi was not an atelier in the accepted sense, with a single famous artist teaching his pupils, but was more of an open facility, useful because of the high cost of hiring an individual model, especially if he or she was required to pose in the nude....
>
> The narrow street bustled with activity—Monday was the jolliest day when a "model-market" was held on the corner of the Boulevard de Montparnasse, where a crowd of hopeful men, women and children, mostly Italian immigrants, would hang around waiting to be selected by the passing artists. It was a convention that if someone was expected to pose nude, they could be taken to the Colarossi and asked to undress for a quick inspection before any deal was finally struck.[1]

The high points of the social season were the artists' balls. They inspired shocking costumes and riotous behavior, and were tolerated, on these special occasions, by the police. Beatrice Hastings, reporting on the Paris art scene for an English journal, evoked the frenetic mood in staccato style. There is "much laughter, much applause for your frock if it is chic, 300 people inside and outside the [Café] Rotonde, very much alive! Models arrayed in [revealing costumes as] a flame or a half-moon dancing down the Boulevard to the bal and absolutely unmolested, an Indian full of war-paint, Spaniards, Chinese, Bacchus, everybody you can think of." The Russian artist Marevna Vorobev, who had had an illegitimate daughter with Diego Rivera and was certainly no prude, was horrified by the naked women and public fornication. There was "debauchery unlike anything I had ever seen before," she confessed. "I was so ashamed and revolted that I wept in spite of myself."

The artists might dress up and dominate the quarter during the festivities, but they usually lived exiguous lives in grim little rooms, where they worked until the light failed. Eager to escape their surroundings, they spent a great deal of time in galleries and at the offices of art magazines, in cafés and humble restaurants. In Montparnasse the cafés were crowded together on the main boulevards and the competition among them was fierce. The lively young artists and their models made them interesting and fashionable, and attracted wealthy customers. The owners, kind hearted or tight fisted, found it good business to give them free drinks. At the tolerant bar and cabaret, the Lapin Agile (the Nimble Rabbit)—frequented by Modi, Picasso, Georges Braque and Juan Gris—clients could drink strong coffee and talk till dawn for only twenty centimes. Severini recalled that the patron, Frédé Gérard, a colorful ex-fishmonger, "dressed like a pirate with a red handkerchief wound tight around his head, always in shirtsleeves, black velvet trousers and boots. Every night he sang typical songs of Montmartre or Vieille France, accompanying himself on the guitar." The Lapin's bad reputation appealed to the artists. In 1911 Frédé's tough young son was mysteriously murdered, just outside the door, by some vengeful thugs known as *apaches*. The Lapin was also the source of a famous hoax. Frédé's pet donkey Lolo, who once hauled fish and now wandered freely through the café, did a painting with a brush tied to his tail. It was called *Sunset on the Adriatic* and exhibited at the Salon des Indépendants in 1910.

A number of cheap *crémeries,* or small restaurants, catered to hungry artists and often fed them on credit. Gauguin's favorite, opposite the Colarossi, was Madame Caron's Crémerie, "immediately recognizable by the two painted-metal panels which flanked the doorway....The somewhat portly Charlotte Caron, who presided over 'her' artists like a dowager, [was] unsuitably dressed in brightly coloured floral gowns. The space for dining was tiny—no more than about ten people could sit down at one time—but the meals cost only a franc, or a franc fifty, coffee was included and the walls of the little room were covered with paintings, offered in repayment for meals."[2] The Crémerie Leduc, around the corner from the Colarossi on the boulevard Raspail, prepared its food in an underground kitchen and served hearty fare to several generations of artists.

Modi's favorite was the cramped Chez Rosalie on the rue Campagne Première. A grateful client wrote that it was run by "a Roman who, after working for many years as an artists' model, had opened, with her savings, a tiny trattoria, uncomfortable and badly equipped, where one could eat Italian food in Montparnasse for only a few francs." Rosalie Tobias felt protectively maternal about Modi, one of her favorites. They spoke in rapid, mellifluous Italian, and she prepared traditional dishes, with strong garlic, especially for him. He often paid for his meals with drawings that Rosalie used to wrap food or simply threw into the cellar. Zadkine vividly recalled that the rats, nibbling on his work, would crawl into the little kitchen in search of more nourishing food, with bits of the drawings still hanging from their mouths.

The carefree gaiety, cheerful poverty and fraternal generosity of the artist's life were idealized in Henry Murger's novel *Scènes de la vie de Bohème* (1848) and immortalized in Puccini's opera *La Bohème* (1896). The English painter and writer Wyndham Lewis, who also lived in prewar Paris, gave a much more realistic and penetrating account of artistic life in his rather grim novel *Tarr* (1918). "Paris hints of sacrifice," he ominously begins. His penniless Dostoyevskian-Nietzschean hero, Otto Kreisler, suffers from emotional extremism, paranoid sensitivity, abject humiliation, manic nihilism and demonic violence. He sleeps with his models and abandons his illegitimate children, insults his companions and (like Modi's painter-friend Moïse Kisling) fights a duel. He's "very touchy about money, like all of a certain class of borrowers," is perennially insulted and injured, and is drawn by "the bitter fascination of suffering...to substitute real wounds for imaginary." His Poe-like room "resembled a funeral chamber. Shallow, ill-lighted and extensive, it was placarded with nude archaic images. These were painted on strips of canvas fastened to the wall with drawing pins....Kreisler, a devout recluse, had taken up his quarters in this rock-hewn death-house."[3]

Modi would later suffer similar violent mood swings, and live in a series of impoverished, gloomy lodgings. He also collected primitive images that would inspire his sculpture and surrounded himself with reproductions of his favorite paintings. Modi would discover for himself the chilling effects of the exile, loneliness and alienation that Lewis described: "Paris is very intelligent: but no friendship is a substitute for the blood-tie; and intelligence is no substitute for the response that can only come from the narrower recognition of your kind."

II

THOUGH ONLY five feet five inches tall, Modi had the darkly attractive looks of the young Marcello Mastroianni and the feverish eyes of a consumptive. He dressed in a corduroy suit, a checkered shirt, red scarf and belt, large black hat and scarlet-lined cape. Fernande Olivier, Picasso's sharp-eyed mistress, admired his commanding presence. He was "young, strong, his beautiful Roman's head compelling attention by the astonishing purity of its features." The critic Michel Georges-Michel, emphasizing his exotic appearance and hot, lustrous eyes, called him "a tall, upright young man, who had the lithe, springy gait of an Indian from the Andes. He was wearing espadrilles and a tight-fitting sweater. And in his pale face, which was shadowed by a shock of thick hair, his eyes burned beneath their sharp, rugged brows."

Zadkine, who worshipped Modi and called him "a young god masquerading as a workman in his Sunday best," saw him with a sculptor's eye: "He carried his head magnificently. His features were pure. His hair was jet black, his forehead powerful, his chin clean-shaven, and there was a blue shadow over his alabastrine face."[4] The writer Charles-Albert Cingria read Modi's noble character in his striking features. He had "a very handsome face, in which slight reserve fought with amusement—in the mobile, ever-changing facial expression natural to Italians, even to Italian Jews.... His laugh was short and dry. He was a fair and good man who flattered no one. I have never known anyone so entirely free from snobbery. He was a man of courage."

Italians were considered more emotional, romantic and sexy than Frenchmen. Modi, enjoying the sexually uninhibited atmosphere typified by the artists' balls, made the most of his good looks and charismatic personality. He once wrote, in imperfect Latin on a drawing of a nude: "The insatiable fiery mouth of the vulva never truly says 'that's enough,'" a challenge that seemed to express his predatory approach. His method of seduction, according to his writer-friend André Salmon, "was to accost a girl with a certain formality, and then take her home with him, gently but firmly." His strange mixture of brooding melancholy and Latin lust was irresistible.

Most of the eager shop girls and models he slept with—Antonia, Adrienne, Rosa, Louise, Victoria, Margherita, Almaisa and Lolotte—have no identity beyond their first names and pretty faces in his portraits. Picasso had a mistress called Madeleine, or Mado, whom he'd persuaded to have an abortion, and she later had a fling with Modi. We know a little more about the girl known as Petite Jeanne. Modi painted two stiffly seated nudes of the moon-faced, high-breasted woman, who had deep-set eyes, a broad nose and thick lips. Jean Alexandre, the brother of Modi's first patron, provided some details of her unfortunate life. She "had come to Paris from the provinces and worked as a model in the drawing schools. She was one of Modigliani's girlfriends, whom he brought to [Alexandre's artists' colony] the Delta." Though not a prostitute, she was treated in a hospital for venereal disease. Jean added that "she'd had a second attack of German measles....She is totally disfigured. She's in low spirits, miserable and terrified she'll never regain her beauty."[5] Modi, in a compassionate mood, visited Jeanne in the hospital and tried to comfort her.

When he first came to Paris he was a handsome, intelligent and cultured man, lively, generous and self-assured. He drank moderately and did not smoke, dressed well and had good manners, looked healthy and prosperous, and loved to discuss art, literature and philosophy. The painter Ludwig Meidner, born the same year as Modi in Silesia, in eastern Germany, the son of a Jewish textile merchant, also arrived in Paris in 1906 and soon befriended him. Meidner praised his attractive qualities, which appealed to both men and women, and recalled that he was "at that time immaculately dressed and a good-looking, ironical, brilliant young man of 22...always lively and enthusiastic; highly-spirited, full of imagination and ever inclined to paradoxical moods....Never before had I heard a painter speak of beauty with such fire."

Fairly soon after he arrived in Paris, however, Modi's personality, dress, behavior and habits changed completely. What accounted for this transformation—from the elegant Italian Dedo to the ragged French Modi? The Parisian avant-garde was notorious for its ability to shock, for its bizarre and often offensive behavior, and he followed the prevailing fashion. In the beginning, Modi's outrageousness (as Picasso later suggested) was something of a pose, an attempt to fit in. He felt he had to renounce his middle-class comforts and conventional values in order to become a real artist. He once told Salmon, with a certain irony, "I used to be a bourgeois!" He deliberately set out to be a Bohemian and then was trapped by poverty. He chose, as Nietzsche and D'Annunzio had urged, to live dangerously.

Modi's paradoxical character made a strong impression on everyone who met him. Many friends were struck by the contrast between his personal fastidiousness and tendency to exhibitionism. He was nervous and rather frail, but also aggressive, truculent and defiant. When drunk, he always looked for a fight. His volatile temper would suddenly flare up and he'd tell his adversaries to go to hell. If he'd been more tactful with dealers and more amiable with clients who wanted to visit his studio, he could have made much more money. But, as Adolphe Basler noted, "never was an artist less interested in financial success. He wanted to stand out only through his intellect, to be accepted as a great painter, to live among people whom he astonished or really loved."

The French writer Francis Carco, with André Salmon, was mainly responsible for creating the image of the dissolute Modigliani who rarely did a stroke of work. Yet Carco also emphasized the spirit-crushing contrast between his aspiration and his failure: "proud and easy-going, he loved his art and served it passionately, but life humiliated him in every way, as if with a sadistic pleasure, made him pay for having the incredible audacity to pretend that he was born to a great destiny."[6] Zadkine's "young god" was like a prince who'd lost his crown but retained his dignity.

Modi's monthly allowance from his mother was 200 francs ($40 or £8). In those days it was enough to live on, if one lived frugally, which the spendthrift Modi refused to do. He could have had a hearty meal, complete with bread and wine, for one franc twenty-five centimes. A glass of absinthe, which he usually preferred, was half the price of a meal. A social historian has calculated the cost of living in prewar Paris. Cramped studios at La Ruche (the Beehive), where Modi and many poor foreign painters would live, were "the cheapest and shabbiest of the artists' dwellings." The minimum monthly living expenses of an urban painter were "between 5 and 25 francs for a studio, 60 francs for meals, and another 50 for drink and incidental expenses—perhaps 125 francs (25 dollars) in all. But this does not include the cost of materials—canvas, paints, brushes—and models' fees. In 1910, skilled Parisian laborers earned comparable sums for working ten hours a day, six days a week." Models, trying to escape from prostitution, earned 4 to 5 francs a session; and the artist had to keep his room warm so that they could pose in the nude.

Twenty years later, George Orwell barely survived in Paris while living on only a few francs a day. In *Down and Out in Paris and London* (1933), he emphasized the sour reek of the refuse carts and the extreme decay of his rooms. He lived on a "very narrow street—a ravine of tall, leprous houses, lurching towards one another in queer attitudes, as though they had all been frozen in the act of collapse." Modi lived at more than thirty such addresses during his fourteen years in Paris and, as if tracking a wild animal through the jungle, one picks up and then loses the spoor of his frequent moves.

To acclimatize himself when he first arrived, he stayed briefly in a respectable hotel, near the Church of the Madeleine, in a fashionable part of town. Salmon described Modi's first room in Montmartre, where he tried to recreate the clean and comfortable surroundings he'd been used to in Livorno. It had "a couch which could serve as a bed, as well as a bed with good cotton sheets, several chairs, an armchair of uncertain style, and what was most surprising to visitors…a broken-down piano covered with a large cashmere shawl.…The walls were decorated with photographs of masterpieces of various Italian schools of painting."

Modi soon abandoned the bourgeois piano he couldn't play and the homely decoration (probably a gift from his mother) of the fringed cashmere shawl. When he moved to the Bateau Lavoir—a cramped tenement, named by Max Jacob after the laundry boats on the Seine—he suddenly came down in the world. Its lopsided square, close to the Lapin Agile, had chestnut trees, benches and a fountain where residents gathered to fetch their water in large pitchers. The Bateau had a peculiar structure. The third floor was on street level; and the artists had to go down a wooden staircase to reach the studios on the second floor and basement, where Modi lived. The tumbledown tenement—smelling of moldy walls, creeping mildew and cat piss—was roasting in summer, freezing in winter and always in wretched condition.

Fernande Olivier, who lived there with Picasso, described their Spartan quarters: "There was a mattress on four legs in one corner. A little iron stove, covered in rust with a yellow earthenware bowl on it, served for washing; a towel and a minute stub of soap lay on a whitewood table beside it. In another corner a pathetic little black-painted trunk made a pretty uncomfortable seat. A cane chair, easels, canvases of every size and tubes of paint were scattered all over the floor with brushes, oil containers and a bowl for etching fluid. There were no curtains. In the drawer of the table was a pet white mouse." The minor poet and financial journalist Louis Latourettes reported that Modi's junk-shop furnishings consisted of "a couple of rush-bottomed chairs—one with its back broken—a makeshift bed, a trunk used as a seat, and a tin basin and jug in one corner."[7] He painted the flowering cherry tree in the courtyard, but children always stole the cherries before he could eat them.

In early 1907 Meidner, who had more money, was shocked by Modi's room in the place Jean-Baptiste Clément, near the Bateau Lavoir: "This studio was a dilapidated hovel on a treeless ugly piece of ground, and although it was as miserable a place as could be imagined, depressing and neglected, like the hiding place of a beggar, one always liked to go there, for it had an artistic atmosphere where one was never bored." Basler described Modi's tiny studio on the boulevard Raspail, where his possessions were even more spartan: "The austerity of these lodgings was pitiful. His furniture consisted solely of a mattress and a jug"—the sad remains of his previous dwelling. When he was living on the rue du Montparnasse, he invited the art critic Florent Fels to see his work. Fels noted that he dwelt in "the square, cold, undecorated, plaster-walled garret furnished with a sofa, a frying pan, and a pitcher and ewer, which I never visited without a shudder."[8] The reaction of his friends, all familiar with Bohemian poverty in Paris, was identical. They all used words like "miserable," "depressing" and "pitiful," and were similarly horrified by his penitential, sacrificial way of life.

Since few artists now live as Modi did, it's hard to imagine how difficult it was for a man, weakened by tuberculosis and without sufficient food, to survive and to work in these grim conditions. When living in the Cité Falguière in the spring of 1909, he had to powder the floor with insecticide to protect himself from the invasive fleas, bedbugs, roaches and menacing rats. Severini remembered that the cold in the cheapest sixth-floor room, without enough bedding, heat or food, was "absolutely murderous." Modi was sometimes forced to stay in bed when he had no money to buy coal or wood to heat the freezing room. Picasso, who was often hungry when he first came to Paris, once ate a filthy sausage that his cat had found in the street and dragged into the room.

Paul Alexandre reported that by 1908 Modi, who had failed to sell his work and was burdened by debts, could not pay his rent, meet his restaurant bills or buy paints. He had nothing to eat and was forced to rely on his mistresses for support. The restaurateurs, however, were rarely as generous as Rosalie. Cheated out of their money, Meidner recalled, they "tracked down our vagabond to his miserable abode and made a hellish row. It was therefore very often necessary in his room to talk in a low voice and, ordered by him, to peep through the keyhole to see whether such a monster was approaching."

Modi lived alone and, apart from his precious mattress and jug, had very few possessions. It was easy for him to change rooms, sneaking out when the vigilant concierge was away from her sentry box, but he often had to leave his art behind. The equally poor Severini was sometimes able to throw his possessions through the window and have them retrieved by a friend in the street, but when he was evicted from his room for failure to pay, the landlord's rent collector seized his furnishings and paintings. Ubaldo Oppi, the handsome young Bolognese painter who ran off with Fernande Olivier when she left Picasso, recalled Modi's tragicomic desperation when he turned up at Oppi's door:

> Someone rang the bell…Modigliani.
> —Oppi, buy this suitcase from me.
> —But I don't need a suitcase.
> —All I need is 18 sous [90 centimes, less than one franc].
> —But I don't even have one sou. Look, I was in bed because I have nothing to eat.
> I was on the doorstep, in my shirt, bare-legged. He'd put the suitcase—canvas with reinforced corners—on the ground and was gesturing with his arms. We looked at each other with sad smiles. Modigliani closed his large, luminous eyes, lowered his beautiful head and bent down to pick up his goods. He stood up sighing, and as he left, downhearted and subdued, whispered: *"alors"* [Well then, that's it].

Modi lived from hand to mouth and, on the rare occasions when he managed to sell a picture, from hand to wall. But unlike many other artists, he refused to support himself with a regular job. He tried to earn a few francs by selling the work of other artists in cafés or to dealers, but was turned away from fashionable galleries because of his shabby appearance. "His once clean coat showed now the marks of numerous meals and paint-brushes," Meidner wrote, "and presented the artist, who had not shaved for several days, in the most unfavourable light....It did not help that he tried to remove the many stains with saliva."9

Referring to Père Angely, a near-sighted lawyer's clerk who sometimes bought one of his pictures, Modi exclaimed, with self-lacerating irony: "I've only got one buyer and he's blind." His constant, gnawing deprivations nearly broke his will to work—and to live—and left him with both physical and psychological scars. As he told a friend in a moment of deep discouragement: "I do at least three pictures a day in my head. What's the use of spoiling canvas when nobody will buy?"10 On those rare occasions when he had enough money to buy paint, it took great courage, willpower and belief in himself to keep on painting.

III

MODI'S BREAKTHROUGH came in 1907 when he met his first patron, Dr. Paul Alexandre. Three years older than Modi, the son of a pharmacist, he'd been educated at a Jesuit college in Paris. He specialized in venereal diseases, treated patients (who sometimes posed for Modi) at the Hôpital Lariboisière in Paris and had just started his own clinic. His younger brother Jean worked for his father while completing his studies in pharmacology. Paul—a handsome, sophisticated, cultivated collector of art—had founded his own small artists' colony. He offered free rooms and studios, as well as a stimulating atmosphere, in a ramshackle building at 7 rue du Delta, on the Right Bank, just west of the Gare du Nord. Paul remembered Modi and his wealthy mistress arriving at the Delta. He was "accompanied by a supremely elegant woman, Maud Abrantès, followed by a car which contained, among other things, *The Jewess*...his sketchbooks, his books and a few old clothes." In 1908 Modi painted a portrait of his intense, dark-eyed, wild-haired companion. Maud, who was pregnant, left for America that year and was never seen again. Modi may have been the father of her child. The Bohemian atmosphere of the Delta was captured in a photo which portrays three men and three women, one of them completely naked except for her high boots and rolled-down stockings, taking part in amateur theatricals.

Paul often took his friend to the nearby music hall at the Gâité-Rocheouart and to the theaters, which Modi loved for their portrayal of life that mixed dreams and reality. In March 1909, for example, they saw two classical plays: Calderón de la Barca's *The Devotion to the Cross* and Marivaux's *False Confidences*. Unlike Degas and Lautrec, Modi was never inspired by the stage. After Paul left for the war, Modi had no inclination or money to buy theater tickets on his own. The only recorded athletic event in his life took place that spring, when he and Paul went canoeing on the Marne.

Paul's supply of drugs and experiments with bitter-tasting, green hashish pills encouraged Modi to resume the habit he'd started in Venice. Jean Cocteau, writing of the similar effects of opium, "preferred an artificial equilibrium to no equilibrium at all" and claimed "the euphoria it induces is superior to that of health." When Modi returned to reality he still had to face the problem of survival. Jean Alexandre introduced him to the editor of *L'Assiette au beurre* (the Butter Dish), an illustrated journal with anarchist leanings that appeared between 1901 and 1912. He could have earned lucrative fees by selling his drawings to the magazine, but claimed it would debase his talent and refused. Jean exclaimed that he "never saw anyone so reluctant to extricate himself from a mess." Instead, Modi sold almost exclusively to Paul, who eventually acquired twenty-five paintings and more than four hundred drawings. The Alexandre family kept them well hidden until 1993, twenty-five years after Paul's death.

Paul posed for four portraits, in 1909, 1911 and 1913. Modi began in a traditional manner, but each of the portraits became increasingly stylized, original and psychologically incisive. In the first, the tall, dashing, cobalt-blue-eyed doctor, with pale skin and ruddy cheeks, has a beard and an elegant mustache that floats off the sides of his face, and wears a high collar and well-cut blue suit. He stands in front of a framed picture of *The Jewess* and, left hand on narrow waist, assumes a swaggering Titianesque posture. In the third, less realistic version Paul, still wearing a high stiff collar, blue tie and suit, stands more naturally with his hands crossed in front of him, before a blue background and brown pillar with an incised geometric design. Instead of confronting the viewer directly, he gazes, with pupilless eyes, downward and to the left. In the final version, Paul is seated, with the spread fingers of his right hand on his heart. A brown curtain hangs on the left and the narrow vertical lines on the blue background frame and intensify his unusually elongated face and pointed red beard. In this portrait his thin neck shows above the wing collar, his eyebrows curve on his forehead and his eyes, with no whites, are pale green. In these portraits, Paul changes from aristocratic to contemplative to withdrawn behind his mask of a face, as if trying to elude the penetrating eye of the artist.

On a drawing of 1913, owned by Paul, Modi wrote the alchemical sign for mercury, a triangle and a six-pointed star, next to some cryptic lines that expressed his interest in the esoteric and the occult:

> Just as the snake slithers out of its skin
> So you will deliver yourself from sin
> Equilibrium by means of opposite extremes
> Man considered from three aspects
> Aour!

The first two lines suggest the possibility of purified rebirth; the third alludes to the balanced mean between extremes (which Modi rarely followed); the fourth and fifth, Paul's son explained, refer to the three aspects of body, soul and mind, and to a version of the Hebrew word for "light."[11] In 1909, after two intermittent years at the Delta, Modi had a violent argument with the sculptor Maurice Drouard, who supervised the colony, and broke with the other artists after wrecking their studio in a drunken rage. Though he retained his friendship with Paul, his departure from the Delta removed a stable and stimulating element in his life.

IV

MODI HAD many friends who belonged to contemporary art movements, but he refused to join any of them. Soffici and Severini were Futurists; Picasso and Rivera, Jacob, Salmon and Apollinaire were Cubist painters and poets; Vlaminck and Derain were Fauves; Brancusi, Zadkine and Lipchitz were abstract sculptors; Utrillo was a naïve artist. Other artists in Modi's time belonged to the Nabis, Expressionists, Surrealists and Dadaists.

The Futurists, for example, were self-conscious iconoclasts, enchanted with the machine age, who wanted to break with, even destroy, the great tradition of Italian painting. Though rebellious and reckless by temperament, Modi rejected their glorification of speed and chic destructiveness. F. T. Marinetti's "Initial Manifesto of Futurism" (1909) bombastically declared: "a roaring motor car, which seems to run on shrapnel, is more beautiful than the Victory of Samothrace.... Italy has for too long been the market of second-hand dealers. We would free her from the numberless museums."

Gino Severini, a year older than Modi, was born in Cortona, in Tuscany, the son of an impoverished clerk. Expelled from school at the age of fifteen, he educated himself by reading Nietzsche, Dostoyevsky and the anarchist Ivan Bakunin. In Paris, in 1906, he met Modi, who introduced him to Picasso and his circle. In *Omaggio a Modigliani,* Severini praised both Modi's character and his art: " He was a gay companion even in the saddest moments. Naturally, we talked about the artistic issues of our time, and he consistently opposed what he called 'Picasso's trick.'" Picasso shattered form, Modi preserved it. Severini noted that Modi's painting, in every phase, "always had a completely Tuscan elegance....If he'd had time to mature, it would have assumed a most elevated form."

Severini said that Modi was "the only person I would have liked to see join our group. [But] he was against such manifestations" and found them ludicrous. Though Modi was passionate about Nietzsche's iconoclastic ideas, he did not believe, with the Futurists, that nudes had to be banned and museums destroyed in order to create something new. An intensely linear artist, he sympathized with Baudelaire's assertion in "Beauty": "I hate the movement that disturbs the lines." Modi could have achieved financial success if he'd joined one of these fashionably popular art movements. As Ehrenburg explained, he was considered retrograde, even backward, by critics and collectors who admired the latest thing: "Those who liked Impressionism could not bear Modigliani's indifference to light, the clean definition of his drawing, his arbitrary distortion of nature."[12]

Modi would have agreed with Picasso who—with all his originality—stressed the importance of working within the artistic tradition and stated that "the art of the Greeks, of the Egyptians, of the great painters who lived in other times, is not an art of the past; perhaps it is even more alive today than it ever was." Like Modi, Picasso's compatriot Juan Gris also felt his work was strengthened and enriched by the work of the great masters. He believed "that the 'quality' of an artist derives from the quantity of the past that he carries in him—from his artistic atavism. The more of this heritage he has, the more 'quality' he has."

Modi's work was influenced, early on, by the sensitive drawing of Art Nouveau (which had originated with the Pre-

Raphaelites and would decorate the entrances of the Paris Metro stations), the satiric line of Lautrec, the solidity of Cézanne, the exotic nudes of Gauguin, the sensuousness and color of the Fauves, the broken planes of the Cubists and the psychological anguish of the German Expressionists. He had the uncanny ability to absorb and transform whatever he needed from each modern movement, but didn't find his own distinct and original style until 1914.

Modi first publicly exhibited seven of his works in the juried and resolutely avant-garde Salon d'Automne in October 1907 and six works in the unofficial, juryless Salon des Indépendants in the spring of 1908. Though mentioned in a review by Apollinaire in the second exhibition, he failed to sell anything, and this pattern continued throughout his life. The Automne of 1907 included a huge retrospective of the work of Cézanne, bringing the painter, who'd died the previous year, into the artistic limelight. Modi took from Cézanne the strong compositions and disparate planes of the face; the gentle bluish grays of the background; the simple clothes, rugged features and placid folded hands of his peasants. His strong-featured, ruddy-complexioned, slope-shouldered *Beggar of Livorno* (1909) has the same pose as Cézanne's work-hardened subjects. The similarly dressed though bearded figure in *The Cellist* (also 1909) bows his head, closes his eyes, fingers the strings and sweeps the bow, whose movement is suggested by streaks of white. The curve of the varnished instrument is subtly echoed in the curved chair as well as in the curved arm and curved fingers of the absorbed and transfigured musician.

Modi's two early Expressionist nudes are entirely different from his later works, which celebrate the beauty of the female body. The angular, anorexic model in *Study of a Nude* (1908) is roughly painted. Her head and jutting chin are twisted backward, her teeth show and her face has an anguished Edvard Munch-like expression. The skinny, flat-chested adolescent model in *Seated Nude* (1909)—painted on the back of a portrait of Jean

Alexandre — has a sloping, thin-shouldered body that seems too frail to support her large head, and a heavy lock of hair that flows along her back and seems to press down upon her.

The fine draftsmanship, angular lines of the face, striking color, erotic immediacy and psychological depth of *Maud Abrantès* (1908), *The Jewess* (1908) and especially *The Amazon* (1909) show the strong influence of the German Expressionists, whom Modi had first seen at the Venice Biennale in 1905. The model for *The Amazon* was the Baroness Marguerite de Hasse de Villers, a girl-friend of Jean Alexandre. She "did not like her portrait very much and recognized herself in it still less when Modigliani decided at the last moment that he had to repaint her red jacket in yellow."[13] She may have objected to the masculine dress and arrogant pose, which resembled the first portrait of Paul Alexandre. After she rejected the portrait, Alexandre snapped it up.

Like it or not, the portrait is a masterpiece. Her high cheekbones narrow to her dainty chin as her wide shoulders narrow to her waist, the curve of her sunken cheek echoes the curve from her shoulder to her waist, and a dark diamond shape (echoing the shape of her torso) appears between the sharp angle of her left arm and her svelte body. She has fine skin; large, almond-shaped, widely spaced eyes; a pert nose and sensual lips. She wears a high stiff collar and dark tie; a tawny, lion-colored, well-cut riding coat, with broad shoulders and nipped-in waist; black kid gloves and a dark skirt. The baroness, assuming an aristocratic stance and strongly silhouetted against the dark background, turns her body to the left, tilts her head slightly and looks disdainfully down at the viewer. This striking portrait shows that Modi could have become a successful society painter, like Degas' friend Giovanni Boldini. Though he had not yet found his mature style, he was beginning to show signs of greatness. His move to the Bateau Lavoir in 1906, a major turning point in his life, would lead to close friendships with some of the most innovative artists and writers of his time.

Four

ARISTOCRAT IN RAGS,
1906–1908

I

⊀ MODIGLIANI HAD charisma and charm, and made friends easily. In Paris he formed close friendships, in two stages, with many of the leading writers and artists: first, at the Bateau Lavoir in 1906; then, after his return from a trip to Livorno, in 1913. In the first decade of the twentieth century Paris was a magnet for foreign artists. The revolution in art and taste achieved by the Impressionists was continued by younger painters, and new movements were emerging. Living was cheap, artistic temperaments were tolerated, society was cosmopolitan and talk was lively in the cafés. There were many art academies, with compliant models; the Louvre was magnificently accessible; and the annual spring and fall exhibitions provided excellent venues for new painters, as well as retrospective shows of recent masters like Cézanne and Gauguin. Most important of all, critics and collectors were seriously interested in contemporary art.

Pablo Picasso and Constantin Brancusi arrived in Paris in 1904, Jules Pascin in 1905, Modi, Juan Gris and Gino Severini in 1906, Jacques Lipchitz in 1909, Marc Chagall in 1910 and Chaim Soutine in 1911. The French and the foreign artists formed two distinct groups, but Modi, with his rich cultural background and extensive knowledge of philosophy and poetry, found it easy to belong to both worlds. He formed literary friendships with the French writers Max Jacob and André Salmon, and through them established artistic friendships with Picasso, André Derain, Maurice de Vlaminck and Maurice Utrillo.

The eastern European artists—Chagall, Zadkine, Lipchitz, Pascin, Kisling and Soutine—were thought of as Jews rather than Bulgarians, Lithuanians, Russians or Poles, but Modi was always considered quintessentially Italian. He liked dishes flavored with strong garlic and ate many of his meals at Rosalie's; he was emotional, dramatic, theatrical and often out of control; he wore flamboyant clothing, enjoyed singing and dancing, loved to declaim Italian poetry and cut a dashing *bella figura;* he was also a great Don Juan. When Severini first saw him from behind on a Paris street, he immediately recognized a fellow-countryman. His speech was full of Italian expressions. Excited and amused as he watched some flirtation, he was heard to exclaim: "*Porca Madonna.*...He's going to grab her ass." Another French writer and friend, Blaise Cendrars, said that Modigliani expressed his emotions even while painting: "His shoulders heaved. He panted. He had grimaces and cried out. You couldn't come near."[1] In his work, however, Modi ignored what was modishly "Italian." Unlike Picasso, Severini and many other artists, he only once portrayed Harlequin, Columbine and other figures from the Italian commedia dell'arte. He rejected the Macchiaioli, the Futurists and De Chirico's Surrealism, and was inspired by Tuscan elegance and the glorious tradition of the Italian Renaissance.

Modi's great friend Max Jacob (1876–1944)—who lived in and gave the Bateau Lavoir its name—was born in Quimper, Brittany, the son of a Jewish tailor. The art dealer Daniel-Henry Kahnweiler said that Jacob's strange, piercing, "admirable eyes, with their extraordinarily tender quality, seemed to contain all the sadness of Israel." Jacob had been severely beaten as a child and as an adult suffered from overwhelming anxieties. At the age of eighteen he entered the Ecole Coloniale, but his training for a post abroad was interrupted by military service—also interrupted, after only six weeks, when he was discharged as a hopelessly incompetent soldier.

To sustain his precarious existence, Jacob took on a series of humble jobs. He was a sweeper in a department store, carpenter's helper and lawyer's clerk; tutor, piano teacher, singer and secretary; art critic for the newspaper *Le Gaulois*. He dabbled in painting and had once shared a room—and even a bed, sleeping in it at night and leaving it to his friend during the day—with the impoverished Picasso. He also had a sideline in magic and mysticism, in fetishes and cabalistic signs as well as in astrology, horoscopes, palmistry, fortune-telling, divination and clairvoyance, and encouraged Modi's fascination with these arcane subjects. Modi's drawing of Jacob included astrological and cabalistic allusions: a crescent moon, a six-pointed Star of David and a French inscription that read: "To my brother very tenderly the night of 7 March the moon grows larger." The hopelessly unworldly and high-minded Jacob inevitably failed in all these ventures. One critic called him an "unemployed artist, unreadable poet, exile from the coteries of Parisian life."[2]

"Short, puny, unprepossessing, and an abject coward," Jacob was a bent-over, sharp-nosed, craggy-faced, gnomelike man, who in 1906 looked much older than thirty. Fernande Olivier wrote that "he was already bald, with a nervous, evasive expression, high colour and a pretty, elegantly curved mouth, which gave a suggestion of delicacy and wit and malice as well." He wore a long raincoat with a bright red lining; and his tiny room always had a peculiarly musty odor, compounded by the overflowing garbage cans just beneath his window. Charles Douglas, the historian of Bohemian life in Paris, recalled that his room was "a mixture of smoke, paraffin, incense, old furniture, and ether. He received [guests] once a week, quite as a man of the world, a curious collection, not of friends only, but sometimes utter strangers."[3]

The French writer Francis Carco captured the multifarious aspects of Jacob's paradoxical character, which so intrigued Modi: "He was gossipy and sublime, obliging, eager, bantering, profound, coquettish, ironical, sophisticated....Max's kindness, his distinguished manners, his readiness to help others and his clever talk inclined people in the [Bateau Lavoir] to put up with him." Other friends noted Jacob's baffling "mixture of genius and ridiculousness, love and hate, sweetness and rage, kindness and cruelty....[He] could be mischievous, dirty, bitter, arrogant, perfidious, thoughtless, insolent and much else, but he also had enormous charm and a sporadically saintly nature."4

Picasso's biographer John Richardson emphasized Jacob's liveliness, learning, and elfish humor: "He was always ready to share the treasures of his well-stocked mind, his poetic imagination, his mystical obsessions and his high camp sense of fun.... He was infinitely perceptive about art as well as literature and an encyclopedia of erudition—as at home in the arcane aspects of mysticism as in the shallows of *l'art populaire*. He was also very, very funny." To amuse his companions Jacob would roll up his trousers, expose his hairy legs and do an animated dance accompanied by an absurd little song. Severini, finally enchanted like Modi and all of Jacob's friends, offered a balanced view of his elusive personality: "[Jacob] is often considered a sort of clown or juggler by some, by others a magician or mystic, and yet others see predominantly his vices and excesses....But what a refined and elegant man!"5

Jacob believed that drugs heightened his poetic imagination and ability to predict the future. In pharmacies he could buy his favorite flasks of ether for only thirty centimes. When Jacob was still an atheist, "he would throw himself on his knees when passing [the cathedral] of Notre Dame and implore: 'God, if by chance you exist, see to it that I am not too unhappy.'" But on October 7, 1909, three years after meeting Modi, Jacob had a vision of Christ (or, according to some dubious friends, a drug-induced prank) and rapturously wrote: "There was something on the red wallpaper. My flesh fell to the floor. I was stripped by lightning....The celestial body is on the wall of my poor room....He is wearing a robe of yellow silk with blue cuffs. He turns and I see that peaceful shining face."

Jacob converted to Catholicism, was received into the church in February 1915 and took the name of Cyprien, a saint associated with magic. Picasso, his sceptical godfather, jokingly presented him with a copy of Thomas à Kempis' *Imitation of Christ,* with the inscription: "To my brother Cyprien Max Jacob. In memory of his baptism." In about 1921 Jacob dedicated a poem, "To Monsieur Modigliani to prove to him that I am a poet," in which he described, in lighthearted fashion, his Catholic conversion and what God meant to him.

Jacob's inability to resolve the conflict between his religious beliefs and his homosexuality and drug addiction deepened his misery and intensified his sense of sin. His homosexual friend Jean Cocteau observed that "Max was unlucky in his love affairs, always getting involved with people who didn't give a damn about him....Max dreamed of chastity, and he was always punishing himself because he could never attain it." Marevna, who'd been shocked by the lascivious behavior at the artists' ball, wrote of her own and Moïse Kisling's sense of shame when Jacob publicly made love to an attractive boy on the floor of Kisling's studio: " 'He's cracked, you know,' Kisling said to me, with a laugh. 'He's turned Catholic, but look how he acts, the swine. And yet, if I asked him for his best coat, he'd give it to me for nothing. He takes drugs, you know. He says he saw Christ in his room, very handsome and smart. Sounds likely! If I were Christ I wouldn't go into Max's room, never fear.' "[6]

The major themes of Jacob's poetry are the pleasures and sadness of rural and urban life, and the consolations of Catholicism. His poems—racy, colloquial, ironic—avoid profound emotion and combine the quotidian with the macabre. One critic wrote that "his work is a paradoxical mixture of fantastic humour and mysticism. While writing poems which combine parody, pun, burlesque and verbal acrobatics of every kind, he lived a life of fervent piety....His most influential work was *Le cornet à dés* [*The Dice Box*] (1917), autobiographical prose poems on apparently gratuitous subjects (a pointless anecdote, a nightmarish vision, a sharp visual perception) in a brilliant style and masterly rhythms which inspired later innovators, particularly the Surrealists."

Two of Jacob's aesthetic ideas influenced Modi's art. Jacob's essay on style, first published in 1916 as a preface to *Le cornet à dés*—whose title alludes to Stéphane Mallarmé's volume of poems, *Un coup de dés,* 1897 (*A Throw of the Dice*)—advocated the use of a classical style in order to place one's work in a broader thematic tradition. This confirmed Modi's frequent pictorial allusions to the tradition of nude paintings. In the same preface, Jacob, who discussed these ideas with Modi, also insisted on the modern idea that "a work of art exists in its own right and not in relation to reality."[7] This aesthetic principle seemed to justify Modi's divergence from realism and his intensely idiosyncratic vision.

Modi's three portraits of Jacob, one of his favorite models, are quite different from Picasso's two pencil drawings (1915 and 1919) of him. Picasso's realistic, incisive works show the vulnerability, pain and sadness in Jacob's character. In Modi's bust-length portrait, painted in 1916, the gray-haired Jacob wears a curved-brim top hat (cut off at the top but covering his bald dome), black jacket, white shirt and blue tie flecked with white dots. One eye, under high-arched eyebrows, is crosshatched over blue; the other is blank gray. Modi gives him a ruddy, even ocher complexion, and captures his long, aquiline blade of a nose, the sly, evasive expression of his small, thin-lipped mouth, and his charming, dandified air. The affectionate portrait makes Jacob more fashionable and self-assured than he really was, but reveals his intelligence, sophistication and wit.

Jacob and Modi were both Jewish, talented, obscure, generous and desperately poor. Jacob valued Modi's extraordinary un-

derstanding of and ability to recite French poetry; and Salmon
hinted that Jacob (like so many others) was actually in love with
Modi. The poet described the painter as a "broad-shouldered
man, with a vaguely Dantesque profile, but short nose. It was
Jewish. His laugh was lively, clear and quick. He was usually discontented, indignant and grumbling. His face and body were
beautiful and very dark. He had the bearing of a gentleman in
rags."

Deeply sympathetic, Jacob related Modi's negative qualities
to his pursuit of an aesthetic ideal: "His unbearable pride, grim
ingratitude, arrogance; all of these expressed nothing else but his
longing for crystalline purity." He praised Modi's character and
lamented his early death: "Modigliani, your work...is savagely
cut in two by a ghost....Death came and our sorrows with it!
Your life of simple grandeur was lived by an aristocrat, and we
loved you. We're left with mourning and you remain sadly close
to us."[8]

Jacob introduced Modi to André Salmon, Picasso and other
young painters. Salmon—Cubist poet, novelist and man of letters—also had a Jewish background, but was born a Catholic, in
Paris, in 1881. His father and grandfather were both minor
artists; and his family, which had anarchist sympathies, was socialist and humanist. From 1897 to 1901, while still in his late
teens, Salmon learned Russian and served as an attaché in the
French embassy in St. Petersburg. He fought with the infantry in
World War I, and was invalided out with scarlet fever in 1916.

Salmon was tall and thin, with a long nose, equine face and
jutting jaw. The American critic Malcolm Cowley interviewed
him after the war and described his dress and habits: "a black
derby hat tilts back on his high angular head. He drinks coffee
in quick gulps, punches with his finger at the bowl of a briar
pipe." Salmon—who looked younger, not older, than his age—
was, like Jacob, an amusing raconteur. Fernande Olivier described him as "distinguished, with intelligent eyes in a very pale

face....His gestures were a little gauche and clumsy: a mark of his shyness....Salmon was a wonderful storyteller. The more scabrous the story, the more explicitly was it told....Salmon got his effects through a kind of wit which was delicate, subtle, fine, elegant and quick."

Salmon admired Modi's literary idol, Lautréamont, and (like Jacob) wrote with a mixture of simplicity and irony, realism and fantasy. In 1919 he published a long Surrealist poem, *Prikaz*, which combined classical precision and contemporary journalism, and was based on his first-hand experience in Russia. John Richardson concluded that Salmon, more phlegmatic and less talented than Jacob and Apollinaire, "was a more conventional *homme de lettres*—a little too polished and a bit of a lackey."[9] Salmon wrote two books about Modi: a brief, vague but enthusiastic account of his art in 1926, and an unreliable, fictionalized memoir in 1961. In *Omaggio a Modigliani,* he elegantly observed that in Modi's work "the dome of Florence was reflected in the Seine."

II

PICASSO—the acknowledged leader of the group—lived in the Bateau Lavoir, that floating ark of talent, from 1904 until 1909. Modi, whose ancestors came originally from Spain, and Picasso, whose mother's family came from Genoa, felt a Mediterranean affinity. Fernande Olivier, who described both of them, was rather critical of her former lover and enthusiastic about the appealing Italian. "Picasso was small, dark, thick-set," she said, "worried and worrying, with gloomy, deep, penetrating eyes, which were curiously still. His gestures were awkward, he had the hands of a woman and was badly dressed and untidy. A thick lock of shiny black hair gashed his intelligent, stubborn forehead. His clothes were half-bohemian, half-workman, and his excessively long hair swept the collar of his tired jacket." Modi, by contrast, "was young and strong and you couldn't take your

eyes off his beautiful Roman head with its absolutely perfect features.…Despite reports to the contrary, Picasso liked him a lot.
How could any of us fail to be captivated by an artist who was
so charming and so kind and generous in all his dealings with his
friends?"[10]

Unlike most artists, who wore either workman's garb or bourgeois dress—"blue or brown overalls, and peaked caps, or
else…classic dark suits and melon-shaped bowler hats"—Modi
wore distinctively Italian attire. Picasso, who favored espadrilles
and plumber's overalls, was criticized not only by Fernande but
also by the stylish Modi, who said: "he might have talent, but
that was no reason why he shouldn't dress decently." Picasso,
conceding this point, called Modi "the only artist in Paris who
knows how to dress." Shortly after, their positions were ironically reversed. Modi, descending deeper into poverty, became a
grubby Bohemian, and Picasso, influenced by his pretentious
first wife, became a respectable bourgeois. Picasso, however, famously exclaimed that "you may find Utrillo drunk anywhere,"
but Modi, whose bad behavior (he felt) was just a pose, was always conspicuously drunk "right in front of the Rotonde or the
Dome."[11]

Both Modi and Picasso loved to draw. And, as Ingres had
told Degas, Picasso told Modi to keep on drawing: "One can
never draw enough. No one has done more drawings than I
have. I recall my father [an art teacher] saying to me: 'I am quite
willing for you to become a painter, but you must not begin to
paint until you are able to draw very well.'" Like Modi, Picasso
painted rapidly and often finished a picture in only a few hours.

Just as Manet, who disliked Degas' unflattering portrait of his
wife, had cut off the offending section of a double portrait, so
Picasso, with far less excuse, once deliberately destroyed one of
his rival's paintings. His biographer Roland Penrose reported
that one day Picasso "searched the house for a canvas on which
to work, and finding none he picked on a painting by Modigliani

which he had acquired. Setting to work on it with thick paint which allowed nothing to show through, he produced a still-life with a guitar and a bottle of port." As if to make amends for his cannibalistic creativity, Picasso later bought another work by Modi, *Young Woman with Hands in Her Lap* (1918), now in the Picasso Museum in Paris.

The two artists were unequal rivals. Both were short, handsome, sexually magnetic foreigners, full of talent and energy. By the time they met the more ruthless and ambitious Picasso already had his own followers, and Modi could not compete with his protean changes in style and his overwhelming genius. Picasso surged ahead and soon achieved fame while Modi remained unknown, but each painter recognized the other's gifts. When an Italian colleague challenged Modi's angry assertion that "there was nobody" of consequence in Italy, "nobody and not a thing" in France, he was forced to concede: "Well, there's Matisse....There's Picasso."[12] He had to admit that the amazingly innovative Picasso was always ten years ahead of everyone else.

Yet Picasso's Cubism remained Modi's bête noire. Salmon (like Severini) recalled him defending the realistic tradition and growling: "I'm not having any of Picasso's little tricks." He felt that Cubist abstraction—with its tediously mechanical stencils, *papier collé* and café bric-a-brac: pipes, tobacco, guitars and old newspapers—was a complete dead end. He believed that the dominance of Cubism prevented buyers from appreciating the merits of his own work, and ruefully declared: "I am another of Picasso's victims." Modi's art was more emotional and now seems more appealing than Picasso's cerebral, dehumanized Cubist works. But Cubism was then in vogue and Modi felt sacrificed—like many of Picasso's women—by his stronger personality and his multitudinous, overwhelming talent.

Despite his condemnation of Cubism, Modi measured his own work against Picasso's and sometimes found it wanting. "Ah, that's no good either," he told the poet and journalist Louis

Latourettes. "Just a misfire. Picasso would give it a good boot if he saw it."[13] Picasso's influence is apparent in some of Modi's paintings. His *Head of a Young Woman* (1908) has the same huge hat, low forehead, prominent eyebrows, purplish skin, ruddy cheeks, thick red lips, strong chin, high blue collar and stern expression as Picasso's *Woman in Blue* (1902), which, in turn, was influenced by Velázquez. The roughly stippled surface in Picasso's *Portrait of Corina Romeu* (1902) influenced the uncharacteristically dotted texture of Modi's portraits of the wealthy French collector and painter, Frank Burty Haviland (1914), and of the girl in the painting he called *Rosa Porporina* (1915), after madder purple, a red dye. Modi's portrait of *Picasso* (1915), also painted in an atypically smeared style, captures, in his round face, what Fernande called his "dark, thick-set, worried and worrying" look. Modi scrawled Picasso's name above his head in large, uneven, black letters and added "savoir" (knowledge) as a tribute to his artistic intelligence.

Derain and Vlaminck—tall, robust men, born in or near Paris and from lower-middle-class families—met in 1900, when both were involved in a railroad accident. Fauve painters, they became close friends and shared a studio, loved fast cars and collected African art. Derain, the son of a pastry cook and town councilor, had a solid education and was associated with Picasso, Jacob (whose books he illustrated) and the painters in the Bateau Lavoir. He served in the war, designed sets for the Ballets Russes and, like Modi, exhibited at Berthe Weill's gallery and with the art dealer, Paul Guillaume.

The balletomane Cyril Beaumont described Derain's high coloring, smooth black hair and dandified English elegance: "He was fair, clean-shaven, very tall and broad, with a massive chest and shoulders and large hands. In dress he affected a broad-brimmed felt hat set at a jaunty angle, soft collar, loose jacket, wide trousers and heavy brown boots. He had the most delightful unassuming manners and radiated the naïve good humour of

a child." The art dealer René Gimpel, noting his cultivated re-
straint, remarked that "Derain has the air of a gentleman of
some learning who has studied a little of everything and therefore knows the limits of knowledge and maintains a wise man's
reserve." John Richardson emphasized his "geniality and charm,
force of intellect and character," as well as his wide-ranging interest in "literature, philosophy, mysticism, comparative religion,
science, mathematics, aesthetics and musicology."

Derain, with typical dynamism, called Fauvism "a trial by fire.
Colours became cartridges filled with dynamite to be exploded
through contact with light."[14] In 1918 he did a portrait of Modi;
the following year Modi did an elegant drawing of him, with a
huge, curving hat, angular nose and curlicue mustache. In *Omaggio a Modigliani,* Derain tenderly recalled that "the memory of my
friend Modigliani is one of the sweetest and noblest in my life."

Vlaminck's father was Flemish, and both his parents were
music teachers. In contrast to the delicate Modi, he was rough-
hewn and powerfully built. An anarchist in politics, and lacking
formal training in art, he painted still lifes and landscapes by day
and worked as a musician in a "gypsy" orchestra at night. He was
a weight lifter and wrestler, loved bikes and motorcycles and had
been a professional racing cyclist. He also earned a precarious
living as a billiards player, oarsman, laborer, postman, and author
of several novels and memoirs. His exuberant, voracious personality loved "movement, noise, sudden fierce desire, laughter,
temper, revolt and violence." Fernande provided a deft summary
of Vlaminck's obstinate character: "He was massive, with blond,
almost red hair, and a rather brutal, stubborn expression, which
made one think that he knew what he wanted. His blue eyes
were sometimes childlike and often astonished. He was very sure
of himself and he always seemed dumbfounded if he was proved
wrong at the end of an argument.... He was so strong that he believed he was naturally invincible."

Like the other artists at the Bateau Lavoir, Vlaminck liked Modi, overlooked his faults, and was impressed by his culture and intellect, his distinguished manner and noble air. He recalled how Modi, with a lordly gesture, would hand over one of his drawings to pay for a drink:

> Modigliani was an aristocrat. The whole of his work is the most positive proof of this fact. His canvases are filled with great distinction; all vulgarity, banality and grossness is excluded from them.
>
> I see again Modigliani seated at a table at the Rotonde with his pure Roman profile, his air of authority, his aristocratic hands with sensitive fingers, intelligent hands which traced in a single line, without any hesitation, drawings which he distributed as a recompense — he was no dupe — to his friends around him....
>
> I knew him when he was hungry. I have seen him drunk. But in no instance did I ever find him lacking in nobility or generosity. I never knew him to be guilty of the least baseness, although I have seen him irascible at having to admit the power of money, which he scorned but which could so hamper him and hurt his pride.[15]

Modi's strangest and most self-destructive friendship was with the tragic Montmartre landscape painter Maurice Utrillo. Born in Paris, a year older than Modi, he was the illegitimate son of an unknown father and of the sometime seamstress, circus performer, model and painter, Suzanne Valadon. The unhealthy-looking Utrillo had dark oily hair, black eyes, sunken yellow cheeks and a drooping black mustache. Like a skeleton at the feast, he provided a terrible warning of what might become of Modi, and helped accelerate his transformation from bourgeois to Bohemian. Comparing the two alcoholics, Charles Douglas wrote that Utrillo "could not carry his liquor and a very slight quantity of drink sent him crazy, yelling and shouting, breaking glasses....Drunk, he was an even greater nuisance and far more often in the hands of the police than Modigliani; moreover, Modi had charm of conversation and manner before he was too far gone, and Utrillo had no powers of conversation."

A hopeless drunkard by the age of eighteen, Utrillo would paint when prompted by wine, but suffered violent seizures and had to be placed in a sanatorium. He was beaten by his mother's lovers, by the police and by his drinking companions, who would leave him unconscious in the gutter. He was also mistreated during frequent confinements in private clinics, prison hospitals and insane asylums. He tried to kill himself by banging his head against a prison wall. But his work later caught on, he was given lucrative contracts by three galleries, and lived with his mother and her lover as "a virtual prisoner in the sumptuous house that his art had provided."

Modi and Utrillo liked to collect the dregs from all the glasses and bottles on the café tables, then toast each other as the greatest living painter. Once, when both fiercely insisted on the other's greatness, they came to blows, wrecked the café and were roughly escorted to the police station. On another occasion, intoxicated and belligerent in Rosalie's restaurant, Modi expressed his affection by pointing to his friend and exclaiming: "'either you throw out that drunk or I won't come in again!' Then Utrillo staggered to his feet and threatened him with a bottle in his hand. 'Don't come in, you know, or I'll smash your head. Rosalie, throw out that piece of trash or I'll slaughter him.'" Utrillo, in a rare, sober moment, nostalgically recalled that he and Modi would be robbed—even when they had almost nothing to steal: "When we met for the first time, back in those bohemian days, to prove our admiration for each other we could think of nothing better to do than to exchange overcoats. Then we got drunk. Then we fought. And, finally, we were found lying almost naked in the gutter because thieves had stolen practically everything from us."

Modi himself wrote only a few letters, and after his early death his friends wrote about him from an elegiac perspective. But in a rare reflection on his friendship with Utrillo, Modi commented rather bitterly on the social and economic problems of the modern artist. He contrasted the splendid lives of the Old Masters, who'd enjoyed the patronage of princes and popes, with his poor friend's desperate condition and depressing subjects: "In the days of the Renaissance, painters lived in palaces, wore velvet and enjoyed the sunshine. But when you think of the squalor a painter like Utrillo lives in, and how many hospitals he has been in, from Picpus to Fontenay, you don't have to ask why he doesn't paint anything but walls, covered with fly-specks, and leprous streets, and an endless series of railings."[16]

Modi's brilliant group of friends, drifting through the dreary Bateau Lavoir, were oppressed by poverty and sordid surroundings, but they managed to encourage and inspire each other, find their own style and create impressive work. While Picasso was the dominant and most successful artist, every one of them — except Modi — eventually achieved in his lifetime critical and financial success.

Five

CARVING DIRECT,
1909–1910

I

⊰ AFTER THREE years in Paris Modi had produced significant work and made important social contacts, but he was depressed and worn out. In 1909 he spent three months, from July to September, in Livorno. Like Picasso on his journeys to Spain, he revived himself in the soothing atmosphere of his own country. Back in his childhood home, coddled by his adoring mother, he seemed calmer, less tormented. He saw his old friends at the Caffè Bardi, painted a portrait of Bice Boralevi, his mother's former pupil, and supposedly wrote articles on philosophy with his aunt Laura—though no trace of them has been found. His brother Emanuele got him a job in the marble quarries of Carrara, but in his weakened state he found the work too exhausting, became discouraged and was forced to give it up. He spent most of the summer sculpting in a rented studio, but none of this work has survived.

On September 5 he wrote an unusually long, confident and cheerful letter to Paul Alexandre, delighting in his physical well-being and love of Italian art. But he had to conceal from his family his eagerness to get back to Paris and suffered a Hamlet-like indecision about exhibiting his work:

It seems to be too late to send in anything for the Salon d'Automne. But please send me some registration forms. You can get them at all artists' suppliers. This shows I have been working a bit. To exhibit or not to exhibit, deep down it's all the same to me but.…You will see me arrive *restored* in both physical and *sartorial* respects. Oh! my dear friend, I am re-joicing—inwardly—at the thought of returning to Paris. I sent you a card from Pisa where I spent a *divine* day. I want to see Siena before leaving. Received a card today from [the Delta painter Henri] Le Fauconnier. He wrote four absolutely extraordinary lines of nonsense about [the sculptor Constantin] Brancusi which pleased me enormously. I am really fond of that man, so give him my regards if you see him. But… you're busy, you're working. Oh, you poor fellow! Give [your brother] Jean my affectionate greetings. In three weeks I shall see you all again. My regards to your parents. At any rate, send me news of the Salon d'Automne.

He returned to Paris with a new Italian wardrobe and once again cut an elegant figure. A photo taken in his studio shows the romantic-looking twenty-five-year-old, with long, wavy hair, casually smoking a cigarette and seated with one leg up on a bench. Wearing an open gray shirt and knotted scarf, dark trousers and thick boots, he stares at the camera with a slightly uptilted chin and an intense, defiant yet vulnerable look.

In 1909 Modi also painted two strikingly realistic portraits of Jewish men. In *The Engraver Weill* the subject, wearing a dark suit and wing collar, has a broad forehead, pouchy eyes, strong nose, drooping mustache and mutton-chop whiskers. The elderly Weill looks straight ahead and suggests, despite his sagging flesh, forcefulness and strength of character. Joseph Lévi, a painter and picture-restorer, also in his sixties, sits in three-quarter view with four pale, vertical columns in the background. His burgundy scarf, gold buttons and dark coat contrast with his pale white forehead; and his baggy eyes, jowly face and double chin are balanced by his thick mustache and stern, self-confident expression. If Modi had cultivated patrons like these, his psychological insight and gifts as a portraitist would have made him famous.

Though Modi painted a few portraits between 1909 and 1914, he came under the influence of Constantin Brancusi and during these years dedicated himself to sculpture. He studied with Brancusi (whom he'd discussed with the artists of the Delta) before the sculptor became famous. When they first met in 1909 Brancusi was known only to a small circle of the avant-garde. Modi worked in his studio at 54 rue du Montparnasse, where he learned how to choose materials and cut blocks of stone. Brancusi taught him that "the work of art requires great patience, and above all a determined struggle against the medium." Like Modi, who also valued the art of the past and remained aloof from the mainstream of contemporary art, Brancusi called himself "neither surrealist, neither Cubist...nor anything of this kind. No, whatever is new in my work comes from something extremely old." The naïve painter, Henri Rousseau, shrewdly told Brancusi: "you want to transform the ancient into the modern."[1]

The fifth of seven children of poor peasants, Brancusi was born in 1876 in the remote village of Hobitsa in southwest Romania, between the Danube River and the foothills of the Carpathian mountains, a region famous for its folk art. As a boy he worked as a shepherd, dyer, grocer's assistant and servant at an inn, and could not read or write until his teens. After impressing a local patron by making his own violin, he was sent to study in Bucharest and in Munich. He then walked to Paris, where he worked as a dishwasher, sang in the choir of the Romanian Orthodox Church and attended the Ecole des Beaux-Arts. After a two-month apprenticeship with the famous sculptor Auguste Rodin, he left the master, explaining that "grass does not grow under the shadow of big trees."

Short and compactly built, Brancusi wore a gray smock and had ruddy cheeks, long black hair and the full beard of a biblical prophet. The American poet William Carlos Williams described Brancusi's cluttered studio as "a barn-like place filled with blocks of stone, formless wooden hunks and stumps for the most part. Work finished and unfinished.... [He] served us cognac, poked up the fire and then began talking of Ezra Pound's recent 'opera,' *Villon*." A critic noted that Brancusi was ascetic and entirely self-reliant: "he made most of his own furniture and equipment—his forge for heating his tools and for casting, his workbenches, brick oven for baking, oil press, and his own gramophone."

Brancusi retained a lifelong, peasantlike fear of the devil and magic spells. For months at a time he eccentrically cultivated monastic isolation and what Modi called "bear-like hibernation." But he would also emerge from his cave and give wild parties, with excellent home-cooked meals of roast lamb and Romanian firewater, accompanied by native folk songs on his violin. He had a lively sense of humor and liked to shock the bourgeoisie. He was fond of music halls and movie theaters, and played an incongruous but well photographed game of golf. Though careful to conceal his homosexuality, he later spent two hedonistic weeks in Corsica with Jean Cocteau's boyfriend, the teenaged prodigy Raymond Radiguet. Brancusi, a sometime bon vivant and roué, described an exuberantly drunken party, which strengthened his friendship with Modi but ended rather badly for himself:

> One evening some artists from the Cité Falguière chipped in to buy two casks of wine and asked some friends over. We caroused, we danced and whirled about the kegs, singing.... Someone suggested going over to Les Halles [the central market] for onion soup. And so we did, washing it down with plenty of wine. As we were all emerging from a tavern, we—Modigliani and I—broke away from the crew and grabbed one of those baskets of vegetables that truck farmers set out on the sidewalks back then. There we were, handing out vegetables to all the passers-by on our way back to Montparnasse. Things got to the point where we were shinning up a street lamp to take down a hairdresser's sign when the police came running. Modi got away, but they nabbed me and locked me up.[2]

The crucial question for the sculptor concerned the choice between modeling and carving. The traditional method, used by most sculptors, was to construct their work with a soft, malleable material like clay or wax. Over an armature made of wire or wood, they shaped and changed the clay model. Once it was complete, they made a plaster cast, then a metal mold, and finally filled the mold with red molten bronze. Rodin was the foremost practitioner of this craft. In contrast to this cautious, careful method, Brancusi and Modi chose a more bold and vital commitment to the material: the self-confident, dramatic, irrevocable direct carving. When the Vorticist painter and writer Wyndham Lewis, for example, first met Henry Moore in the early 1930s, he went directly to the point and asked: "How do you carve and with what? Do you go straight for the wood, like an African?" Brancusi, who changed from modeling to what he felt was the true path of carving in 1907—a major turning point in his career—rejected the prevailing technique and asked: "What good is the practice of modeling? It leads to sculpturing cadavers." He taught Modi that only material which had been cut and carved from beginning to end by the artist's own hand could be called real sculpture.

Between 1909 and 1912, when he and Modi worked intensely together, Brancusi produced several carved heads—*Naiade, Baroness R.F., Sleeping Muse* and *Muse*—that were influenced by ancient sculpture. They each had the essential characteristics of African art: stylized hair, broad foreheads, almond-shaped eyes set close together, long narrow noses, tiny mouths, pointed chins, elongated necks and what the sculptor Sidney Geist called "a force of personality emerging from its compact stoniness." In 1912, as Brancusi turned from human to animal forms, from realistic figures to his smooth statues, polished and purified into abstraction, he and Modi chose different subjects and styles and began to drift apart. The influence, however, was mutual: Brancusi's art was also shaped by Modi's early portraits. One critic concluded that in Brancusi's sculpture, "the attenuated grace of so many figures, the long curving necks and stylised features of the *Mlle. Pogany* and *The Princess* series, testifies to Modigliani's continued presence long after 1914, when the creative part of the friendship was over."[3]

In 1909, on the back of his study for *The Cellist,* Modi did a hastily executed portrait of Brancusi (now divided by the supporting frame). Wearing his familiar gray smock, with heavy eyebrows and shaded eyes, thick black hair and beard, the sculptor—model for the bearded cellist on the other side—looks contemplatively downward, and inward.

II

AFRICAN ART, a major influence on the sculpture of both Brancusi and Modi, had a powerful attraction for many Parisian artists in the years before the war. African sculpture, which first began to appear in France a few years after the conquest of the kingdom of Dahomey in 1893, was exhibited at the Musée d'Ethnographie du Trocadéro. The carved wooden figures, masks and ritual objects had a shocking and energizing effect on contemporary artists, who were drawn to their stylized simplicity. Archaic and primitive art eliminated extraneous detail and reduced the human form to essential lines and volumes. It suggested a way for sculptors to break away from the idealized figures and perfection of technique that had dominated art since the Renaissance. Modi's contemporary, the German painter Franz Marc, insisted that artists had to "look for the rebirth of our artistic feeling in this cold dawn of artistic intelligence, and not in the cultures that have already run a thousand-year course." Baulé sculpture from the Ivory Coast, whose style Modi closely followed, was "the most refined and linear, the most aesthetic and the least daemonic of African work." This refined art, primitive yet sophisticated, also allowed sculptors like Brancusi and Modi to escape the overpowering and now outmoded influence of Rodin. "The new sculpture," Geist wrote, "proclaimed its freedom from Rodin by the abandonment of theatricality and an accumulated sculptural rhetoric of touch and gesture, and the adoption of formal hardness and clarity."[4]

Several of Modi's close friends—Derain, Vlaminck, Frank Burty Haviland and Paul Guillaume—admiring the archaic austerity, expressionistic passion and barbaric intensity of African art, became serious collectors. Vlaminck first discovered the statues in 1905, Picasso in 1906, and they took a powerful hold on the art world after Picasso completed the masked figures in *Les Demoiselles d'Avignon* in 1907. (Carl Einstein published the first book on this subject, *Negerplastik,* in 1915.) Since African culture was then unexplored, the artists were unaware of the religious and iconographic significance of the fetishistic idols, but they intuitively responded to the emotional expression and aesthetic harmony in their depictions of the human body. They admired "the highly refined, often intricate workmanship, beautifully polished or patinated surfaces, and restrained, stylized realism." Picasso, who believed the pagan statues were both revolutionary art and protective talismans, wrote that "the masks weren't just like any other pieces of sculpture. Not at all. They were magic things.…The Negro pieces were *intercesseurs:* mediators.…They were against everything—against unknown, threatening spirits." They revealed a world of originality and strangeness, and seemed to put Western artists into direct contact with magical powers.

African sculpture, by making the face concave rather than convex, by reversing the actual appearance of the human head, shifted modern art from styles based on visual perception to those based on the artist's particular view of the world. Picasso stressed the nervousness and violence of the African statues. Modi, by contrast, emphasized the masks' tranquility rather than their savagery. The Tahitian statues of Gauguin, another important but unrecognized influence on Modi, had combined Peruvian, Egyptian and Oceanic art. Modi's sculpture fused and purified elements of archaic Greek, Khmer and African art.

Robert Goldwater observed that for Modi, "almost alone among modern artists, the primitive connoted neither force nor mystery....The simplified charm he discovers in the primitive is closer to the linear grace which the archaizing neo-classicist extracted from the tradition of Greece and Rome."⁵ Modi absorbed African art into his fundamental traditionalism. These exotic statues gave him the freedom to be highly stylized, yet remain true to his own vision.

His sculptor-friend Jacques Lipchitz recalled how Modi had passionately rejected the traditional "soft" modeling used for bronze statues and tried to rescue his art with "hard" direct carving: "[He] was very taken with the notion that sculpture was sick, that it had become very sick with Rodin and his influence. There was too much modeling in clay, 'too much mud.' The only way to save sculpture was to start carving again, direct carving in stone....The important thing was to give the carved stone the feeling of hardness, and that came from within the sculptor himself." The German critic, Curt Stoermer, who visited Modi's studio in the Cité Falguière in 1909, noted his dedication to work and artistic technique: "Just as there were times when he loved idleness and indulged in it with the greatest sophistication, there were also times when he plunged himself deep into work. He cut all his sculptures directly into the stone, never touching clay or plaster. He felt destined to be a sculptor. There were certain periods when this urge started, and thrusting all painting tools aside, he snatched up the hammer."

Gino Severini had also observed Modi's progress from painting to sculpture, which Modi considered his true calling. This, in turn, affected his portraits during and after the war:

Modigliani disappeared from Montmartre. Later we learned that he had moved [across the river] to Montparnasse and was busy sculpting. I went to see him in his new studio, another glass cage like the one he had in Montmartre, but with a nicer garden. In the midst of the plants were already some stones roughly shaped by his hand. He explained, in his typical outburst, "I wanted to renew myself completely, so...." He appeared at the next Salon d'Automne, in 1912, or perhaps at the Indépendants, exhibiting those elongated stone heads inspired by African art, which formed a basis for him to better and more completely satisfy his calling as a painter.

Since Modi had no money to buy the expensive materials, he had to steal stone from building sites and wood from a nearby Métro station that was then under construction. All his narrow, rectangular figures had exactly the same dimensions as the oak sleepers on the train tracks.

Just as portraits dominate Modi's painting, so twenty-three out of twenty-five surviving statues portray the human head. The other two are a standing female figure, apparently pregnant, and a caryatid, or sculpted female used as a supporting column in a building. Both suggest the theme of maternity. The caryatid, crouching in a near-fetal position, has one knee resting on the ground, the other raised, rounded and echoing her ample breasts. An art critic, summarizing the essential characteristics of the caryatids in his statue, paintings and numerous drawings, wrote that "they all have sensual bodies, with full breasts, well-rounded thighs and hips, and waspish waists, consisting of perfectly formed opposing curves...[and] oval-shaped blank eyes."[6]

His carved heads range from rounded spheres to elongated ovals, from those scarcely emerging from the stone to those deeply incised, from the very rough to the completely finished, from the rich textures of Rodin to the egg-like smoothness of Brancusi. Though it's impossible to date the untitled statues precisely, they probably evolved from round to oval, rough to finished. They all have elaborate and richly decorated coiffures, with one face marked by African tribal scars. The hair, straight or wavy, is usually piled high on the head. The razor-like noses merge with the eyebrows and the pursed, sometimes button-like lips, protrude from the face. The most unusual statue—which has a high headdress, large, bulging, downcast eyes and a beatific smile—was clearly influenced by Khmer sculpture from French Indochina. Modi was interested in depicting the mood and atmosphere of his subjects. His statues, like his paintings, seem mysterious yet serene.

The Russian sculptor Ossip Zadkine gave a vivid description of the technique Modi used to liberate, almost magically, the statue from the stone: "I would watch his progress, and little by little I would see the oval of the head lengthen and become reduced to sharp angles. The nose took the shape of a fine blade, bent back at the tip. The lips would practically disappear. The olive-like eyes seemed to protrude more and more, as though they were about to burst from the stone." Alluding, perhaps, to Baudelaire's "Luxe, calme et volupté" in "L'Invitation au voyage," Modi dreamed of creating a "Temple de la volupté"—a temple of pleasure, supported by "columns of tenderness." Lipchitz, elucidating this concept, recalled him "stooping over those heads of his, explaining to me that he had conceived all of them as an ensemble. It seems to me that these heads were exhibited later the same year [1912] at the Salon d'Automne, arranged in step-wise fashion like tubes of an organ, to produce the special music he wanted." Modi's work, as always, received scant attention at the Salon. A few of the heads, perhaps because of their oddity, were illustrated in the press, but there were no significant reviews and no sales.

In April 1913, after working without recognition for four years, Modi finally sold his first carvings. He was helped by the rough, burly, blunt-featured sculptor Jacob Epstein, who brought the British painter Augustus John to his studio. Born in New York in 1880, the son of Russian-Jewish immigrants, Epstein had studied at the Académie Julian in Paris and then moved to London. He was involved in major scandals about his nude figures for the British Medical Association building in 1907 and for his tomb for Oscar Wilde in Père-Lachaise Cemetery in Paris in 1912. He'd met Modi that year; and in 1913 returned to London, joined the Vorticists and created his famous *Rock Drill* statue. Epstein found Modi sympathetic, and rejoiced in the verbal assaults on his enemies: "His geniality and *esprit* were proverbial. At times he indulged himself in what he called *'engueling'* [abusing]. This form of violent abuse of someone who had exasperated him was always, I thought, well earned by the pretentiousness and imbecility of those he attacked, and he went for them with gusto. With friends he was charming and witty in conversation, and without any affectations."[7]

The Welsh-born Augustus John, who bought two stone heads, was a great draftsman and fine portrait painter. A princely figure, with impressive amorous as well as artistic achievements, he swaggered about in a large black hat and led a flamboyant yet patriarchal life, surrounded by his beautiful wife, adoring mistresses and brood of unkempt, cheeky children. In his autobiography, John recalled meeting Modi and the powerful effect of his statues: "In his less inflated moods, he would describe himself as a 'decorator.' 'I make garden statuary,' he would say modestly.... I visited his studio in Montmartre [i.e., Montparnasse] one day, and bought a couple of the stone heads he was making at the time. The floor was covered with them, all much alike and prodigiously long and narrow....The stone heads affected me strangely. For some days afterwards I found myself under the hallucination of meeting people in the street who might have posed for them....Can 'Modi' have discovered a new and secret aspect of 'reality'?"

Nina Hamnett, an artist's model and memoirist, explained how John paid for his purchases. She described Modi's ambivalent attitude about living in France, and captured the essence of his unsettled existence. Livorno seemed more appealing when he was impoverished and depressed in Paris; Paris more desirable when he was bored to death in provincial Livorno:

Augustus John knew him very well and bought two of his sculptures.…He gave him several hundred francs for them.… Modigliani said that he was tired of Paris and the vile existence that he lived, and pined for Italy. He asked John not to give him all the money but enough to get to Italy, where he could live very cheaply, and send him the money in small sums at a time. He went to Italy and, after, wrote to say that he was well and happy, enjoying the pure atmosphere and the sunlight, so far away from the temptations of Paris. John sent some more money and Modigliani took the next train back to France.

John was always attracted to the primitive, and his painting *In Memoriam: Amedeo Modigliani* (c.1920) celebrates the work as well as the man. It portrays one of Modi's sculpted stone figures— based on the long, oval statues that John had bought—wearing a black, lace-trimmed headdress, resting on a table covered with a patterned cloth, and surrounded by a guitar, a thick, leatherbound book and a pot of large white flowers. John's letter of December 27, 1944, explained his symbolism: "The book represents his Bible—*Les Chants de Maldoror;* the cactus [in flower], *Les Fleurs du Mal;* the guitar, the deep chords he sometimes struck; the fallen tapestry, the ruins of time."

Despite the extraordinary sale to John, Modi's grandiose plan for a temple of pleasure was constantly frustrated and never completed. In a heartbreaking incident that also took place in 1913, he spotted some suitable blocks of stone on a building site, and "late on summer nights he took his chisels and secretly began to carve." When he'd nearly finished the statue, he saw "the callous workmen burying his beautiful carving—that is, of course, placing the stone in its due place in the foundations. He had protested and apparently made a scene, but they had laughed, said he was crazy, and driven him away." The hardnosed French workmen didn't care if this half-mad Italian, with his wild gestures and emotional *"Porca Madonna,"* was a great artist. They had to get their stone back, clean or cut, or pay for the loss. Now, somewhere in the heart of Montparnasse, there's a building with Modi's lost statue buried within it.

Zadkine poignantly added that Modi, in deep despair, was forced to abandon his precious statues — as if they were corpses — in the wet earth: "these stone heads, which all got left outside, unfinished, [were] bathing in the mud of the little court-yards of Paris, embracing [their] magnificent dust. A big stone statue...was lying, face and stomach upward, under the grey sky. The unfinished mouth seemed full of unexpressed terror."[8] Modi had left his work behind in Carrara and would throw other pieces in the Livorno canal. In Paris, once again, he lacked the means to preserve his most ambitious sculptures.

The problem of finding a ground-floor studio (few landlords were willing to rent to a sculptor who hammered away day and night); the sudden scarcity of stone and wood after the Great War broke out; the impossibility, for someone with tubercular lungs, of moving the heavy materials; the danger of breathing toxic dust from the cut stones; the amount of time needed to create statues; the difficulty of exhibiting and selling them; and the pressure to earn some money forced Modi to give up his beloved sculpture and take up drawing and painting again. In the course of his career he abandoned carving three times: in Pietrasanta in the summer of 1902, in Livorno in the spring of 1913 and, finally, in Paris in August 1914.

III

THOUGH THE two artists never met, the tragic career of the ex-ceptionally gifted and heroically impoverished French sculptor Henri Gaudier-Brzeska (1891–1915), his close contemporary, illu-minates Modi's character, his struggles and his art. Gaudier had a slender build, thin lips and nose, long dark hair and an ascetic-looking, hawklike face. He spoke English with a heavy French accent, and had a tolerant smile, delicately moving hands and an abundance of nervous energy. Though Gaudier was desperately poor, he refused (like Modi) to work in a pleasing, saleable style. Wyndham Lewis wrote that "Gaudier, though I knew him very little, I always liked. This little sharp-faced, black-eyed stranger… lived under a railway arch with a middle-aged Polish sister who was not his sister.…He was gentle, unselfish and excitable." Ezra Pound, in a memoir of his dynamic friend, alluded to Gaudier's famous vulpine drawing and compared him to "a well-made young wolf or some soft-moving, bright-eyed wild thing."[9]

Modi and Gaudier had equally short, chaotic lives, marked by emotional intensity and disastrous relationships with women. They were bilingual émigrés: both lived in Montparnasse in 1909–10, and Gaudier worked for three years in England. Both raided building sites for materials, and had all-too-brief careers as sculptors from 1908–09 to 1914. Gaudier's spartan, gas-lit studio was horribly like Modi's. It "contained the barest of necessities, working benches, a table and a few odd chairs, and was in a state of disorder with dirt, stone dust and the appalling stench of Gaudier's less than fresh *pot-au-feu*." Both artists had astonishing virtuosity as sculptors, draftsmen and portrait painters, but endured extreme cold and discomfort, suffered breakdowns in health from malnutrition and anemia, and had to return home to recover.

Like Modi, Gaudier was volatile, discontented and impatient; energetic, ambitious and apparently self-confident; talkative and full of fiercely held opinions; subversively witty and contemptuous of bourgeois values; and had the contradictory qualities of aggression and gentleness, good humor and penetrating intensity. Evelyn Silber's description of Gaudier's character sounds very like Modi's: "he displayed precocious brilliance and an unswerving sense of mission; his chronic poverty and disregard for comfort could be seen as emblematic of his fanatical devotion to his art; [he was] undismayed by the continual rebuffs and lack of comprehension of his work, [and] his inherent qualities and disturbing but charismatic presence eventually attracted the recognition of his peers; though he sold little, he had just begun to achieve critical recognition when he succumbed to what appeared a predestined but avoidable fate."

Both men enjoyed the favors of the promiscuous Nina Hamnett, who had posed for Gaudier's *Torso* and, proud of her slender figure, like to strip off all her clothes and dance naked in public. In 1913 she visited Modi's large, untidy studio on the rue St. Gothard, noted his generosity, and was fascinated by both his art and his unusual pet: "Round the wall there were gouache drawings of caryatids. They were very beautiful and he said, 'Choose one for yourself.'...Attached to the end of the bed was an enormous spider-web and in the middle an enormous spider. He explained that he could not make the bed as he had grown very much attached to the spider and was afraid of disturbing it."

Her biographer described Nina's ambivalent feelings about Modi, whose alcoholism and poverty never obstructed his love life: "She was rather proud of the fact that Modigliani wanted to sleep with her, but she told Gaudier that she had refused him because he was always drunk and penniless....She was careful to go only once to his studio because she was rather frightened of what she called his 'eccentricities of behaviour.' However, had Modigliani really wanted her, it does not seem likely that Nina would have refused him."[10]

Both artists—frustrated in their careers, degraded by poverty and seriously ill—had volatile, often violent connections with women. The Polish-born Sophie Brzeska, whose name Gaudier companionably attached to his own, was a foreigner in England just as Modi's lover, the South African-born Beatrice Hastings, was a foreigner in France. Like Beatrice, Sophie was "angrily feminist in her emphasis on the humiliations...experienced by women in their family, social and working lives." After the deaths of their lovers, Sophie went insane and Beatrice also had a tragic end.

Modi and Gaudier shared a romantic, Nietzschean concept of the artist who, by virtue of his extraordinary powers, transcends the conventional rules of society. Both were influenced by Brancusi and by African art, and used Jacob Epstein as their intermediary. It's ironic that in 1912 Gaudier, a Frenchman living in London, should learn about the Parisian avant-garde from the Russian-American Epstein, who also lived in London but had been working in Paris. Gaudier and Modi agreed about the extreme emotions and natural purity of African art. "This sculpture," Gaudier rather awkwardly wrote, "has no relation to classic Greek, but is continuing the tradition of the barbaric people of the earth (for whom we have sympathy and admiration)....The very conventional form of the primitives, which gives only an enormous sensation of serene joy or exaggerated sorrow—always with a large movement, synthesized and directed toward one end—had a comprehension more true, more one with nature." Both artists believed, according to an art historian, in "the rejection of the classical ideal of beauty; the freedom to create sculpture based on intense feelings and [released from] anatomical accuracy."

Modi would certainly have agreed with Gaudier's statement: "The sculpture I admire is the work of master craftsmen. Every inch of the surface is won at the point of the chisel—every stroke of the hammer is a physical and mental effort."[11] In the first issue of Wyndham Lewis' Vorticist magazine *BLAST,* Gaudier, insisting on the need to seek new sources beyond Western culture, naturally included Modi among the most talented contemporary sculptors: "And WE the moderns: Epstein, Brancusi, [Alexander] Archipenko, [Xawery] Dunikowski, Modigliani, and myself, through the incessant struggle in the complex city, have likewise to spend much energy. The knowledge of our civilisation embraces the world, we have mastered the elements."

Gaudier returned home and enlisted in the army when the war broke out. On June 5, 1915, at Neuville-Saint-Vaast, near Arras in northern France, he was one of ninety-five soldiers killed in a pointless attack that captured a few houses on the main street. Pound, mourning his loss, said that "Gaudier was the most absolute case of genius I've ever run into, and they killed off an awful lot of sculpture when they shot him." Another writer, John Cournos, exclaimed: "it is hard to believe that a man so gifted with genius, so abundantly endowed with aliveness, should [die with]...his work undone, his creative secret untold." His biographer concluded that "like his contemporary, Modigliani, Henri Gaudier's bohemian life-style and early death has given rise to an extensive mythology, rich in anecdotes and in its almost operatic storyline of tragically unfulfilled genius and tormented love."[12] Both artists, loved and mourned by their friends, became cult figures soon after their deaths. Though Gaudier's life was taken in war, Modigliani's by disease, both lost the struggle to create and sell their innovative sculpture.

Six

ARTIFICIAL PARADISE, 1911–1912

I

◁ IN 1909 Modi had left Montmartre and moved across the river. Frédé's cabaret, the Lapin Agile, where Lolo the donkey painted with its tail, had helped turn the quarter into a crowded tourist attraction, and artists now found Montparnasse more congenial. As one critic wrote of the change: "Montparnasse with its new bridges and broad avenues contrasted strikingly with the winding streets and picturesque seediness of Montmartre.…The small, essentially private, bohemian world of 19th-century art had given way…to the expansive but uncomfortably public and unrelenting 20th-century [art world]."

The social centers became the Café Dôme and the Café Rotonde, both on the boulevard du Montparnasse, where it crossed the boulevard Raspail. The Dôme, which opened in 1908, had marble-topped tables, soft leather booths and large mirrors on the walls. Victor Libion, the owner of the Rotonde, welcomed the lively artists and their girlfriends, who drew richer clients to the café. He provided foreign newspapers (attached to wooden rods and held in racks) for his cosmopolitan clientele, and allowed poor artists to sneak rolls from the breadbasket, pay their bills with drawings and linger for hours over a single cup of coffee.

Modi spent most of his free time with friends in these cafés, scraping by on allowances from his family and infrequent sales of his and others' work. On May 18, 1910, the talk centered on the rare appearance of Halley's Comet, a portent that was said to foreshadow the end of the world. He wrote ironically to Paul

Alexandre: "Carissimo. The comet has not yet arrived (by ten to six). *Terrible.* I'll definitely see you on Friday—*after death* of course....Modigliani." Not patriotic and uninterested in politics, he ignored more momentous events in September 1911: Italy's glorious victory against the Turks, conquest of Libya and expansion of its empire into North Africa. In November 1912 he wrote an optimistic letter to his engineer-brother, Umberto, who'd just sent him some money, mentioning his exhibit of seven carved heads in a "decorative ensemble" (a significant achievement) and his plan to show at the Salon des Indépendants the following spring:

> Thank you first of all for the unexpected help. I hope in time to disentangle myself; the important thing is not to lose my head. You ask me what I plan to do. Work, and exhibit. In the depths of my heart I feel in that way I shall end up sooner or later by getting on the right track. The Salon d'Automne was a relative success, and it is comparatively rare for those people, who pride themselves on being a closed group, to accept things *en bloc.* If I come out of the Indépendants well, it will be a definite step forward.[1]

Prewar Paris was full of Russian students, anarchists and revolutionaries, including Lenin and Trotsky, who banded together, stern and self-absorbed. The French were discovering and translating the great Russian authors of the previous century, from Gogol to Chekhov. In 1905 Anatole France had publicly argued for the release of Maxim Gorki from prison, and French intellectuals imitated the fierce polemical style of the Russians. In 1909 the impresario Sergei Diaghilev brought Nijinsky, Pavlova and the Ballets Russes to Paris. The premiere of Igor Stravinsky's ballet *The Firebird* took place in June 1910, shocking and delighting Parisians with its explosive music and exotic costumes; the following June, Diaghilev presented Michel Fokine's choreography of Stravinsky's *Petroushka.* By 1910, Ida Rubenstein was dancing in *Schéhérazade,* and the fashionable Ballets Russes, challenging traditional performances, would become a theatrical staple for the next twenty years.

In May 1910—in this intellectually exciting atmosphere, when being Russian conveyed a certain attractive mystery—Modi met the immensely talented young Russian poet Anna Akhmatova. Both had studios at the Cité Falguière, a building named after a well known French academic sculptor who had built a suite of studios for his assistants. Young, struggling artists, many of them Jews from eastern Europe, lived there. When Modi and Anna met, he was twenty-six; she was twenty-one, just married and on her first trip to Paris. They were immediately attracted to each other, and though she soon returned home, they corresponded all that winter.

Born in 1889 near Odessa, in the Crimea, the daughter of a naval officer, Akhmatova grew up near St. Petersburg. Tall, elegant and attractive, with a striking Dantean profile, she wore dark bangs and exotic shawls. Isaiah Berlin, who met her in Leningrad (formerly St. Petersburg) in 1945, remembered her as "immensely dignified, with unhurried gestures, a noble head, beautiful, somewhat severe features, and an expression of immense sadness." Joseph Brodsky, her poetic protégé, described her as "five feet eleven, dark-haired, fair-skinned, with pale gray-green eyes like those of snow leopards, slim and incredibly lithe, she was for half a century sketched, painted, cast, carved, and photographed by a multitude of artists starting with Amedeo Modigliani."

Anna wrote dramatically powerful love lyrics and clear, intense evocations of the Russian countryside. In one of her poems, "White Flocks," she rhapsodically declared:

> Everything is for you: my daily prayer
> And the thrilling fever of the insomniac,
> And the blue fire of my eyes,
> And my poems, that white flock.

In his cultural history of Russia, Orlando Figis wrote that she "returned to the classic poetic principles of clarity, concision and the precise expression of emotional experience." He quoted her "Prayer, May 1915, Pentecost," written five years after she met Modi and during the war, when she was prepared to sacrifice everything for the patriotic cause:

> Give me bitter years of sickness,
> Suffocation, insomnia, fever,
> Take my child and my lover,
> And my mysterious gift of song —
> This I pray at your liturgy
> After so many tormented days,
> So that the stormcloud over darkened Russia
> Might become a cloud of glorious rays.[2]

When she returned alone to Paris in May 1911, after her marriage had fallen apart, she and Modi had a love affair. She embodied his aesthetic ideal and he drew her in the attire of an Egyptian queen. She often modeled for him, and recalled: "You see, it was not likeness that interested him. It was the pose. He made some twenty drawings of me," portraying her slender, graceful body and her handsome face with its aquiline profile, short fringe and hair done up in a knot. A critic noted that her memoir, which emphasizes their intuitive understanding, reflects her own character as well as his: "in describing Modigliani she describes what she herself was like — with her ability to guess other people's thoughts, have other people's dreams, to hold conversations that had little or no connection with events of the ordinary day-to-day world."

With her poet's eye, Anna perceived that Modi, despite his circle of friends in the Bateau Lavoir, suffered the melancholy and loneliness of a foreigner in Paris, and had sacrificed everything for his art. But he believed in himself and, despite many failures, had the courage to keep on working: "I knew him when he was poor, and I did not understand how he survived — he didn't possess even a shadow of recognition as an artist.... All that was divine in Modigliani only sparkled through a sort of gloom."

Modi, who wanted to keep Anna all to himself, avoided his friends but also revealed his isolation: "He seemed surrounded by a dense ring of solitude. I don't recall that he exchanged greetings with anyone in the Luxembourg Gardens or the Latin Quarter, where everyone more or less knew one another. I didn't hear him mention the name of any acquaintance, friend, or artist, nor did I hear him tell a single joke.... He was courteous, but this was not the result of his upbringing, but of his exalted spirit."

They visited the Louvre, where he talked passionately about Egyptian art. As the horse-drawn cabs clattered by, he took her to see the real Paris, by moonlight, in the old streets of the Latin Quarter. She remembered that "we would sit under his umbrella on a bench in the Luxembourg Gardens, a warm summer rain would be falling, and nearby slumbered *le vieux palais à la Italienne* [the old Luxemburg palace, built in the Italian style]. Together we would recite Verlaine, whom we knew well by heart, and we were glad that we could remember the same things." Their mutual love of Paul Verlaine's poetry sealed their love for each other. They seemed to look at the world in the same way and with the same belief in their destiny as artists. Verlaine's poems, with their heady mixture of nostalgia and torment, their images of statues, moonlight and rain, were just the sort of thing Modi might have written if he had been a poet. His affair with Anna was romantic, poetic and intensely literary, and he recited Verlaine as he'd once recited Dante and Lautréamont.

Verlaine's "My Recurring Dream," with its opposition of hot fever and tears to cool hands and stone, suggested their own guilt-ridden, bittersweet passion:

> She does understand...
>   and the fever of my pale brow
> Only by her can be cooled, as she weeps....
> Her gaze is like the gaze of statues,
> And her voice, distant, calm, and low,
> Has the inflection of dear voices that are stilled.

"Moonlight," mixing dreams and passion, also conveys the melancholy mood of their ephemeral love:

> With the calm moonlight, beautiful and sad,
> That brings dreams to the birds in the trees
> And the sobs of ecstasy to the fountains,
> To the tall fountains slender among the statuary.

Sitting under his enormous old black umbrella, they surely would have remembered Verlaine's famously heart-wrenching "Tears Flow in My Heart," with its doleful vowels and persistent rhyme of *pleure* and *coeur* (weep and heart):

> Tears flow in my heart
> As rain falls on the town;
> What languor is this
> That creeps into my heart?
>
> Gentle sound of the rain
> Of earth and roofs!
> For an aching heart
> Is the song of the rain![3]

Verlaine transformed the pity and sadness, the sobs, tears and heartbreak of love into poignant lyrics. His poetry connected art with grief (*"les sanglots longs / Des violons"*—"the long sobs of violins") and made Modi's poverty and melancholy seem beautiful, even dignified. For Modi, the poems recalled his wasted youth; for Anna, they suggested the willing self-sacrifice (for art and for others) that she would endure throughout her life.

Anna recalled an incident that symbolized their magical understanding and intimacy, even when apart:

> Once, when I went to call on Modigliani, he was out; we had apparently misunderstood one another, so I decided to wait several minutes. I was clutching an armful of red roses. A

window above the locked gates of the studio was open. Having nothing better to do, I began to toss the flowers in through the window. Then, without waiting any longer, I left.

When we met again, he was perplexed at how I had gotten into the locked room, because he had the key. I explained what had happened. "But that's impossible — they were lying there so beautifully."

Using those few minutes very well, she left the studio, but left the flowers in her place. The red roses in this fable not only flew over the gate and through the window, but also — like two embracing lovers — fell into an exquisite pose.

Modi, completely absorbed in his sculpture, did not paint Anna, who would have been a ravishing subject, but he made many sketches of her. "I didn't pose [or did she?] for his drawings of me," she recalled, "he did them at home and gave them to me later. There were sixteen [or twenty] in all, and he asked me to mount and hang them in my room at [her family estate] Tsarskoe Selo. They vanished in that house during the first years of the Revolution." Anna's biographer, Roberta Reeder, reproduces two slight sketches of her, with thick, dark hair and a thin, elongated body. In one, she's standing and seen from behind; in the other, she's seated, with extended arms, and seen from the front.

Four other drawings are now in Paris and Rouen. Two of them, more finished versions of the earlier sketches, have shaded outlines that give depth to the form of her figure. The first shows the strands of her high, black hair, the delicate features of her face and, in profile, her distinctive, unmistakable nose. The second shows her bent head, fingers, navel and uptilted breasts, and shows, framed on the back wall, a childlike sketch of a little house. The other two drawings, cut off beneath the buttocks, are more interesting. In one, Anna lies on her belly, her arm tucked under her cheek, apparently asleep. In the fourth drawing her reclining body is unnaturally elongated. A dark, curtained, slightly menacing window appears in the background and a headless man, with muscular left arm, stands over her as protector—or voyeur. Modi's cool, objective drawings contrast with the intensity of his love.

Reeder connects Modi to one of Anna's early poems, which shows that she decided to end the affair by returning to her husband and to Russia, the source of her poetic inspiration: "When you're drunk," written in 1911 when Anna was close to Modi, juxtaposes "images that convey how the everyday world was transformed in the mind of the poet through her guilty love" (she was still married to the poet Nikolay Gumylov):

> When you're drunk it's so much fun—
> Your stories don't make sense.
> And early fall has stung
> The elms with yellow flags.
>
> We've strayed into the land of deceit
> And we're repenting bitterly,
> Why then are we smiling these
> Strange and frozen smiles?
>
> We wanted piercing anguish
> Instead of placid happiness
> I won't abandon my comrade,
> So dissolute and mild.

"The poem shifts suddenly," Reeder adds, "from the speaker talking to her lover to the metaphor of yellow autumn leaves resembling flags fluttering in the wind—then abruptly returns to the speaker's feelings of guilt and joy." In this poem, the transient moment of drunken fun (Modi needed alcohol to shake him out of his somber mood) is immediately undercut by the guilt and regret that makes the lovers awkward and frozen. Anna must have had her share of "piercing anguish" with Modigliani, who seemed doomed to suffer, and could not possibly provide "placid happiness." The poem ends with her decision to extinguish their future for the sake of her dissolute comrade and husband.

After returning to Russia in 1911, Anna joined the circle of Acmeist poets and became the brightest star of the prerevolutionary avant-garde. She was later cut off from the West by World War I, the Russian Revolution and the Soviet dictatorship. But she learned of Modi's death from an obituary that compared him to Botticelli, and she discussed him with Ilya Ehrenburg and read about him in a book by Francis Carco. She later recalled, with some exaggeration and nostalgia: "I was lucky. I met him before everyone else. Everyone who remembers Modigliani now made friends with him in 1914, 1915. Whereas I knew him in 1910 and 1911."[4]

A legendary seductress, Akhmatova had deep romantic attachments with many talented men. But her life, like Modi's, was tragic. Under Stalin, her work was suppressed, two husbands and her son were sent to prison camps in the Soviet gulag, and Gumylov was executed on a false charge. She was expelled from the Writers Union, had her books pulped and was completely silenced for more than thirty years. She was deprived of her food rations, and forced to eke out a living as a translator. Nevertheless, she memorized her poems until they could finally be published after Stalin's death, bravely bore witness to the horrors of twentieth-century Russia and became the wintry conscience of her country. "Requiem," her major poem, "preserved in poetic memory the torments of a generation."

When Isaiah Berlin visited Anna at the end of World War II, she spoke of her friendship with Modi and still had one of his drawings hanging over the fireplace. The others, along with his love letters (not one of Modi's words about her has survived) were lost during the terrible three-year siege of Leningrad. Berlin admired "her intellect, critical power and ironical humour [which] seemed to exist side by side with a dramatic, at times visionary and prophetic, sense of reality." He concluded that "her entire life was one…uninterrupted indictment of Russian reality." Anna died after a lifetime of suffering, forty-six years after Modi, in 1966.

Modi and Anna met at the height of their physical beauty and creative powers, and at the threshold of their careers. Her return to Russia averted the disaster that would inevitably have occurred if they had remained together. Young, gifted and full of hope, they couldn't imagine the tragedies that would soon overwhelm them, though she later wrote that "the future, which as we know casts its shadow long before it appears…cut through our dreams." Anna was, along with Picasso, the only real genius in Modi's life. She was his ideal love—never again to be realized—the only woman with whom, despite the undertones of sadness, he had a joyful and harmonious attachment.

In August 1911 Modi's health broke down and his devoted aunt Laura decided to take him away from Paris. She planned a healthy summer holiday in the country and rented a small house for them at Yport, in Normandy. He made some excuse for not leaving Paris with her, and though she sent his traveling expenses three times, he still had not turned up by the beginning of September. Reckless, as always, about his health, the tubercular finally arrived in an open carriage, soaking wet. He'd impulsively decided to visit the beach at Fécamp, a few miles up the Channel coast, and went there, despite the downpour, without bothering to cover the carriage. His foolish behavior placed a great burden on Laura, who wrote to a friend in Livorno, with considerable exasperation: "I felt that I had made an enormous mistake in bringing to such a damp climate an invalid who calmly exposed himself to all weathers. I was haunted by the terrifying idea that I would find myself with no means of heating the house, with no means of avoiding a return of his illness.…It was absolutely impossible to do anything to help him. We left

Yport—Dedo thought, because of a whim of mine—without, so far as I can remember, having spent even a week together."[5] This tragi-comic incident shows how difficult it was to help Modi and how he hid the love affair with Anna that kept him tied to Paris. The emotional upheaval of tearing himself away from her may explain his impulsive and rather absurd expedition to stormy Fécamp.

II

BACK IN PARIS, Modi began to move from dissipation to disaster, from the well-bred bourgeois to the drunken madman. His years of carving statues had ended in failure and loss. Now, driven by his inner demons, he began the precipitous descent into drink and drugs that would ruin and shorten his life. The tradition of the *artiste maudit,* to which Modi belonged, went back to the medieval poet François Villon and included many nineteenth-century French poets, from Charles Baudelaire to Paul Verlaine and Modi's beloved Lautréamont. As Vlaminck wrote, emphasizing the cursed fate of the contemporary artist: "One is born a painter, as one is born a hunchback. It is a gift or an infirmity."

In 1884 Verlaine had published *Les Poètes maudits.* Modi, Utrillo, Soutine and Pascin—"grouped together as though violence of temper and proneness to trouble constituted a school of art"—were later called *les peintres maudits.* Modi's self-destructive drinking gave him a double personality. When drunk, the gentle, charming and intelligent man would suddenly become nasty, aggressive and violent. Like Edgar Allan Poe and Scott Fitzgerald, Modi was unable to hold his liquor and became intoxicated after only a few drinks. As soon as he got drunk, he felt compelled to start fights and humiliate himself. He drank anything he could get down his throat, the stronger the better, including *mominette,* the cheap absinthe based on potato alcohol. The highly toxic, addictive absinthe (now illegal), usually made with bitter-tasting wormwood, acted powerfully on the nerve centers, intoxicated rapidly, and could cause hallucinations and delirium tremens. Modi demanded drink as his right, even when he couldn't pay for it. When refused a glass of gin in exchange for some drawings that nobody wanted, he would emphasize the urgency of his addiction by angrily exclaiming: "There are needs which demand immediate satisfaction."[6]

Alcohol did not usually make him relaxed, congenial or content, and all his friends told stories about his drunken antics. His delirium tremens, one of them recalled, "released his razor-sharp wit, and made his lips seem to sparkle." Adolphe Basler, thinking of Modi declaiming Dante's *Inferno,* compared his cries while drunk to those of "a sinner condemned to eternal torment." The sculptor Hans Arp remembered Modi in Picasso's studio, drinking a whole bottle of the licorice-based Anis del Mono and lying "prostrate on the floor whimpering about all the savageries he had seen."

His humiliations were sometimes pathetic. One morning, after a heavy drinking bout, "he was awakened by someone pulling his arm. He tried to move but could not. It was broad daylight. Above him were standing a couple of street cleaners, laughing and jeering. Then he perceived to his astonishment that his knees were just under his chin. He had been forcibly thrust into a large ash-bin" and had spent the whole night there. When yanked out of his little-ease, his limbs were half-paralyzed, he stank and was covered in filth, and had lost his pale-blue-covered sketchbook and his identity papers. Modi professed to find it all rather funny and called himself "a god in a dustbin!"[7] A few friends were amused by his behavior, many felt sorry for him, and most were appalled by his self-pity and public degradation.

Modi's specialty when drunk was to strip naked in public, as Nina Hamnett also liked to do. Marevna described how Modi astonished the demure Anglo-Saxon ladies with his theatrical striptease and the narcissistic exhibition of his beautiful body: "Sometimes, when drunk, he would begin undressing under the

eager eyes of the faded English and American girls who frequented [Marie Wassilief's] canteen. He would stand very erect
and undo his girdle, which must have been four or five feet long,
then let his trousers slip down to his ankles, then slowly pull his
shirt up over his head and display himself quite naked, slim and
white, his torso arched. 'Hi, look at me!' he would cry. 'Beautiful as a new-born babe or just out of the bath. Don't I look like
a god?' "

Lipchitz, though fond of Modi, found him trying. He once
woke Lipchitz up at three o'clock in the morning by pounding
on the door and demanding a volume of Villon's poetry. Lipchitz
got up, lit a kerosene lamp and gave him the book. Instead of
leaving, Modi settled into an armchair and began to recite in a
very loud voice:

> Soon my neighbors began to knock on the walls, on the ceil-
> ing, on the floor of my room, shouting, "Stop that noise!"
> This scene is still vivid in my mind: the small room, the dark-
> ness of the middle of the night, interrupted only by the flick-
> ering, mysterious light of the kerosene lamp, Modigliani,
> drunk, sitting like a phantom in the armchair, completely
> undisturbed, reciting Villon, his voice growing louder and
> louder, accompanied by an orchestra of knocking sounds
> from all around our little cell. Not until he exhausted himself,
> hours later, did he stop.

Maddened by his lack of recognition, Modi was determined to
prove that the artists and the public might ignore his work, but
could not ignore *him*. If they would not pay attention to his
paintings, he would upset, disrupt and shock them, force them
to pay attention to himself. His outrageous behavior created a
personal reputation that began to swamp and obscure his art.

But there were deeper reasons for his addiction to alcohol.
As William James observed: "Sobriety diminishes, discriminates,
and says no; drunkenness expands, unites and says yes.... It

brings its votary from the chill periphery of things to the radiant core." He drank to induce euphoria, extinguish remorse and compensate for his failures. Liquor provided useful if temporary comfort and gave the illusion of happiness. He indulged in alcoholic binges in times of emotional stress—which were almost constant. He drank to sustain his morale, to shield himself from tormenting memories, intolerable loneliness and a fear of impending doom. He used alcohol, as the novelist William Styron said of himself, both "as the magical conduit to fantasy and euphoria and...as a means to calm the anxiety and incipient dread that I had hidden away for so long somewhere in the dungeons of my spirit."[8]

Yet Modi's painting thrived on chaos. As his life went downhill and his personality disintegrated, his artistic genius developed, and his patrons actively encouraged him to drink. From Paul Alexandre at the beginning of his career to Léopold Zborowski at the end, they practiced a kind of artistic slavery, stoking him with wine and whisky to increase his output. In 1913 the art dealer Georges Chéron would lock him up in a basement with a model and a bottle of cognac.

Modi had two kinds of dealers: drug and art. Sometimes, like Alexandre, they conveniently served both functions—supplying one and buying the other. Modi probably sniffed ether, readily available in the pharmacies of Paris, under the guidance of the accomplished addict Max Jacob. Though he enjoyed its hot, sweet taste and pleasing sensation of intense cold and numbness, he preferred hashish pills, which he'd first tried as a teenager in Venice. Before World War I (when meals cost 1.25 to 2 francs, models 4 to 5 francs a sitting) the drug habit could be sustained for as little as twenty-five centimes a day—about the same price as English or American tobacco. These soft, green pellets were not smoked, like opium or marijuana, but popped in the mouth like pills. In his authoritative "Poem of Hashish" (1860), based on long experience with the drug, Baudelaire wrote that the unappetizing sweetmeat, the size of a nut, looks "like a yellow-greenish hair-oil and retains a disagreeable odor...of rancid butter." He suggested strengthening the dose by melting it in a cup of black coffee. He also described the kind of artistic personality (exactly like Modi's) that would be most responsive to this kind of experience: "a temperament half nervous and half choleric...a cultivated mind, practiced in the study of form and color; and a tender heart, wearied by unhappiness but still ready for rejuvenescence."

Modi's favorite source was Pigeard, a notorious dope peddler. His house on the Impasse du Delta (next to Alexandre's artists' colony), decorated like a Chinese opium den, was a rendezvous of hashish addicts. Modi had urged Severini to take a bit of hashish to bolster his courage and to drink it with strong coffee. The drug had the desired effect, distorting reality and making everything "sumptuous and sublime." Severini thought Modi took it "to counteract the failure surrounding him when he had even lost faith in himself." Vlaminck, emphasizing the fashionable aspect of the addiction, said that for artists "the done thing was to be or at least look abnormal or strange." Many of them smoked opium, chewed hashish, and topped them off with plenty of alcohol and ether. Charles Douglas recalled that Modi "loved to be told that he was mad...liked to indulge in cocaine as well as hashish...[and] said that hashish enabled him to see and compose extraordinary combinations of colours."[9]

Baudelaire, the high priest of intoxication, did for hashish what Thomas De Quincey had done for opium. By describing its effects in highly charged poetic prose, he persuaded artists that hashish would heighten their imagination and strengthen their powers of creation. After taking the drug, attacks of irresistible hilarity and ceaseless mirth, of overwhelming languor and disturbing dreams, gave way to a feeling of "well-being and plentitude of life." The rush of mental images and the intensity of colors that flowed into the brain, transporting the artist into unknown realms of experience, were particularly appealing to Modi, who was always searching for new sensations. As Baudelaire declared: "All surrounding objects are so many suggestions provoking in him a world of thought, all more highly colored, more vivid and more subtle than ever before....External objects acquire, gradually and one after the other, strange new appearances; they become distorted or transformed....A new subtlety or acuity manifests itself in all the senses....The eyes behold the Infinite."

Baudelaire rapturously portrayed the surrealistic expansion of time and space, and the exhilarating, irresistible antidote to depression, "the pitch of joy and serenity at which he is *compelled* to admire himself." He emphasized that "hashish spreads over the whole of life a sort of veneer of magic, coloring it with solemnity and shining through all its depths. Scalloped landscapes; fleeting horizons; perspectives of towns blanched by the cadaverous pallor of a storm or illumined by the concentrated glows of sunset, depths of space, allegorical of the depths of time.... The universality of all existence arrays itself before you in a new and hitherto unguessed-at glory."

Like De Quincey, Baudelaire vividly described the appalling nightmares and increasingly negative effects of the drug, as well as the difficulty on the "terrible morrow" of creating art while under its influence. The hashish-eater experiences "a sensation of chilliness in the extremities...and a great weakness in all the members. In your head, and throughout your being, you feel an embarrassing stupor and stupefaction....All the body's organs [are] lax and weary, nerves unstrung; [there are] itching desires to weep, the impossibility of applying oneself steadily to any task. It is in the nature of hashish to weaken the will."[10] Lured by the prospect of delightful sensations, Modi forgot about the aftereffects. While the visions lasted, it was impossible for him to paint; when he returned to a normal state, the wondrous visions had vanished. The hashish did not help his work, and certainly undermined his already frail health.

Italian friends who were visiting Paris and had not seen Modi for several years were horrified by his dramatic physical decline and his change of temperament, from charming geniality to sarcastic bitterness. In 1912 Anselmo Bucci heard him, like a ghoulish character out of Poe, proclaim his own appalling failure: "We found Modigliani at the Café de la Rotonde, where he practically lived; he was dead drunk as usual....He came forward, dirty, with a foul breath, glazed eyes. He was laughing, with a sardonic, monotonous simper. He was laughing, running his hands through his battered curls and showing his black teeth.... 'It appears that I am one of Picasso's victims!' he kept on saying." At about the same time Ardengo Soffici, who'd known Modi as a promising art student in Venice in 1904, felt the Bohemian persona had collapsed and that he now reeked of decay: "Dressed in extreme disorder, the shirt unbuttoned and the neck bare, the hair ruffled and the eyes staring and febrile, he seemed obsessed. His face, once so beautiful and clear, had become hard, tormented, violent; his sensual mouth was twisted into a bitter, mocking smile, and the words he spoke were vague and full of sadness."

In 1914 Carlo Carrà, who noticed Modi's feverish disease, "was particularly struck by the deterioration in his physical condition. His eyes were ablaze, his mouth set in a bitter twist. Untreated tuberculosis and alcohol abuse had ravaged his face." At the end of that year, his brother Emanuele, a Socialist member of parliament who was opposed to Italy entering the war, visited Modi in Paris. He was terribly upset to see his brother's condition and blamed it on his dissolute companions at the Rotonde.

A bright photograph, taken by Jean Cocteau on August 12, 1916, captured Modi and his close friends. The sinister-looking Max Jacob—small, bald, wearing a pince-nez and absorbed in a thin volume (perhaps his own)—sits on a park bench in a deserted street. Seated next to him, the burly, long-haired, thick-lipped Ortiz de Zarate smokes a pipe, leans on a walking stick and gazes at Jacob. The tall, horse-faced André Salmon, leaning on the back of the bench, peers over Jacob's shoulder and down at his book. All three are neatly dressed in summer suits. Modi, by contrast — standing next to Jacob, smoking a cigarette and staring straight at the camera — is shabbily dressed. He wears a crumpled black velour hat, ragged tie, shirt with its collar points bent upward and a badly wrinkled, ratty-looking linen jacket whose bulging pocket may contain a copy of his constant companion, *Les Chants de Maldoror*. His eyes are shadowed by the hat and his enigmatic smile seems slightly forced.[11]

When Lipchitz, disturbed by Modi's crazy behavior and chaotic existence, "began to urge him to be less self-destructive and to put some kind of order into his life, he became [as] angry as I've ever seen him." It was, as his Aunt Laura had said, "absolutely impossible to do anything to help him." Why did Modi refuse to heed the pleas and warnings of his friends? Between Anna's departure in 1911 and his relationship with Beatrice Hastings in 1914, Modi, cut adrift from the anchor of women, declined dramatically. Deracination and exile (as Anna perceived) made him a perpetual outsider. The *maudit* tradition and the Parisian milieu offered too many temptations and too much freedom. He had come to rely on drink and drugs to stimulate his creativity, but they inevitably took away the disciplined routine he needed to get his work done.

Modi lacked recognition not only from the public and the critics, but also from many of his fellow artists. They resented his stubborn independence, and thought his work was too traditional, even reactionary. Accustomed from childhood to middle-class comforts, he felt degraded by his exiguous way of life and was compelled to punish, even destroy himself for his failures. When they became successful, artists nostalgically remembered the days when they were poor. Modi, who never became successful, felt bitter about his humiliating poverty. Picasso wanted to live like a poor man, but with a lot of money; Modi, his "victim," had to live like a poor man with no money at all. As he saw it, friends like Picasso, with his "little tricks," achieved astonishing success, while he was tortured by constant failure.

Modi had sworn, "you will see, Mama, that in the end I shall give you more than the others."[12] He wanted to honor her with his paintings and repay her for all the love she had given him and all the care she had taken when he was ill. He was now forced to admit that he'd disappointed the family who'd supported him for so many years and would never fulfill his promise. He was often in pain, lacked medical treatment, knew he had an incurable disease and believed he would die young. Like the *artistes maudits,* he chose to have a brief but intense life.

In the winter of 1912 Modi became seriously ill, collapsed and went into hospital. In mid-April 1913, when he was well enough to travel, he returned to Livorno, as he'd done in 1909, to recover in the protective warmth of his family. The once-proud Modi, his thick black hair cropped in the hospital, now reeked of failure. A friend, shocked by his tattered appearance, recalled: "His head was shaven like that of an escaped convict, and more or less covered with a small cap with the visor torn off. He was wearing a miserable linen jacket and open shirt, and his trousers were held up by a string tied around his waist. He said that he had come back to Leghorn for the sake of the *torta de ceci* [chickpea tart, a local specialty] and to get some more of those convenient and comfortable shoes."

On April 23, a week after he arrived, he asked Paul Alexandre to collect one of his statues from Brancusi's studio and keep it safe in his own home. As usual in his letters, he was upbeat about his prospects, and was enthusiastic about his plan to work, as he'd done in 1902 and 1909, in a village near Carrara:

My dear Paul, a favour—go to the Serbo-Croat's [Brancusi], fetch the head and take it to the av. Malakoff and look after it for me. Drop me a line when this is done. Fulfilment is on its way. The keystone won't have been placed in the arch till

I have done another fortnight's work. . . . I will do everything in marble. The village near where I shall quite literally pitch my tent—a tent for shelter—has dazzling light and air of the most luminous clarity imaginable. Very best regards to you while waiting to hear from you and to write again to you. Modigliani. Received *Maldoror* with thanks. I shall send you photos.

It's a great pity that Modi, dedicated to sculpture during his two trips to Livorno, never recorded his affection for his family by painting their portraits. The family wanted him to stay nearby and get well. Emanuele had found what seemed to be an ideal place for him to rest and work: a small house, surrounded by a garden, with plenty of marble nearby. At first Modi seemed pleased with the idea, but then became agitated. After looking at it, he suddenly changed his mind and told his brother: "Yes, yes. You are right, it's all true, but this place is not for me. It's too remote. I can't stand that. I need a big city to be able to work."[13] His family did their best to rescue him from his way of life, but lost the struggle. He had to have the excitement of Paris, the conversation of friends, the stimulation of drugs, the proximity to the abyss.

On June 23, 1913, just before leaving Livorno after a three-month stay and returning to Paris, Modi sent Alexandre two small sculpted heads (not included in Alexandre's catalogue of drawings) as samples of his current work. He also wrote: "My dear Paul. Soon I shall be back in Paris. I am sending you at av. Malakoff two little pieces of marble as *advance scouts*. I am paying all the costs here but if by chance there were a few centimes to pay, you can be sure to be reimbursed on my return. I won't say much more about it, as we shall soon have the pleasure of talking to each other again in person. In all friendship. Modigliani."

Jean Alexandre died of tuberculosis, aged twenty-six, in 1913. When war broke out in 1914 Paul Alexandre enlisted, served in the medical corps for the next five years and did not return permanently to Paris until May 1919. Though the two friends were not as close in 1912–14 as they had been during the early years of their friendship, it's surprising that they never met again after the war. Modi's postcard to Paul, sent from Italy on May 6, 1913, defined himself, with poetic perception, as a melancholy angel. His resentment of his benefactor suggests that they may have parted on bad terms: "Toady and friend. Happiness is a grave-faced angel. The resuscitated man."[14] This new-born man, like Modi himself, now felt more able to lead an independent life.

When Paul came back to Paris he readjusted to civilian life and resumed his medical practice, but did not contact his old friend. He might have found it hard to track down Modi, who was constantly on the move, and may have been put off by his notorious reputation. Despite new patrons, Modi had had a very hard time, and was too proud to search for Paul. He didn't want to acknowledge his failure to serve in the war or to achieve artistic success.

The small heads he sent to Alexandre were, unfortunately, all that survived from his carvings in Livorno. According to one story, his Italian friends, jealous perhaps of his exciting life in Paris while they remained stuck in the provinces, condemned his strange stone carvings. On a dare, he put them in a wheelbarrow, pushed them over the high walls of the old canal and dumped them into the Fosso Reale, which curved around the original town of Livorno. If nobody wanted his artistic creations, he preferred to destroy them—painful as it was—in a theatrical gesture of symbolic infanticide.

Seven

JEWS IN PARIS, 1913

I

﹖ MODIGLIANI, whose family had lived in Spain, France and Italy, was a Sephardic Jew and a son of the Mediterranean. His charm and sociability (when sober) were thoroughly Italian, but his Marseillaise mother gave him a knowledge of France that led many acquaintances to assume he was French. Living in xenophobic and anti-Semitic Paris heightened his consciousness of being Italian and Jewish. Yet he was not a "Jewish" painter: he had the cultural background of a secular Jew, but was heir to the art of classical Rome, Renaissance Tuscany and modern Italy.[1] As he got to know the group of Jewish artists, Ashkenazi émigrés from eastern Europe and Russia who also lived in Montparnasse, he better understood what it meant to be a Jew, and formed a close bond with the poverty-stricken and half-crazy painter Chaim Soutine.

Modi was assimilated and appeared at ease in France. But his Jewishness was intensely valuable to him, and the disdain and persecution meted out to Jews were never very far from his mind. He identified with Rembrandt, a contemporary of Spinoza in Amsterdam, who painted many fine portraits of Jews. Jacob Epstein wrote that "Modigliani was intensely proud of his Jewish origin, and would contend with absurd vehemence that Rembrandt must have been Jewish on account of his profound humanity." The Russian-Jewish writer Ilya Ehrenburg recalled two examples of Modi's conversation that revealed his knowledge of Jewish poetry and Italian history: "Modi read me some sonnets in Italian by Emanuele Romano, a Jewish poet of the fourteenth century [and contemporary of Dante]: mocking, bitter poems that were nevertheless full of the love of life." He also told the story of how in the fifteenth century the Romans had celebrated carnival by having a Jew stripped naked, mocked by the crowd and "forced to run three times around the city."

In 1906, the year Modi arrived in Paris, Captain Alfred Dreyfus, a Jew who been falsely accused and convicted of treason in 1894, was exonerated and restored to his army rank. Modi was shocked by anti-Semitism, almost unknown in Livorno but then rampant in France. To most friends, both Gentile and Jewish, he went out of his way to emphasize his Jewish identity. Augustus John wrote that "on one occasion Modi, feeling low, complained a little of his lot, with an allusion to racial prejudice. I said 'So, it's wretched to be a Jew?' 'Yes,' replied Modi, 'it's wretched,' but Jacob Epstein exploded in violent dissent."[2] Epstein, living in England, did not fully understand what Modi was up against.

According to Louis Latourettes' frequently repeated story, Modi, while dining with friends in a Parisian restaurant, overheard a group of noisy young Royalists pounding the table, shouting virulent anti-Semitic slogans, and lamenting the betrayal of France by Dreyfus and the rest of the Jews. Suddenly, he became furious. He jumped to his feet, rushed to the table and stood over the group. Shaking with rage, he screamed: *"Je suis juif et je vous emmerde"* (I am a Jew and I shit on you). Stunned and cowed by his ferocious anger, the Royalists backed down, changed the subject and soon left. The story seems convincing enough about Modi's impulsive behavior when drunk, but its triumphant outcome is no doubt mythical.

Modi informed another Italian painter, Anselmo Bucci, of his race and religion. He mentioned it to stress the comparative freedom of Jews in Italy and his close ties, despite their physical distance, to the family that continued to support him:

> "I'm Jewish you know," [Modi] declared.
>
> "I had never thought about it."
>
> "It's true. In Italy, there is no Jewish question. I'm Jewish, and you know the family bond we have among us. I can say that I have never been destitute, my family has always helped me. Even if the money order was for five francs, they have never abandoned me."

With women he could be confrontational or brazen, but never shy, about his origins. He once offhandedly said to Anna Akhmatova, in case it hadn't occurred to her: "I forgot to tell you that I'm Jewish." On his first meeting with Nina Hamnett in Rosalie's restaurant, he dramatically and very oddly declared himself in both French and English, as if daring her to reject either him or his low-priced work: "Suddenly the door opened and in came a man with a roll of newspaper under his arm. He wore a black hat and a corduroy suit. He had curly black hair and brown eyes and was very good looking. He came straight up to me and said, pointing to his chest, *'Je suis Modigliani, Juif, Jew,'* unrolled his newspaper, and produced some drawings. He said, *'Cinq francs.'* They were very curious and interesting, long heads with pupil-less eyes. I thought them very beautiful. Some were in red and blue chalk. I gave him five francs and chose one of a head in pencil." When the drunken Modi exhibited himself as well as his art by stripping naked in public, there was an extra surprise and shock: unlike most French men, he was circumcised.

Despite his secular life, Modi clung to some remnants of Jewish ritual. Though he never had running water in his squalid rooms, he told the art dealer Paul Guillaume that "it was a Jewish practice, standing up, to wash oneself as completely as possible and that rinsing the mouth with cold water made one lucid."[3] Charles Douglas recorded another operatic and strangely moving scene. Stressing his bond with the self-destructive Maurice Utrillo and with Utrillo's mother (and Modi's mother-substitute), Suzanne Valadon, Modi once "informed the whole restaurant that Valadon was the only woman who understood him, because she had had such a lot of trouble with Utrillo.... After a few drinks he began to sing the 'Lamento,' a Jewish dirge, which depressed the company, although nobody dared protest. He finished the lament sobbing on Valadon's shoulder." When Modi wanted to mourn his own miserable failures, he sang Kaddish, a prayer for the dead, as if anticipating his own death.

Like many secular Jews, Modi was ambivalent about his background. Léon Indenbaum, a Russian-Jewish sculptor whose portrait Modi painted, wrote that Modi, desperate for recognition, was proud of a newspaper story in a Yiddish newspaper. Since he couldn't read the Hebrew letters, a friend must have translated it for him. "One evening he took a newspaper out of his pocket. He read, in *Yiddish,* an article praising him. He was visibly moved, folded the paper and put it back in his pocket." On other occasions, as if to deflect hostility, he pretended to be the usurious Jew of folklore: "'I am the son and grandson of bankers,' he proclaimed. (He added, smiling, 'Jewish bankers')." When Picasso, offering him a 100-franc note to repay a small debt, said, "'here is the five francs I owe you,' Modi crumpled [it] and laughed. 'Thanks,' he said, 'but as I'm a Jew I'll keep the change.'"[4]

Paul Guillaume's statement that Modi "liked to think of himself and his art as Jewish," is misleading, and has been taken up by critics who wish to claim (and limit) him as a Jewish artist. In this respect there's a deep divide between the man and his art, between "liked to think" and actually was. In the catalogue of a recent exhibition of Modi's art at the Jewish Museum in New York, Emily Braun recycled some unconvincing clichés that could easily apply to many other artists: "Critics frequently read 'Jewish' content in details of his close family ties, his melancholic

disposition, the sensuality of his nudes, and his respectful adoration of women." Modi was the first Jewish artist, not simply of
modern times, but of all time, to paint sensuous nudes, so that
they cannot be called characteristically Jewish. "Respectful adoration" is exactly the opposite of his attitude toward his casual
mistresses and the most important women in his life: Beatrice
Hastings, Simone Thiroux and Jeanne Hébuterne.

Another critic, Mason Klein, wrote that in Modigliani "the inability of Jews to escape their condition...is given literal, formal,
and symbolic expression: literally, in the case of the caryatid
locked in its column; formally, as in the 1915 *Portrait of Juan Gris,*
with the embrace of elemental geometric forms within whose
deceptively simple universality the artist introduces the speci-
ficity of the individual; and symbolically, in Modigliani's real-life
assumption of the role of pariah."[5] But this interpretation is unconvincing: *all* caryatids are locked in their columns; Juan Gris,
a Gentile, is a poor subject to represent Jewish art; and the Gentile Utrillo was just as much a pariah as Modi. This catalogue
overstates Modi's artistic debt to Judaism. His work has significant Christian elements, and almost no Jewish content. In this
sense, Rembrandt was much more of a "Jewish" artist than
Modigliani.

In fact, the emotional power of Modi's stone caryatid comes
from images of Christ bent under the weight of the cross on the
Via Dolorosa; and the drooping heads in many of his portraits
recall the dead Christ in the descent from the cross. A series of
1916 drawings inspired by the Italian Renaissance as well as by the
recent Catholic convert, Max Jacob, portray specifically Christian
figures, some of them kneeling with clasped hands: *Young Man
in Prayer, The Monk in Prayer,* the tonsured *Ecstatic;* the naked
Léopold Zborowski as *St. John the Baptist* (a voice preparing the
way for Modi, but also crying in the wilderness), *Beata Matrix*
(Blessed Mother of God, with a satiric allusion to Beatrice Hastings), *Virgin and Child; The Crucifixion* (with "Christ" in Greek let-

ters on the drawing), two *Dies Irae, Dies Illae* (Days of Wrath, or Judgment Day) and *Purgatorius Animus* (Soul in Purgatory).

Modigliani's work does contain some specifically Jewish imagery. In a 1913 drawing owned by Paul Alexandre, he transcribed the word "aour," for "or," which means "light" in Hebrew. Alexandre's drawing, as well as the *Head of Woman* (1915) and *The Young Rabbi* (1917), include the Star of David. Modi wrote Hebrew words, probably copied from a printed text, on *The Young Rabbi* and on the 1916 drawing of the Ukrainian-Palestinian sculptress, Chana Orloff. The rabbi's first two names, in Hebrew, are "Yehoshua Yoram"; the words on the drawing of Chana mean "Chana, the daughter of Raphael."[6]

As for paintings of Jewish subjects, besides the early portraits of *The Engraver Weill* and *Joseph Lévi,* whose names suggest they were Jewish, Modi did two portraits in 1908 of the same model, called *The Jewess.* These were his versions of Goya's *Naked Maja* and *Clothed Maja.* The dressed, seated, long-nosed, thick-lipped woman wears a high-crowned purple and green hat that covers most of her hair. The Fauvist stripes of green color in her eyes and on her pale sallow face emphasize her cadaverous look and sullen expression. The half-length, standing nude wears the same large, tilted, saucer-shaped black hat and has thick dark hair, heavy eyebrows and beady eyes. Modi grotesquely exaggerates her nose, mouth and chin as well as her enormous, sagging breasts. Both portraits, the fierce-looking clothed woman and the brutally sensual naked one, are ugly and repulsive. At best, they seem to suggest dislike or disgust with the model; at worst, Jewish self-hatred.

II

IN THE YEARS before the war, the first truly international group of painters in France, known as the Ecole de Paris, lived and worked in Montparnasse. Modi befriended artists from Spain, Italy, Germany, Romania, Mexico and Japan, as well as

from eastern Europe. Among the Jewish artists, he was ac-
quainted with Marc Chagall, Léon Indenbaum, Pinchus Kremegne, Elie Nadelman and Chana Orloff; his closest friends
were Ossip Zadkine, Jacques Lipchitz, Jules Pascin, Moïse
Kisling and Chaim Soutine.

Assimilated Italian Jews felt equal to or even intellectually superior to their Christian neighbors, while poor eastern European
Jews, confined to the ghetto, living in remote villages or *shtetls,*
and victims of persecution, often felt distinctly inferior. They
spoke Hebrew in the synagogue, Yiddish at home, Russian or
Polish in their village or town. The men wore untrimmed beards,
long black caftans and wide-brimmed velvet hats; the women
kept kosher kitchens. They went weekly to the bathhouse, sent
their children to Hebrew school and arranged their marriages.
They respected the rabbi, worshipped on the Sabbath and observed the Jewish holidays. Such closed communities, bound by
the rituals of Orthodox religion, tried to shut themselves off
from the outside world.

Marc Chagall, whose grandfather was a butcher in Russia,
described the ritual slaughterer who followed the Mosaic law
and killed suitable animals according to Talmudic prescription.
Chagall remembered it as an event that combined the sacred
and spiritual with the sight and smell of spurting blood: "One
scarcely hears the prayer as, drawing taut [the cow's] neck, he
plunges the blade into her throat. Pools of blood...jets of fat
and blood...rosecolored blood" quickly filled the basins held
out to receive it. More blood was spilled when Cossacks with
drawn swords rampaged through the village and slaughtered
every Jew they could find. These Jews, as Kenneth Silver said,
were "endemically poor, implicitly segregated, paranoid before
Gentile sensibility, fearful of pogrom, and religiously orthodox
and conservative."[7] Though most of Modi's friends did not
grow up in the poverty of a *shtetl,* that experience was part of
their cultural heritage and had bitten into their souls. Even

Eugenia Modigliani, mother.
Klüver/Martin Archive

Emanuele Modigliani, brother, 1908.
Archivio Centrale dello Stato, Rome

Modi with nursemaid, c.1886.
Klüver/Martin Archive

Modi with slight beard, 1901.
Klüver/Martin Archive

Modi with long cravat, c.1908.
Klüver/Martin Archive

Anna Akhmatova, 1920s. Anna Akhmatova
Museum, St. Petersburg

Modi seated in his studio, 1915.
Klüver/Martin Archive

Beatrice Hastings, 1922, photo by Man Ray.
Artists Rights Society, New York

Modi, Max Jacob, André Salmon and Ortiz de Zarate, Paris, August 12, 1916, photo by Jean Cocteau. Artists Rights Society, New York

Modi with hands on hips, 1917. Klüver/Martin Archive

Modi in his studio with foot on bench, 1918. Klüver/Martin Archive

Jeanne Hébuterne, 1919. Klüver/Martin Archive

Modi in profile, seated in front of Japanese screen, 1919. Klüver/Martin Archive

Paul Alexandre, 1909. Collection of Yamazaki Mazek Corporation, Japan

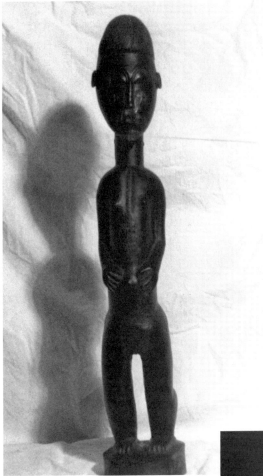

Baulé statue, Ivory Coast.
Jeffrey Meyers Collection,
Berkeley, California

Head, 1911–13,
Solomon Guggenheim Museum,
New York

The Amazon, 1909.
Mrs. Alexander Lewyt

Max Jacob, 1916.
Kunstsammlung
Nordrhein-Westphalia,
Düsseldorf

Jacques Lipchitz and His Wife,
1917. Art Institute, Chicago

Bride and Groom,
1915. Landau Fine
Art, Montreal,
Canada

Moïse Kisling, 1915. Pinacoteca di Brera, Milan

Chaim Soutine, 1915. Staatsgalerie, Stuttgart

Paul Guillaume, 1915. Réunion des Musées Nationaux/Art Resource, New York

Beatrice Hastings as *Madam Pompadour*, 1915. Art Institute, Chicago

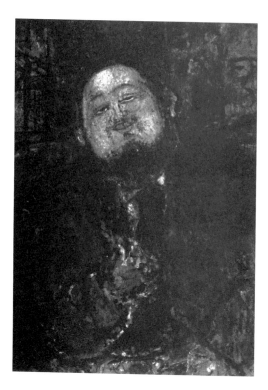

Diego Rivera, 1914.
Kunstsammlung
Nordrhein-Westphalia,
Düsseldorf

Jean Cocteau, 1916.
Princeton University Art
Museum, Princeton,
New Jersey

Léon Bakst, 1917.
National Gallery of Art,
Washington, D.C.

Léopold Zborowski, 1919.
Museu de Arte de São Paulo Assis
Chateaubriand, Brazil

Lunia Czechowska with a Fan, 1919.
Musée d'Art Moderne de la Ville
de Paris

Seated Nude, 1916.
Courtauld Institute of Art Gallery,
London

Simone Thiroux as *Girl in a Green Blouse*, 1917. National Gallery of Art, Washington, D.C.

Jeanne Hébuterne, 1918. Norton Simon Art Foundation, Pasadena, California

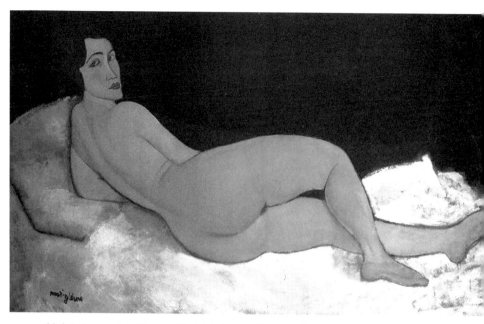

Nude Reclining on Left Side, 1917. Christie's Images, Private Collection

Gipsy Woman with Baby, 1919.
National Gallery of Art,
Washington, D.C.

Crouching Nude, 1917.
Koninklijk Museum voor Schone
Kunsten, Antwerp

Self-Portrait with Palette, 1920.
Museu de Arte Contemporânea da
Universidade de São Paulo, Brazil

Nude with Eyes Closed and Necklace, 1917. Solomon Guggenheim Museum, New York

those who'd left for the city carried the indelible memory of *shtetl* life.

The eastern European Jewish artists came from an austere religion, rich in Hebrew text and theology, but which, like Islam, proscribed graven images. They created splendid decorative arts, but had almost no pictorial or sculptural tradition. Modigliani had been born into a rich artistic culture; they had to invent one. Jews with artistic ambitions had a special reason to escape the *shtetl* and ghetto. Chagall recalled that "in our house there wasn't a single painting, not a single engraving on the walls.... At Vitebsk up to 1906 I had never in my life seen drawings or paintings." The Jewish artists who came to France (including the Impressionist Camille Pissarro) created more painting and sculpture in the twentieth century than all the painting and sculpture that Jews had produced since biblical times.

Unlike Modigliani, the eastern Europeans looked and behaved like foreigners. His friends spoke ungrammatical French with heavy Slavic accents and were outsiders by virtue of their poverty, religion and Bohemian way of life. (Max Jacob and Constantin Brancusi were also homosexual.) Many of them first came to Paris as lonely teenagers and formed their own distinct, protective group. At the turn of the century, when the Salons as well as the patronage of Church and State were beginning to be replaced by art dealers, most of the Jewish artists — except Modi — were taken up by Jewish dealers: Adolphe Basler, Daniel-Henry Kahnweiler, Léonce and Paul Rosenberg.

When he met the Russian sculptor Ossip Zadkine in the spring of 1913, Modi had left Montmartre for Montparnasse, had recklessly abandoned his paintings and was devoting himself to sculpture. Zadkine was born in Smolensk (between Moscow and Minsk) in 1890, to a Scottish mother and a Jewish father, a professor of classical languages who'd converted to the Orthodox Church. In 1906 he studied art in Sunderland, in the north of England, and in London; then worked as an assistant in a London woodcarver's studio. At the age of nineteen he settled in Paris. In 1915 he volunteered for the French Foreign Legion (which would give him French citizenship) and drove an ambulance. Two years later he was gassed and invalided out.

The wild-looking Zadkine was typical of the emotional and primitive set of eastern European Jews who became Modi's friends. With his full lips and thick mop of hair, he resembled one of the Three Stooges. The elegant art dealer René Gimpel described his bizarre looks: "He has brows like lianas in a virgin forest; his hair is too tight-woven and lusterless, giving him a somewhat rough appearance; his upper jaw comes down like a roof; keen eyes are creased by movement. He loves the gigantic, as people of small stature do." Charles Douglas recalled Zadkine's meager quarters: "He occupied a small cellar, and his inseparable companion was an enormous dog, a Great Dane....It seemed impossible that both could find room in the tiny studio crowded with sculptures. Zadkine...wore a Russian smock and had his hair cut à la Russe and fringed over the forehead, which gave him a startling resemblance to his own images in wood."

Zadkine visited Modi's "studio on the ground floor in a courtyard [at 216] Boulevard Raspail. The roof and the wall were glass. [He] remembered seeing Modi lying there asleep, naked. He had drawings pinned up all along the walls, together with photographs of Italian paintings....Zadkine saw them all fluttering slightly with the wind as though they were the waves of the ocean, and Modigliani lying asleep as though he were drowned."[8] In this foreboding scene, the delicate drawings seem about to disappear off the wall and Modi looks as if he were dead.

Another sculptor friend, Jacques Lipchitz, was born with the forenames Chaim Jacob in Druskieniki, Lithuania, on the banks of the Nieman River, between Vilna and Warsaw. His father, a building contractor from a wealthy family, sent him to Paris at the age of eighteen in 1909. Four years later he was introduced to Modi by Max Jacob. Like Zadkine, he greatly admired Modi and called him "a *riche nature*—so lovable, so gifted with talent, with sensitivity, with intelligence, with courage."

In 1917, after signing a contract with the dealer Léonce Rosenberg, Lipchitz had some extra money. He asked Modi to paint a double portrait of himself and his new wife, the Russian poet Berthe Kitrosser. The portrait—painted in Brancusi's former flat at 54 rue du Montparnasse—was based not only on the subjects themselves, but also on a formal wedding photograph that Lipchitz had taken to send to his parents in Russia. After quickly making some exquisite preliminary drawings, Modi set to work. Lipchitz described his alcoholic inspiration, his astonishing speed and his negligible fee:

> Modigliani came with an old canvas and his box of painting materials, and we began to pose....[He was] sitting in front of his canvas which he had put on a chair, working quietly, interrupting only now and then to take a gulp of alcohol from the bottle standing nearby. From time to time he would get up and glance critically over his work and look at his models. By the end of the day he said, "Well, I guess it's finished."... I felt some scruples at having the painting at the modest price of ten francs; it had not occurred to me that he could do two portraits on one canvas in a single session. So I asked him if he could not continue to work a bit more on the canvas, inventing excuses for additional sittings. "You know," I said, "we sculptors like more substance." "Well," he answered, "if you want me to spoil it, I can continue."

He took two more weeks to finish it.

Modigliani's portrait of *Jacques Lipchitz and His Wife* shows Lipchitz standing, with one hand in his pocket and the other resting affectionately on the shoulder of his seated wife. He has a large round head, wide forehead, strands of hair hanging over his ears, narrow slits of blue eyes, swerving nose and faint mustache. He wears a dark green, high-collared turtleneck sweater, circling his neck like the rings of Saturn, under a buttoned-up, broad-shouldered brown jacket. Berthe, leaning back against her husband, is endowed with a large, perfectly oval head. She has black hair, blank dark sloping eyes, ruddy cheeks, spatulate nose and full lips, and wears a scalloped white collar to adorn her open-necked dress. Three small green triangles—below his buttoned jacket, above her head and along her cheek—form a larger triangle that subtly surrounds and balances her. The dreamy figures, slightly withdrawn into each other, seem perfectly harmonious and content.

Modi's picture was partly inspired by another wedding portrait, Rembrandt's dignified and reverential *The Jewish Bride* (1666). Kenneth Clark observed that the work expressed the artist's "profound humanity" in the sweetness of the husband's touch and the affectionate response of the wife: "These are two individual souls, who nonetheless embody certain universal and enduring truths: that we need one another, that we can achieve unity only through tenderness, and that the protection of one human being by another is a solemn responsibility."

Modi also drew on his earlier, satiric and witty *Bride and Groom* (1915) in his treatment of the Lipchitz wedding picture. In *Bride and Groom,* his only other double portrait of adults, the rigidly standing man in formal dress—top hat, tiny bow tie, stiff collar and starched shirt front—is much older and taller than his consort. His ruddy face, bisected by a vertical line, reflects the disparate planes of Cubism. He has squinting eyes, a flat triangular nose and an elegantly twisted gray mustache above a glimpse of rosy lip. The woman faces slightly to the right and shows her pale forehead between dark bangs. She has asymmetrical eyes, a tiny pursed mouth and large round dangling earrings (though only one is shown). Unlike Jacques and Berthe, they seem stiffly remote from each other. Modi seems to have captured this unknown, newly married couple in a café after the opera rather than in a church or town hall. The painter who managed to evade marriage made a caustic comment on marital bliss.

Once the Lipchitz portrait was complete, Modi, the notorious seducer, boldly asked Berthe to pose nude and she reluctantly agreed—as long as her husband remained in the room. Modi "carefully instructed Berthe to assume the pose he wanted....[He] then proceeded to draw Berthe beginning with the eyes, continuing slowly and carefully to recreate and represent the sinuous curves of her body."[9] Lipchitz sat for hours as Modi sketched, and though he was acutely uncomfortable, dared not leave the room, even to relieve himself. The result was worth the suffering. The gorgeous drawing of the seated nude leaning backward on her hand, with her realistically drawn face tilted downward and wavy hair flowing along her body, is charged with sexual excitement.

Jules Pascin (born Julius Mordecai Pincas) was, like Modi, one of the most exotic and colorful characters among the Jews of Montparnasse. Both the Pincas family (who came from Salonika, Greece, then under Turkish rule) and, on his mother's side, the half-Serbian, half-Italian Russos (from Trieste, Italy, then under Austrian rule) were, like the Modiglianis, Sephardic Jews who'd originally come from Spain. The immensely wealthy family were merchants and bankers with close connections to the kings of Bulgaria and the sultans of Turkey. Pascin was born in 1885, the seventh of eight children, in Vidin, Bulgaria, a small town of 15,000 on the banks of the Danube River, between Sofia and Belgrade. It was a trading center for the neighboring Romanians, Yugoslavs, Greeks and Turks.

When Pascin was six years old the family moved to Bucharest, and he was educated in Vienna. After getting entangled in a sexual scandal, he left home and lived in Budapest, Vienna, Berlin and Munich, where he signed a lucrative contract as an illustrator with the German satirical magazine *Simplicissimus*. He moved to Paris in 1905 and lived there for the next decade. When the Great War broke out, Pascin, at home everywhere in the world, went to New York to escape military service in Bulgaria, became an American citizen, and traveled to Charleston and Havana.

A short, thin man with a large nose and thick lips, Pascin was physically unattractive, yet his sophistication and self-confidence, wealth and well-cut clothes, reckless generosity and famous champagne parties made him a great ladies' man. Gaudier's friend Horace Brodzky gave a staccato description of Pascin's sinister appearance and melancholy temperament. He had "a head that seems too big for his body, topped with a mop of Levantine hair; a pointed nose, heavy Oriental eyes, and a wisp of a mustache. His lips full and sensual. A hard bowler hat, precariously balanced on a head much too big for it." He seemed to be a "shady character from the Mediterranean shores, a greasy-looking character, mysterious and subtle." He was "a queer person, dark, brooding and elemental. He often appeared glum....His voice was soft and low, almost colorless."

The American expatriate writer Robert McAlmon, who met Pascin in the Parisian cafés in the 1920s, was fascinated by his fashionable clothing, poetic sensibility and corrupt character. He was "always elegant, vital, restless, inevitably on his way to somewhere else, speaking of the look of the evening beyond the *terrasse* as if speaking of a desirable woman's flesh....Although it was summer, Pascin usually wore a handsome black felt hat, with a snap brim, and at times very good leather gloves, buttoned at the wrists, and pleated shirts, even his way of dressing the most exquisite refinement of depravity. The charm of his manner had nothing to do with the restless grief in his eyes, his urgent hospitality, his worldliness and wit."

McAlmon's sometime friend Ernest Hemingway, fresh from the puritanical Midwest and the horrors of war, was also intrigued by Pascin's mysterious air and impressed by his heartlessly macho attitude toward women. His description of Pascin in *Islands in the Stream* recalled the criminals in his story "The Killers": "He was small and very tough and very strange. He used to wear a derby hat most of the time....He always acted as though he knew a great secret, as though he had just heard it and it amused him." In *A Moveable Feast,* his memoir of Paris in the twenties, Hemingway wrote that Pascin looked "like a Broadway character of the Nineties." Lounging in the Café Dôme with compliant models on each arm, Pascin threw down a few drinks with Hemingway and brutally disillusioned one of the girls: "'You want me to paint you and pay you and bang you to keep my head clear, and be in love with you too,' Pascin said. 'You poor little doll.'"[10]

Pascin painted in the satirical, linear tradition of Degas, Lautrec and Egon Schiele. The German artist George Grosz remembered him sitting in a Paris café and drawing "elegant little obscenities with uncanny skill" on the margins of newspapers. Like Modi's, his draftsmanship was impulsive yet precise, and he usually finished his paintings in one afternoon. He specialized in "monstrous women, deformed criminals, emaciated vicious children, uncanny animals" and sensual *demimondaines.*

Unlike Modi, Pascin traveled widely, was wealthy and had a worldly sophistication that compensated for his lack of looks and charm. But like Modi, he suffered from a sense of failure and always believed he would die young. The tough survivor used to exclaim, *"Je veux une morte rigolette"* (I'd like an amusing death)—but he didn't get one. On the eve of his one-man show in a prestigious Paris gallery, he became deeply depressed and said, "I've done what I set out to do and there is nothing more."[11] He felt that his creativity was exhausted, that his manner was too facile and that he was merely repeating himself. On June 2, 1930, in a Montmartre studio, he slashed the veins in his wrists and then, to make doubly sure of his death, hanged himself with a thin cord that cut deeply into his neck. In *Tarr,*

Wyndham Lewis gave an imaginative description of such a death when his fictional artist, Otto Kreisler, hangs himself: "The same throttling feeling returned: the blood bulged in his head: he felt dizzy.... [But] he did not resist: he gently worked the bed outwards from beneath him, giving it a last steady shove. He hung, gradually choking—the last thing he was conscious of was his tongue." When Pascin's mistress, married to a Norwegian painter, discovered his corpse three days after his death, she was confronted with the grim valediction, *"Pardon, Lucie,"* written on the wall with his own blood.

Pascin's clear artistic decline and disappointment in his work did not fully account for his death. McAlmon, puzzled by the suicide of a successful and apparently happy man, wrote that "the case was a tragedy, for Pascin had genius, a market for his paintings, friends, and appeared to enjoy life, although in a strangely morbid and exotic way." Moïse Kisling, a friend of both Modi and Pascin, also searched for an answer. He blamed the suicide on heavy drinking and a mysterious childhood trauma: "I see Pascin again, pale and suffering, thin, brown, somber. He has killed himself at the moment when fame and fortune have arrived. Was alcohol the reason for this? I believe he carried with him a secret wound which life aggravated every day—a taste for suffering, a morbid desire for obliteration amidst fog and ashes." Charles Douglas, in the most convincing explanation, noted both physical and psychological causes. Pascin suffered from diabetes, insomnia, despondency and an obsession with suicide: "He was sick, used up by excess of every kind, his work was unfinished, his life already at an end, his mental qualities were sinking, his organs played out. Even alcohol forsook him, he could not stand it any more."[12]

Moïse (Moses) Kisling, another of Modi's close friends, was the grandson of a well-known lawyer and son of a tailor. The same age as Jacques Lipchitz, he was born in the ghetto of Cracow, Poland, in 1891. After studying at the Warsaw Academy of Art, he moved to Paris in 1910 and lived in the Bateau Lavoir. In

1913 he shared his paints, models and studio at 3 rue Joseph Bara, off the boulevard du Montparnasse, with Modi. The Russian artist Marevna described Kisling's attractive appearance and feisty character:

> There was something Asiatic and exotic about his face, with its smooth, olive-tinted skin, its beautiful black eyes shaded by long lashes, and its firmly outlined red mouth; but it was the quivering nostrils of his small, well-shaped nose which revealed the turbulent and passionate character of the artist. He enjoyed great success with women, from artists' models to the society ladies whose portraits he painted.... [He was melancholy yet had] an irresistible gaiety that sometimes became wild, to the extent of shattering vodka glasses at parties. In addition, he had the Polish spirit of combativeness, and was quick to provoke quarrels, fights and even duels.

René Gimpel gave an example of Kisling's physical strength and violent temper, which would have appealed to Modi: "One night, when he was arguing with his wife on the doorstep, a police officer hit him over the head from behind. Turning around, our painter laid him out with a terrific punch that broke the officer's jaw. He was hauled off to the station house in handcuffs, roughed up, put in the black maria, and kept in prison for three days. Six thousand francs settled the matter."[13] He became notorious in June 1914 when he fought a duel with the Polish painter, Leopold Gottlieb, provoked by some obscure "point of honor." They began with pistols and, when neither bullet hit its mark, switched to swords, though Kisling had never handled a sword in his life. After his nose was cut and face sliced, Kisling alluded to the tragic history of his country, split apart by Russia, Austria and Prussia, and wittily called the duel "the fourth division of Poland." Nina Hamnett recalled that a cinematographer filmed the duel and that they saw it in a theater that evening.

When the war broke out Kisling, like Zadkine, joined the French Foreign Legion and became close friends with another volunteer in his unit, the Swiss-French writer Blaise Cendrars. In 1915, after being wounded in the chest in the battle of Carency, on the Somme, Kisling was invalided out and convalesced in Spain. After the war he unexpectedly inherited $5,000 from an American pilot named Chapman, who'd often visited his studio and had been shot down in combat.

Modi's friends were convivial and gave parties in their own idiosyncratic style. Brancusi's were warm, intimate and musical; Pascin's were open-handed, lavish and fueled by champagne; Kisling's were drunken, violent—and underfinanced. At one of his raucous parties, Marevna recalled, Ortiz de Zarate, "a mountain of a man…picked up a heavy marble table with one hand and prepared to hurl it at the head of his opponent, who had fallen to the floor. Certain murder was prevented only with difficulty." Chana Orloff described Kisling's 1917 wedding party, which provided a rare feast for the hungry artists: "Kisling, *en grand seigneur,* invited everyone to dinner. Such openhandedness worried me a little, but my husband and Modigliani next to me merely remarked: *'On va bien manger'* [We'll eat well]. In the midst of the meal, when Kisling was sufficiently ripe, 'I shall,' he said to us, 'dance the dance of chastity.' He pulled his shirt out of his trousers and he galloped around us; after which he declared, 'You take care of the bill,' and he skipped."

As he painted in Kisling's studio one day, Modigliani drank the entire contents of the bottle of gin that Kisling had used in a still life (as he had once drunk a whole bottle of Picasso's Anis del Mono). He repentantly wrote on his drawing of Jean Cocteau: "I, the undersigned, author of this drawing, swear never to get drunk again for the duration of the war"—and actually remained sober for an entire day.

Modi painted two portraits of Renée Kisling and three of Moïse, and in both cases his first ones were the best. In Renée's portrait of 1916, she has thick brown hair, cut short but with bangs hanging down to her cloudy green eyes. Her nose and mouth, square jaw and chin, and head tilted sharply to the left are painted in a realistic rather than stylized manner. She wears a man's dark jacket, white shirt and red tie, has an androgynous appearance and brooding expression, and resembles the long-faced Austrian singer Lotte Lenya. The portrait of Moïse, painted in 1915 when he was twenty-four, captures his brawny yet boyish look. The close-up of his massive head, supported by a broad pillar of neck, occludes the background, fills the frame and directly confronts the viewer. He has a short monk's fringe of hair, large uneven wide-open eyes under thick eyebrows, the hint of a mustache over a delicate amusing mouth, a broad face with square jaws and notched chin. Like Renée, he's dressed in a white shirt and (slightly darker) red tie, and seems intense and explosive.

Kisling's reciprocal painting, *Modigliani's Studio* (1918), portrays a framed copy of Modi's *Crouching Nude* (1917). She has a luxuriant cascade of hair on her shoulders, full, melonlike breasts, and a white cloth across her loins (yet shows her pubic hair). Leaning on her hands, she sits on a striped red and brown bedcover with her legs folded beneath her. Her pretty face tilts downward and to the right, her large, lustrous eyes look to the left. Kisling's tribute, like Augustus John's memorial to Modi, includes the artist's work, materials and possessions: a carved stone statue, paint brushes in a jar, fruit and knife, pipe and playing cards, bottles of wine and olive oil (an allusion to Italy). After Modi died, Kisling did several drawings of his closest friend, made his death mask and arranged his funeral. In *Omaggio* he tenderly asked Modi, "Why aren't you here to see your fame grow? It will always increase," and once again revealed the powerful emotions that Modi aroused in his friends: "he was like a brother to me, I loved him and admired him."[14]

III

CHAIM SOUTINE, Modi's intimate friend, was the complete antithesis of Modi and of urbane, polished, multilingual painters like Jules Pascin. The tenth of eleven children, Soutine was born in 1893 in Smilovitchi, a small Jewish village of 400 souls on the

Berezina River, twelve miles from Minsk, in Russian Lithuania. The village, not far from where Lipchitz was born, was a brown mass of broken-down wooden houses scattered along an unpaved and often muddy street. His father, a clothes mender (not a tailor) was the poorest of the poor.

Soutine sometimes told stories of his traumatic childhood. When he was seven, he stole a utensil from his mother's kitchen in order to buy a colored pencil and was punished by being locked in a dark cellar for two days. When he dared to ask the village rabbi to pose for him, he was beaten up by the rabbi's son. But the rabbi had to pay damages to Soutine's family, and he used this money to study art in Minsk and, later on, in Vilna. He reached Paris in 1911 and, always hungry, barely survived by digging ditches and loading railway cars. During the war he enlisted in a work brigade, dug more ditches and was discharged for poor health. When Lipchitz suggested sending money to his impoverished family during the war, the old resentments boiled up and "Soutine's harsh reply was '*Qu'ils crèvent!* [Let 'em starve!]…. You don't know how they treated me.' His father seems to have taken repressive measures against him such as locking him overnight in the poultry cage as punishment for wrongdoing and Soutine nursed an implacable hatred of him."

Soutine was a crude, boorish barbarian, whose ugliness, filth and coarse manners became legendary in Montparnasse. When his dealer advised him to wear a hat, he replied: "I can't go around like the Tsar every day." He took tea like a Russian, sucking it out of a saucer and through a lump of sugar in his mouth. He slurped water right out of the bottle, ate with his fingers and tore his food apart with his teeth. Pathologically afraid of washing, sometimes covered with vermin, always ragged and dirty, he was a kind of walking palette, with hair as well as clothes splattered with paint. Later on, small, stooping and shabby, like an insulted and injured Dostoyevskian hero, he crept around in a furtive fashion with his hat covering his face and his eyes wet with tears. A painter friend described his inner anguish: "His dark face and burning eyes created a tormented expression; his body huddled into his coat, he seemed a frightened, suspicious man imprisoned within himself, wanting only to be left alone, distrustful of everyone."[15]

Many companions left accounts of his repulsiveness. René Gimpel, in staccato phrases, vividly described the coarse features that Modi captured in his portraits of Soutine: "A clumsy man. A singsong voice rising from deep to shrill. The flattened face of a muzhik [Russian peasant]; his nose comes out in a rectangular cube and his nostrils move like wings; large sensual lips that speak as fish breathe out of water, with the same rapid tragic beating. He seems always to be looking into the air, the way large dogs do."

Marevna made him seem like a higher primate:

He had a short neck, high shoulders, and he stooped. His face was broad and jowly....His thatch of coarse, dark hair was cropped like a Russian peasant's, but a fringe came down to his eyebrows and concealed his large, protruding ears and low forehead. He had expressive dark eyes, sunken and tilted upward; the lids were red and swollen. His nose, narrow at the bridge, widened into a thick wedge. He smacked his thick lips when he talked, and flecks of white foam gathered at the corners of his wide mouth....The smile exposed his unhealthy, dull, dead-looking teeth, greenish at the gums.

Yet Marevna took pity on him, overcame her physical revulsion and slept with him.

Modi's friend, the French writer André Salmon, testified not only to the disgusting conditions in which Soutine lived, but also to his ability to endure them: "There was too much about the physical presence of the man himself which revolted me. Not only the filthy state in which he stumbled through life, but above all his slobbering speech....I just couldn't come to terms with

the poor fellow who incidentally gave the ear-specialist quite a
surprise when he finally decided to consult him about his terrible
earache. In the canal of the painter's ear the doctor discovered,
not an abscess, but a nest of bed bugs."[16]

Scarred by the ghetto, Soutine felt life was nothing but pain
and suffering. He was grateful for the smallest pleasure in Paris
where, in contrast to Russia, he could sit quietly on a public
bench without fear of being beaten by the police. Moody, solitary and demanding, capricious, tyrannical and often enraged,
he suffered from stomach ulcers and epileptic fits, and was a
mass of illnesses, obsessions, delusions, jealousies and fears. The
American novelist Henry Miller, who knew him in the 1930s, recalled that a measure of success did not make him any happier:
"Soutine lived right downstairs from me in the Villa Seurat. By
that time his Bohemian days were finished. And he was suffering from stomach and liver troubles and whatnot, and lived like
a recluse. I used to go down to borrow a knife and fork or salt
and pepper from him now and then. Once in a while he came
upstairs to my place when we had a party. He had an obsession
with Rembrandt, whom [like Modi] he idolized." Soutine would
take a train to Amsterdam, spend the day studying the Rem-
brandts in the Rijksmuseum and then rush straight back to Paris.

It was strange that the cultured, socially adept and usually fas-
tidious Modi, should befriend this irascible man who carried his
misery like a hunchback and antagonized everyone else. He recognized Soutine's genius, sympathized with his self-denial and
sacrifice for art, and tried (with slight success) to civilize the barbarian by teaching him table manners and personal hygiene. In
1917 the two artists shared a filthy garret at 2 passage Dantzig,
an octagonal warren of artists' studios nicknamed La Ruche
(the Beehive), built near the Gare Montparnasse in 1900 by the
academic sculptor Alfred Boucher. On his way home one hot
summer night, Léon Indenbaum dropped by La Ruche and discovered a scene out of Henry Murger's *Scènes de la vie de Bohème*:

"Near the door he found Modigliani and Soutine lying next to each other on mattresses, with water splashed all around their little island to discourage the bedbugs. Both had candles beside them and books in their hands." Modi was reading Dostoyevsky and called him a great writer.

Though Soutine never portrayed Modi, Modi made ten drawings of Soutine and painted him four times between 1915 and 1917. In the second portrait he's seated, with hands on his knees, eyes raised and a mournful expression. The third, more elongated figure is also seated, with hands joined, in front of a pale green background and a table supporting a glass of wine. The fourth was painted in an unusually rough impasto style on the back of a wooden door in Zborowski's flat. When Zbo complained about the desecration of his door, Modi prophetically said: "Some day you will be able to sell the door for its weight in gold." To which Zbo's wife Hanka, who loathed Soutine, replied that until then "we have to live with that portrait."[17]

As with the pictures of Kisling, Modi's first portrait of Soutine was the best. The seated portraits are dominated by brown and green tones; the first one, by Soutine's ruddy complexion and red lips, reflected in the red background. Like the portrait of Kisling, also painted in 1915, Soutine's close-up head nearly fills the frame and looks straight out at the viewer. His high thick parted hair falls over his ears; his brown eyes, with tiny dots of white, are asymmetrical; his nose is broad and spadelike; his lips, parted in a smile, show strong white teeth; his head rests on a long column of neck. Modi, revealing Soutine's naiveté and intensity, his sensuality and peasant strength, compassionately portrays him as an amiable country bumpkin rather than as a tortured soul. In his grotesque self-portraits, Soutine exaggerates his own ugliness and looks like the village idiot.

Modi's elegant draftsmanship and classical harmony were quite the reverse of Soutine's Slavic excesses and convulsive Expressionism. Unlike Modi's sensuous nudes, Soutine's *Reclining*

Woman (1919) looks like a corpse mangled in a car crash. But both artists usually completed their pictures in a single session; and Soutine's *Valet* (1927–28) was clearly indebted to Modi's 1917 portrait of Blaise Cendrars. The figures in both paintings have short bangs, broad foreheads, prominent ears, wide noses, slightly opened mouths, elongated necks and thin, triangular, Fred Astaire-shaped heads with pointed chins. Both have startled expressions, as if wondering how their portraits will turn out.

The tragic element in Soutine's art was powerfully connected to his traumatic life. As a child he often saw the ritual slaughterer cut the neck of a bird or beast and drain out the liquid, and he remained as haunted as Lady Macbeth by the smell of blood. His thick, flowing, viscous pigment portrays explosions of cadmium red and hemorrhages of carmine color. Attracted to carrion and to death, Soutine painted many dead birds and animals. Even his triangular ray fish (inspired by Chardin) has an anguished expression. He bought calf's heads from a butcher, but always wanted to choose his own specimen. "You don't understand," he would say. "I want a calf's head of distinction." He sometimes revved himself up by deliberately fasting with a piece of meat in front of him, waiting to paint until his hunger became intense.

His *Flayed Ox,* inspired by Rembrandt's painting with the same title, later inspired the shocking, hideous slabs of raw meat in the art of Stanley Spencer and Francis Bacon. After hauling the huge carcass from the local slaughterhouse into his studio, Soutine paid a model to sit next to it and fan away the swarms of flies. When the beef dried out, he splashed it with a pail of fresh blood. Finally, the stench of rotting meat became so overpowering that the neighbors called the police and forced him to remove it.

Soutine impressed his friends with the manic intensity of his art. Painting in a frenzy of inspiration, he'd use forty brushes in a single work and throw them wildly around the room. "One

eye-witness said that he 'flung the colours on the canvas like poi-
sonous butterflies,' another that he 'threw himself from a distance *bang bang bang* at the canvas.'"[18] Zbo saw him slash and tear
at his pictures like a madman. He came to hate almost all his art
before 1923, tried to repossess it and managed to destroy most
of it. When his indulgent patrons, the Castaings, wanted to buy
a picture, Soutine ordered them to find two works painted in
Céret in the French Pyrenees in 1919–22, and demolished them
before he would sell his clients a new one.

Soutine's weird, twisted figures seem to have been painted in
Rimbaud's "drunken boat." His uniformed cooks and page boys
look like madmen in an Edgar Poe House-of-Usher hotel. His
paintings, even more extreme than the tormented distortions of
van Gogh, are molten, horrific, demonic. His houses, tottering on
the edge of an abyss, are about to collapse into ruins and cascade
off the edge of the earth. A French critic described "a certain
wildness of rhythm loosed on the canvas, twisting in every linea-
ment of nature and human nature: 'It bends and shakes his figures as though they had St. Vitus' dance. Harmonious still lifes,
flowers and fruits, it reduces to rags and tatters. Houses oscillate
on their foundations and move ardently hither and thither in the
landscape, turning it topsy-turvy as in a series of seismic shocks.'"

Soutine's hopeless neediness appealed to Modi, but his art,
which laid bare the personal torments of a ghetto childhood,
also had a deep meaning for him. Modi had sublimated his sorrows and tensions in his own classically inspired work, yet felt a
kinship with this wildly Expressionist art that came from a bleak,
poverty-stricken eastern Europe. In certain intoxicated moods
he'd declare: "Everything dances around me as in a landscape by
Soutine." In *Omaggio,* Soutine wrote, with profound gratitude,
"Modigliani gave me confidence in myself." As he lay dying,
Modi still felt responsible for his manic friend and told his
dealer, Léopold Zborowski, "It is all up with me, but I am leaving you Soutine."[19]

Eight

WILD COLONIAL GIRL,
1914–1916

I

⁊ THE GREAT WAR broke out on August 2, 1914 and the gaiety of Bohemian Montparnasse soon came to an end. It took four years of murderous trench warfare, fought on a 400-mile front from Switzerland to the Baltic Sea, for the Allies to prevail. In the process millions of people perished, and a whole way of life was utterly swept away. A historian described the persistent stalemate on the Western front. In 1916 "the British and French had gained only a few miles in the mud of the Somme, churned up mercilessly by artillery fire. There the British lost 400,000 men, the French 200,000; at Verdun the French casualties mounted to 350,000." Eventually victory came, but at great cost to France: "some million and a quarter military, and half a million civilians, dead or soon to die, and three quarters of a million permanently injured, invaded departments looted and devastated, and a national debt of huge proportions."[1]

During the war years impoverished émigré artists led an even more marginal existence. Though the pictures Modi painted seem as tranquil as before, the hardships and privations of his life increased. Short of coal and wood to heat his studio, he haunted the Dôme and the Rotonde, where the terraces were heated by charcoal braziers and protected by large glass screens. The cafés now closed at eight P.M., tobacco was scarce and absinthe outlawed. Gas and electricity were rationed, food was hard to find, and black market prices were beyond his means. Travel was severely restricted, male civilians were scorned, foreigners treated with suspicion and hostility. Early defeats on the battlefield and the constant news of death and bereavement caused French morale to sink. Wounded and mutilated soldiers, back from the front and seen on the streets in every French town, presented a heartbreaking spectacle. Frenchmen were humiliated to see their women consorting with the German invaders.

Many of Modi's friends—the writers Salmon, Apollinaire and Cendrars; the artists Gaudier, Derain, Vlaminck, Zadkine, Kisling and Soutine—joined the army, and most of them went straight into combat. Even the precious Jean Cocteau signed up, through he wore a special uniform, designed by himself, and secured a safe post far from the front. Drawn out of the rarefied Bohemian world and thrown into close contact with ordinary soldiers in the trenches, the artists became increasingly aware of social and political realities. One critic noted that during the war Cendrars, for example, "would discover and rediscover with renewed intimacy the common people, outside artistic cliques and ivory towers, classical or modernist. It was a re-education. He turned down promotions and years later wrote scathingly of the officers' aristocratic disdain for the ordinary soldier." The Delta artists Maurice Drouard and Henri Doucet, Gaudier and Apollinaire, the Italian Umberto Boccioni, the Germans Franz Marc and August Macke were all killed in the war.

De Chirico, who was four years younger than Modi and outlived him by fifty-eight years, returned to Italy. But Modi and several other foreign artists remained in wartime Paris: Ortiz de Zarate, Brancusi, Picasso, Juan Gris, Lipchitz, Rivera and Foujita, as well as the permanently drunk Utrillo. The charming and beautiful Marie Wassilief tried to ease their plight by founding an artists' canteen in 1914. The same age as Modi, she'd been born (like Zadkine) in Smolensk, Russia, came to Paris in 1905 on a grant from the czarina, studied with Matisse and founded her own academy in 1909. The canteen helped in a small way. But during the war, when few people could afford the luxury of pictures, the art market collapsed and most painters found it difficult to survive. The annual Salons were cancelled and many galleries closed, as French dealers and collectors enlisted and foreign ones left Paris for home.

Modi spoke of returning to his mother in Livorno, where he retreated in difficult times, but stayed on in wartime Paris. Italy did not enter the war on the Allied side until May 1915 and Modi, living in France, was safe from the draft. In any case, his chronic tuberculosis would certainly have exempted him from military service. In November 1915 he wrote to his mother in French apologizing for his silence, giving his latest address (to receive her remittances, now increasingly difficult to send) and striking an optimistic note, though he wasn't selling much. He also noted that his brother Umberto supported the war, which Emanuele opposed, and that his parents were still separated: "My dear mother, I am a criminal for having let so much time pass without sending news. But...but so many things have happened.... Change of address first: new address 13 place Emile Goudeau XVIIième. But in spite of all the disturbances I am relatively happy. I am painting again and selling them. I'm very pleased that my brother [Umberto] is working in the munitions industry.... Give my love to my father when you write to him. Letters and I are enemies, but don't think I forget you and the others."

Modi, absorbed in his daily struggle to survive, was also psychologically affected by the war. As the Spaniard Juan Gris wrote late in 1916: "Ever since the war broke out, all the civilians I come into contact with have their minds warped by events. There's not one of them intact; all have broken down under the pressure." Modi felt uneasy about remaining safe while friends risked their lives in the trenches. As he guiltily and rather absurdly told the militant Anselmo Bucci: "I wanted to go on foot all the way up to the front, but when I reached the end of the Boulevard I was dissuaded. What about you though? Gone and been a hero with the Futurists?"[2] He was unfit to serve, but by not fighting he seemed to have failed a crucial test of manhood. His civilian status intensified his deep sense of personal and artistic failure.

Modi defiantly declared, *"Io me ne frego della politica"* (I don't give a damn about politics). But the apparently apolitical artist was, like his brother Emanuele, a socialist and pacifist. In conversations with Ilya Ehrenburg he expressed shrewd, even prescient political ideas. Lenin and Trotsky, lurking in Montparnasse cafés, were plotting the Revolution and the withdrawal of Russia from the war, which would put tremendous pressure on France and Italy as Germany shifted their armies to the Western front. Ehrenburg—a Russian poet, novelist and journalist from a middle-class Jewish family in Kiev—reported with considerable surprise that "when the first news of the revolution in Russia arrived, Modi ran to me, embraced me, and began screeching enthusiastically (sometimes I could not make out what he was saying)."

Influenced, no doubt, by the mystical Max Jacob, Modi had been reading the doom-laden prophecies of the sixteenth-century French astrologer and physician Nostradamus. His remarkable cures during an outbreak of plague and his obscure rhymed predictions in *Centuries* (1555) brought him fame and secured him a position at court. Though finally condemned by the Catholic Church, his fierce prophecies regained some currency in these troubled times. Sensitive to the political atmosphere, and afraid, like everyone else, of the dangers of German militarism, Modi believed Nostradamus was right: "people will be exiled to islands, a cruel ruler will seize power, everyone who does not learn to be silent will be put in prison; and the extermination of mankind will begin."

France had suffered at the hands of the Prussians in 1870, but had been peaceful and prosperous for forty years. No one in 1914 could have foreseen the barbaric tyrannies that would take power in Europe in the 1920s and 1930s. When artists anxiously discussed the dangerous present and uncertain future, Modi would mock anyone who thought life could return to the way it was before the war:

> You're all a lot of bloody innocents. Do you think anyone's going to say to you: "My dear fellows, take your choice?" You make me laugh. The only people who make a choice today are the ones with self-inflicted wounds, and they get shot for it. When the war is over, everyone will be put in prison. Nostradamus was right. Everyone will have to put on a convict's uniform. At the most, the academicians will be entitled to wear checked trousers instead of striped ones.[3]

Though Modi died before the rise of Hitler and Mussolini, his obscure rantings now seem amazingly clear-sighted about conditions in postwar Europe.

After Paul Alexandre joined the medical service and left Paris, the art dealer Paul Guillaume became Modi's patron. The son of a humble bank messenger from the Jura in eastern France, Guillaume was born in Paris in 1891. He began his career as clerk in a garage that imported African rubber for car tires. The suppliers also offered him African statues, which he began to collect and sell. Suave and self-confident, with a talent for attracting publicity, he soon met Apollinaire and Max Jacob, who introduced him to Modi. He opened his own gallery on the fashionable rue de Faubourg St. Honoré in 1915 and continued to sell art as competition faded during the war. He said that "in 1914, during all of 1915 and part of 1916, I was the only buyer of Modigliani and it was only in 1917 that Zborowski became involved with him."

Modi painted four portraits of Guillaume in 1915–16, all stylized but clear likenesses of the handsome and dapper young man. In the best portrait, his large square head, under a black felt hat and supported by a cylindrical neck, is tilted to the right. The triangle of his nose matches the triangles of his mustache (separated in two elegant halves) and of his half-open mouth, which seems to be inhaling smoke from the cigarette between the fingers of his gloved hand. His white cuff peeks out of his sleeve, and a dark tie with a touch of red extrudes from his stiff white collar. On the portrait of this arrogant and rather supercilious dealer, Modi wrote "NOVO PILOTA" and "STELLA MARIS." Guillaume was to be the new pilot of his ship and would guide him, like a star of the sea (a name of the Virgin Mary), to his long-awaited wealth and fame. The word "NOVO" and the allusion to the Virgin also suggest the rubric in Dante's *La Vita Nuova* (1293): *"Incipit Vita Nova"* (The New Life Begins).

A 1918 photo of the smart, stylish Guillaume leading the shabby, grubby Modi along the Promenade des Anglais in Nice reveals why the portrait was satirical. Modi painted all the pictures, Guillaume had all the money. Yet Guillaume deserves credit for taking a chance on the difficult and drunken Modi when he was an unknown failure. Recalling Modi's special appeal, he later wrote that he "was all charm, all impulsiveness, all disdain, and his aristocratic soul remained among us in its many-coloured, ragged beauty."[4] His risk paid off when he sold the artist's work for tremendous profits after his death.

II

MODI STAYED on in Paris, despite the wartime gloom, his serious illness and his dependence on alcohol. In May 1914 he met Beatrice Hastings, who would become his lover and supporter for the next two years. He thrived on chaos and a roaring girl, even wilder than himself, was just what he needed to fire him up. The alarms of war, his tense relations with Guillaume and emotional upheavals with Beatrice coincided with the development of his mature style and the creation of his greatest portraits and nudes. Hardly a Dantean Beatrice, she was sexually voracious, short-tempered and alcoholic, but also bright, stylish and well off. At thirty-five, five years older than him, she was wiser and tougher than her successors and could recognize real talent, stand behind her man and provide the necessary "stiffening." Nina Hamnett claimed to have introduced them and they may have met through Jacob Epstein, but the ubiquitous procurer and go-between, Max Jacob, probably brought them together.

When she arrived in Paris in 1914 Beatrice had come a long way, literally and figuratively. Born Emily Alice Haigh in 1879 in Hackney, East London, she was the seventh of eleven children of a prosperous fruit and wool merchant. Her parents were visiting England at the time and soon returned to Port Elizabeth, between Capetown and Durban, South Africa, where she grew up. At age twelve she was sent to an English boarding school in Kent, near Hastings, from which she adopted her similar-sounding name (Haigh-Hastings). Though she was a good pupil, she was bullied by the headmistress' husband, hated school and went home the following year. In adolescence she was a solitary misfit and rebel, resentful of adults and alienated from her parents.

Beatrice had a convoluted past. In February 1897, at the age of eighteen and partly to escape her stifling Victorian home, she was briefly married to Edward Tracy Chamberlain. He was heir to a fortune based on laxative pills, and soon died of a heart attack. The wild colonial girl, sent packing by her family and given a generous allowance, left South Africa in 1899 at the outbreak of the Boer War. She inspired many colorful stories. She was rumored to have ridden horses in a Transvaal circus, worked as a nurse on a hospital ship to England and had a brief career as a showgirl in New York. Her second marriage, to the boxer Lachlan Thomson, was equally ephemeral. At some point she gave birth to a child who died in infancy; she had also seen a younger sister die in childbirth and always vehemently denounced the horrors of maternity. Though claiming the right to sexual freedom, she loathed the degrading mechanics of sex and thought childbirth the ugliest fact of human life. She was sexually attracted to both men and women, and had many stormy affairs.

In London in 1907 she met A. R. Orage, a tall, formidable-looking Yorkshireman of Huguenot ancestry, during a talk on Madame Blavatsky at the Theosophical Society. He was six years older, married and editor of the highbrow radical journal the *New Age*. She soon became his contributor and mistress. "Lively, dark, and outspoken; and remarkably well read," she also had a ferocious temper. Edgar Jepson, a colleague on the journal, called her "a very pretty and clever woman...who, I have always believed, put the stiffening into [Orage]...a posing sentimentalist...and made him the successful editor he was." Another colleague rightly noted that her mind lacked balance. Orage's devoted secretary shuddered to recall that "B.H. was a very violent person if she failed to get her own way, mostly resorting to hysterics."⁵ The wild girl could have escaped from one of Soutine's vertiginous pictures. Daring and defiant, independent and iconoclastic, she was also "vivacious, amoral, venomously articulate...an indomitable brawler and fire eater."

Totally lacking in the traditional English reticence and reserve, Beatrice was a sexual juggernaut, physically aggressive and determined to take her pleasure in the same way as a man. A London acquaintance said that before she left for France her sexual frankness and sexual appetite had amazed and excited Robert Frost, then living in England: "Frost told of an evening at T. E. Hulme's flat in, I suppose, 1913. I suppose Pound took him there. Orage was in the group but Frost, the country man from New Hampshire, was more impressed by Orage's mistress, Beatrice Hastings. I believe she talked anti-feminism and declared that she had notches on her bed for every man who had slept with her. This talley of men impressed Frost no end." No doubt Frost would have liked to earn a notch, which resembled a gunslinger's mark on a six-shooter. While accounting for her numerous lovers, she'd nearly whittled away her bed.

In July 1914, just before the war began, their affair ended and Orage sent Beatrice to Paris to write a weekly article for the *New Age*. She knew Max Jacob, who introduced her to many artists and writers, and her accounts of wartime Paris, written from the inside, were vivid and perceptive. Jacob, whose limited knowledge of English made him overestimate her talent, was clearly impressed by her dress, behavior and exotic background. He declared that "I've made the acquaintance of an authentic great English poet: Mme. Hastings, drunkard, pianist, woman of fashion, Bohemian, dressed Transvaal-fashion and surrounded by bandits who do a little art and dancing on the side."[6] Beatrice was far from being a great poet. Her copious prewar contributions to *New Age* included some prettified verse, feeble fiction and vitriolic commentary. Oscillating between emotional and ideological extremes, she would suddenly and quite unexpectedly change from defending to attacking Catholics, Jews, suffragettes, pacifists and mystics.

Though an English colleague called Beatrice an "elegant, sylphlike beauty," in Man Ray's 1922 photograph she seems nice looking but not especially beautiful. She wears a pale blouse under a loud checked jacket and has strands of short dark hair drooping over her broad forehead. Her brown eyes are wide set, her nose uptilted and pudgy, her jaw firm and her mouth half-open (showing even white teeth) in a reluctant smile. Beatrice's dress was as flamboyant as her character. Dispensing with the de rigueur hat and constrictive corset, she astonished the French by wearing soft sandals and loose Liberty frocks, and by smoking in public. At a fancy dress ball she turned up as an eighteenth-century shepherdess, with a tall crook, long-ribboned hat and basket of live ducks. At the Quat'z' Arts (Four Arts) ball she appeared in a stunning trompe l'oeil dress that Modi had painted onto her naked body.

Besides her art criticism and literary journalism, Beatrice's works included *The Maids' Comedy,* "a very strange book, narrat-

ing in self-conscious ninetyish language the adventures of a female Quixote ('Dorothea') and her black female Sancho Panza
in the uplands of Beatrice's youth, above Port Elizabeth." *Madam
Six* (alluding to the number of her hospital bed in a clinic for the
poor) fictionalized her grim confinement in a Paris cancer ward
in 1920. She also appeared as a colorful character in French fiction. In Francis Carco's *Les Innocents* (1916), a popular novel of
lowlife in Montmartre, a character named Beatrice (alter ego of
another woman based on Katherine Mansfield) is a reporter,
painter and pervert who had once, back in Africa, strangled her
lover to see how it felt to be a murderer. As Mlle. R. in Jean
Cocteau's *Le Livre blanc* (*The White Book*), published in 1928, she
tries desperately to possess and dominate her rival's lover.

In both London and Paris Beatrice had an intensely emotional friendship with Katherine Mansfield. The two women
looked a bit like each other and had striking similarities: a colonial background, a wealthy, oppressive father and an adored
younger brother, killed in the Great War. Both were bisexual, intelligent, caustic and high strung. Beatrice helped Katherine have
an abortion in 1911. Mansfield's pathetically devoted friend, Ida
Baker, wrote that Katherine found it "stimulating to be clever,
amusing and even bitter and cruel with Beatrice. As she herself
said, Beatrice brought out the worst in her. Perhaps she took on
the worst of Beatrice?" Beatrice and Katherine both wrote under
pseudonyms and collaborated on several articles in *New Age* that
satirized their pretentious friends.

In March 1915 Katherine, in wartime France to continue her
affair with Francis Carco, described her visit to Beatrice, who
had by then been with Modi for eight months. She gave a keen-
eyed account of Beatrice's arty and comparatively luxurious flat,
where she created her own little world—sustained by regular remittances from South Africa and with the loyal Max Jacob as
majordomo—at 13 rue Norvins in Montmartre, just north of
the Bateau Lavoir. When in residence there, Modi could escape

the squalor that had horrified his friends and enjoy the bourgeois comforts of his youth. Katherine wrote:

> Beatrice's flat is really very jolly. She only takes it by the quar-
> ter at 900 francs a year—four rooms & a kitchen—a big hall,
> a cabinet and a conservatory. Two rooms open on to the gar-
> den. A big china stove in the salle à manger heats the place.
> All her furniture is second hand & rather nice. The faithful
> Max Jacob conducts her shopping. Her own room with a grey
> self colour carpet—lamps in bowls with Chinese shades—
> a piano —2 divans, 2 armchairs—books—flowers, a bright
> fire was very unlike Paris—really very charming. But the
> house I think detestable—one *creeps* up and down the stairs.

Katherine also provided, with a certain grim satisfaction, a
clinical account of her rival's drunken deterioration (under
Modi's expert guidance), and managed to capture Beatrice's
satirical wit and ingenuous egoism:

> Strange and really beautiful though she is still with the fairy
> air about her & her pretty little head still so fine—she is ru-
> ined. There is no doubt of it—I still love her, but I take an
> intense, cold interest in noting the signs. She says—"it's no
> good me having a crowd of people. If there are more than
> four I go to the cupboard & nip cognacs until it's all over for
> me, my dear." —or "Last Sunday I had a fearful crise [cri-
> sis]—I got drunk on rhum by myself at the Rotonde & ran
> up & down this street crying and ringing the bells & saying
> 'save me from this man.' There wasn't anybody there at all."
> And then she says with a fairish show of importance—"of
> course the people here simply love me for it. There hasn't
> been a real woman of feeling here—since the war."

A week later, to arouse the jealousy of her future husband,
Katherine described dancing in Beatrice's flat with an attractive
woman. This episode had also aroused the jealousy of the

drunken Beatrice and led to yet another "final" quarrel: "At B's this afternoon there arrived 'du monde' including a very lovely young woman—married & *curious*—blonde—passionate—We danced together.... It ended in a great row. I enjoyed it in a way, but Beatrice was very impossible—she must have drunk nearly a bottle of brandy & when at 9 o'clock I left & refused either to stay any longer or to spend the night there she flared up in a *fury* & we parted for life again."

In May 1915 Katherine commented ironically on Beatrice's friendship with Max Jacob, her familiar spirit and Modi's emotional rival. Referring to Modi by his Italian nickname, she also mentioned that he and Beatrice had thought of moving to Italy, which he considered a safe haven in times of crisis: "I wonder if Beatrice Hastings has maxed her jacob yet or if she flew to Italy with her Dedo. I am not really curious [though she *was*] and I'll never seek to know."7

Katherine always spoke of Beatrice with a strange mixture of fear and admiration. The fear was well founded and they sometimes had violent fights. The English poet Ruth Pitter once "called on Beatrice and Orage to find the floor scattered with beads, and was told Katherine and Beatrice had come to blows with their necklaces." Katherine's description of one of her dreams, inspired by the recent row, caught Beatrice's tone of voice and speech. In the dream Beatrice exclaimed that Katherine, for all her superior pretensions, was just as immoral, though less candid, than she was: "Vile people came into my room. They were drunk. Beatrice Hastings led them. 'You don't take me in old dear' said she. 'You've played the Lady once too often, Miss—coming it over me.' And she shouted, screamed *femme marquée* [whore] and banged the table. I rushed away."

In a journal entry of January 13, 1922 (a year before her early death), Katherine recorded her feelings about the terrifying yet intriguing Beatrice, to whom she'd sent many sexually compromising letters: "In some way I fear her.... There was a peculiar recklessness in her manner and in her tones which made me feel she would recognise no barriers at all. At the same time, of course, one is *fascinated*." She also remembered that Beatrice must have had a large number of her letters which didn't bear thinking about. Her fears were fully realized after her death, when Beatrice cruelly and jealously wrote that Katherine had "twittered her way out of a world she had fouled wherever she went."[8]

Despite her fiery feminism Beatrice could be emotionally vulnerable. In London in 1914, between leaving Orage and becoming Modi's mistress, she had a brief, tempestuous affair with Wyndham Lewis. Shortly before she left for Paris, she wrote him a pitiful, self-abasing farewell letter, which revealed her convulsive feelings and her craving for punishment: "I cannot see you again for a long time. My love for you is altogether beyond me. You become more adorable every time I see you & when I realise how things are I am near fainting; I am just recovered from one of a hundred bursts of pain and tears....You see I am quite lost. It will be no use if you behave ever so badly because of this. I should never believe you meant to hurt me now I have told you beyond any doubt of my perfect admiration."[9]

III

IF BEATRICE was precisely the stimulus that Modi needed, he was exactly what she was looking for—an attractive man and artistic genius. She wanted someone she could influence as well as love. In the *New Age* she described her first, ambivalent impressions of his personality. When she met him at Rosalie's, Modi was repulsively drugged and drunk. When she saw him in a café and in his studio, he carried his favorite book and discussed his most famous sitters. Though he was mad, bad and dangerous to know, his seductive charm soon overwhelmed her: "A complex character. A pig and a pearl. Met in 1914 at a 'cremerie.' I sat opposite him. Hashish and brandy. Not at all impressed. Didn't know who he was. He looked ugly, ferocious, greedy. Met again at the Café Rotonde. He was shaved and charming. Raised his cap with a pretty gesture, blushed to his eyes and asked me to come and see his work. Went. Always a book in his pocket, Lautréamont's *Maldoror*. Despised everyone but Picasso and Max Jacob. Loathed Cocteau."

Their liaison unfolded amidst bitter reproaches and burning retaliations, between Zeppelin raids and the German advance on Paris. Like Kreisler in Lewis' *Tarr,* they "approached a love affair as the Korps-student engages in a student's duel—no vital part exposed, but...at least stoically certain that blood would be drawn." Calling Modi "the pale and ravishing villain," Beatrice noted the contrast between his personal fastidiousness and his tendency to exhibitionism. He was "slight, somewhat fragile, and extremely reserved until he was drunk." Then, in a rather alarming way, he would pass out in public. Their violence was so common that neighbors in the quarter, hearing her scream "Help, he's killing me," would merely shrug their shoulders and keep on walking.[10]

Ehrenburg reported that when Modi was suddenly seized by a fit of horror and rage, Beatrice would try to pacify him by referring to his distinguished family. This would work like a charm until he realized how he'd come down in the world, and would begin to destroy instead of create: "[She] kept saying, with a pronounced English accent: 'Modigliani, don't forget that you're a gentleman. Your mother is a lady of the highest social standing.' These words acted on Modi like a spell. He sat in silence for a long time. Then he could not bear it any longer and started breaking down the wall. First he scratched away at the plaster, then he tried to pull out the bricks. His fingers were bloody and in his eyes there was such despair that I could not stand it."

Both Beatrice and Modi enjoyed public displays and operatic emotions. She had sparred with her boxer ex-husband, an experience that came in handy when she went a few rounds with

Modi. One night she turned up at the Café Dôme with her new dress ripped to shreds and coyly explained, with a hint of sexual delight: "Modi's been naughty." Foujita's first wife, Fernande Barrey, recalled that "when Modi saw [Beatrice] coming to the Rotonde to fetch him, he said in a panicky voice, '*Cachez-moi, c'est une vache!*'" (Hide me, she's a bitch!) Fernande added that Beatrice, the stronger of the two, was the one who eventually ended the affair.

Beatrice's tragicomic account of her departure from the Gare du Nord, on a short trip to England, illustrated her emotional dominance and captured his self-deprecating, ironic humor. In the *New Age* of July 16, 1914, she vividly described how Modi dramatically passed out in front of some English travelers. When he came to, she forced him to admit that he'd wasted several years on his sculpture:

> He arrested the taxi as it was crossing the Boulevard Montparnasse and implored to be allowed to ride with me — it was so chic, like being his rich uncle [Amedeo] who was dead of the gout! But I didn't know what to do with him at the station when he fainted loudly on the grubby side of the carriage and all the English stared at me.... Modigliani was gasping, "Oh, Madame, don't go!" I said, "Modigliani, someone says you've been three years fiddling about with one type of head and you'll be another three on the new design." He came round. "Crétin!" he glared at me as though I had said it. "Mais, ma-a-a-is, ma petite, he is right! I might have grown some asparagus in the time."[11]

Beatrice confessed that she rather enjoyed their ferocious combats, often fueled by alcohol: "'Once we had a royal battle, ten times up and down the house, he armed with a pot and me with a long straw brush.... How happy I was, up in that cot on the Butte.' Max Jacob spoke of '*scènes avec revolvers*.'" Marevna, often appalled by the artists' behavior, described another fight which ended with a defenestration that shattered a window. Modi blamed Beatrice for provoking him and kept protesting that it was not his fault:

> Modigliani and Beatrice Hastings, far gone in drink, began one of their arguments. It quickly turned into a fight, with the two of them pommelling and kicking each other. The next thing we knew, he had seized her and hurled her through the closed window. A shattering of glass, a scream, and all that remained visible of Beatrice Hastings was her legs, dangling over the window sill—the rest of her was in the garden.... Beatrice Hastings was carried in and laid on the sofa. Her long, flat breasts were daubed with blood; she was sober now, and utterly wretched. She wept, while Modigliani repeated, *"Non mea culpa, non mea culpa."*...Beatrice Hastings was given some coffee and wrapped up in a Scotch plaid, and Modi began telling her jokes to distract her.

But what sort of jokes could have soothed her? Their relationship depended on extreme swings of mood—though this time it went a bit too far—and could sometimes be salvaged (as in the railroad station) by ironic, earthy jokes.

Their notorious and widely reported fights were clearly a form of sexual foreplay that—as with D. H. and Frieda Lawrence—aroused both combatants and led to passionate reconciliations. As Frieda wrote: "I hit back or waited until the storm in him subsided. We fought our battles outright to the bitter end. Then there was peace, such peace." Thora Klinckowström, who sat for Modi, said Beatrice had told her "she had a child by Modi, a little girl who died at birth or soon after."[12] Though Thora may have confused this death with the death of Beatrice's first child, the story could be true. They were often drunk in bed together, and Modi took no precautions about conception. But given Beatrice's previous trauma, her hatred of childbirth and doctrinaire defense of abortion, she probably did not have a child with Modi.

Beatrice's descriptions in the *New Age* of her life with Modi are uniquely valuable. They were written on the spot and in the heat of the moment, before his tragic death and the growth of his *maudit* legend. On July 9, 1914, right after they first met, she emphasized his attractive appearance and the ritualistic bathing he associated with Jews: "He is a very beautiful person to look at, when he is shaven, about 28, I should think, always either laughing or quarreling à la Rotonde....He horrifies some English friends of mine whose flat overlooks his studio by tubbing at two hour intervals in the garden, and occasionally lighting all up after midnight apparently as an aid to sculpturing [the Tower of] Babel."

In the same issue she expressed irritation with the reckless generosity that left him permanently impoverished. If no one would buy his work, Modi, desperate for recognition, would rather give it away to connoisseurs than hoard it in his studio: "The Italian is liable to give you anything you look interested in. No wonder he is the spoiled child of the quarter, enfant sometimes—terrible but always forgiven—half Paris is in morally illegal possession of his designs [drawings]. 'Nothing's lost' he says, and bang goes another drawing for two-pence or nothing, while he dreams off to some café to borrow a franc for some more paper!"

Beatrice believed in his genius—as important to him as her love—and was the first to praise his work in print. In the *New Age* of February 11, 1915 she wrote that she treasured his sculpture, that its "unfinished" quality enhanced its aesthetic value and that there was an essential sadness in his statues ("In much wisdom," said Ecclesiastes, "is much grief"):

I possess a stone head by Modigliani which I would not part with for a hundred pounds even at this crisis; and I routed out this head from a corner sacred to the rubbish of centuries, and I was called stupid for my pains in taking it away.

Nothing human, save the mean, is missing from the stone. It has a fearful chip above the right eye, but it can stand a few chips. I am told that it was never finished, that it never will be finished, that it is not worth finishing. There is nothing that matters to finish! The whole head equally smiles in contemplation of knowledge, of madness, of grace and sensibility, of stupidity, of sensuality, of illusions and disillusions — all locked away as matter of perpetual meditation. It is as readable as Ecclesiastes and more consoling, for there is no lugubrious looking-back in this effulgent, unforbidding smile of intelligent equilibrium.

The following week Beatrice repeated one of Modi's firm beliefs: that it was easier to maintain friendships with men than to live harmoniously with women — his natural enemies. Their domestic intimacy inevitably led to violence with plates and pots and brooms. But Beatrice also described the amusing side of their conflicts: "A creature [Modi] said that all he knew about love was from his friends and that he supposed it to be a business of eating from the same plate so as to be close enough to prevent each other from being the first to get it as a weapon. We picked enormous holes in this theory, but he stuck to it, that they do eat off the same plate and break it on each other's head afterwards. I never did anything with a plate exactly, but what *is* love?"

Beatrice complained that Modi used to come home drunk and if the door was locked would break the windows to get inside. Max tried to play the peacekeeper: "if I happened to be drunk too [and she often was], there was a great scene! But I was writing, usually, and just plagued to hear him ring. If Max was there when Dedo arrived the chances were not altogether against a peaceful conversazione and the witty exit of Modigliani to his own atelier close by." Even before her bout with cancer, after the war, Beatrice complained of poor health, and (quoting

Lord Byron's "The Destruction of Sennacherib") called herself
a poor lamb, beginning to dread and hate "the swoop of the As-
syrian on my fold."[13]

Beatrice also wrote of her relations with Modi in a long-lost
novella, recently discovered in the archives of the Museum of
Modern Art. Composed in awkward French, it was corrected by
Max Jacob. The surrealist text, influenced by *Les Chants de Maldoror* (but without its horror and ugliness), has hallucinating
characters that may have been created under the influence of
drugs. The novella, to escape the horrors of war, "drifts in and
out of dream-like passages."

The name of the eponymous heroine (based on Beatrice),
Minnie Pinnikin, suggests "manikin," "pinafore" and the baby
rhyme "Minnie-Pinnie." Pâtredor (based on Modi) suggests
Maldoror and, literally, "father of gold," or artist. The dominant
images are of sun, dance and drink. The childish fantasy imitates
the down-the-rabbit-hole episode in *Alice in Wonderland* when
Minnie says, "Let's go and see what there is on the other side of
the hole," and asks, "Do you wish to leave or jump into the
world?" Pâtredor replies: "I would not mind jumping if there is
no other means of knowing the future."

Pâtredor colors Minnie's dress with pastels, just as Modi
painted Beatrice's costume for the Quat'z' Arts ball, and gives
her a swanlike neck, as Modi did in his portraits. Beatrice expresses her strong attraction to Modi by having Minnie observe
that "he was really beautiful. The sun that danced in his hair
leaned forward to look into his eyes." Ignoring the harsh realities of their life, she abandons her hostility to marriage and fan-
tasizes about the future: "One could tell that they would be
married one day but no one ever mentioned it simply because it
was not yet time. They were still playing the first love games."[14]
Despite her age and her wealth of experience, Beatrice was attracted to the adolescent aspect of Modi's character. She retreated into a childish fantasy of the future—when she was not
actually bashing him with a broom.

Modi did innumerable drawings and fifteen mostly unin-
spired portraits of Beatrice between 1914 and 1916. The realistic
drawings do not look like the photo of Beatrice, nor do his more
stylized portraits. Proud to be his model and muse, she described the casual way she posed for him: "[He was] inspired
every day with something about me—'voilà, encore une' he
would say—I never knew what he meant and was too arrogant
to ask. I never posed, just let him 'do' me, as he pleased, going
about the house. He did the Mary portrait [*Beata Matrix*] of me
in a café where I sat thinking what a nuisance he was with his
perennial need for more pastels." His 1915 drawing of Beatrice,
with eyes closed in a "beatific" look, and with the words *"La
Vita Domestica,"* (Domestic Life), *"Santa"* (Saint) and *"Soeur Charitable"* (Charitable Nun) written on the image, is clearly ironic. An
exceptionally beautiful standing nude drawing of Beatrice portrays her with hair coiled on her head and falling on one shoulder, eyes closed, face tilted downward, high breasts, elongated
torso and pubic hair showing above the cloth, held in the traditionally modest *Venus pudica* pose. He used a variant of this vulnerable nude figure on the cover of the catalogue of his one-man
show in 1917.

The three best portraits, in which Beatrice looks quite different, are *Madam Pompadour* (1914), *Beatrice Hastings in Front of a Door*
(1915), *Beatrice Hastings with a Mauve-Checked Blouse* (1916). Madame
de Pompadour (1721–64) was a French beauty, mistress of Louis
XV and until her death the virtual ruler of France. Her middle-
class origin made her insecure at court, but she maintained
power over the king by her talent and wit. She favored Voltaire
and other writers and employed many artists to decorate her
residences, but her enormous expenditures made her unpopular
with the masses. The spelling of *Madam* suggested Beatrice's
English origin and her dominant role in their common-law
marriage.

In *Madam Pompadour* Beatrice looks more like the bride in
Bride and Groom than like Modi's portraits of her. The checked

screen in the top right corner, the feathered hat and the pale green panels (like an abstract painting) on both sides of the dark brown door foreshadow the later portraits. She wears a huge, buckled, feathered, boatlike hat, with curls of dark hair falling beneath it, a dark V-necked, green-sleeved dress on her sloping shoulders and a crimson brooch hanging from a delicate white-beaded necklace. Beatrice's wide nose and cupid's-bow lips are bisected by vertical lines, and she has an appropriately haughty demeanor. On *Les Pampas,* an elegant 1916 drawing of a man, Modi puns on the title of Beatrice's portrait by writing "Les Pampas pompadour" and signing it "Pinarius," another name for Pâtredor in "Minnie Pinnikin."[15] Modi's portraits of Beatrice are satiric, while her novella, largely about him, retreats into sentimental fantasy and is far less revealing than her reportage.

Modi's second portrait of Beatrice is tender, full faced, and enhanced by the puffy purplish feather beneath her low, square black hat, the parted strands of brown hair on her pale forehead, the rosy cheeks and demure red lips. She has one blank and one open brown eye, a firm oval chin and a long swanlike neck. She's dressed in a dark jacket over a brownish-gold blouse, adorned with an olive-shaped, olive-green brooch that picks up the pale green panel to the right of the closed door.

In the third portrait, Beatrice's mauve-checked dress echoes not only the loud-checked jacket in her photo, but also the checked background in Modi's *Lola de Valence* (1916). The title comes from Manet's 1862 portrait of Lola de Malea (of Valencia), the star of a fashionable Spanish dance troupe. The features of Modi's Lola were clearly inspired by the masklike faces and jagged teeth of his African statues. Against a smudged, cloudy gray background Beatrice, in three-quarter view but with her nose and pursed lips in Cubist profile, has long wavy light brown hair, high forehead, blank gray eyes, square jaw and stiff neck rising out of a pointed white collar. In contrast to Modi's usually round or oval heads, her head is compressed between two

straight vertical lines. Her face, turned to the right, is more angular, her expression more withdrawn, than in the previous
portraits.

Beatrice genuinely admired Modi's genius and had tried to
save him from his descent into alcoholism. But she found it increasingly difficult to sustain their fantasy life, soon became as
haggard as he was and began to look out for a more promising
candidate. Frightened by his need to destroy himself, she decided to leave him before he destroyed her. "Modi suspected
me," she said, "but he never knew distinctly of what until I
abandoned him." In August 1916, after two tumultuous years together, she replaced Modi with the equally handsome though
less talented Italian sculptor Alfredo Pina. The affair ended ex-
plosively at a banquet that Marie Wassilief gave at her canteen
for the painter Georges Braque, who'd returned from the war
with a head wound. Knowing that Beatrice would bring Pina,
Marie said she inadvertently provoked Modi by telling him: " 'for
heaven's sake don't come tomorrow. I haven't invited you. Do
me this one favor and I'll give you three francs instead of your
[daily] fifty centimes. I don't want a scandal.' Well, at the end of
the meal the doors burst open, and there was a whole band of
painters and models who hadn't been invited. Pina, when he saw
Modigliani, drew a revolver, and pointed it at him. I seized the
gun by main strength, forced him out the door, and he rolled
down the stairs." It seems unlikely that the elegant Marie could
wrestle a revolver from a man and throw him down the staircase.
But Modi's suspicion and jealousy, his threats and eruptions of
violence had frightened Pina and led to what Max Jacob called
"*scènes avec revolvers.*"

Pina was duly succeeded in Beatrice's series of notches by the
teenage novelist, Raymond Radiguet, friend and perhaps lover
of Max Jacob. Radiguet was simultaneously sleeping with Jean
Cocteau and would have an affair with Brancusi in 1921 before
dying of typhoid, at the age of twenty, in 1923. Beatrice's love

letters to Radiguet contain the same extremes of masochistic adoration and vitriolic self-abasement as her letters to Wyndham Lewis, and show how exciting it must have been to get involved with her and how difficult to escape from her grasp: "When you've really killed me I'll become a nun. I'm dying from not seeing you. I'm impatient for the *coup de grace.*... I kiss you on...hard to choose when everything is perfect.... You cross Paris at night to be with me...and when I hold out my hands to you and my entire heart, not to mention a shoulder against which you sleep very well—then you run away leaving a little hissing snake instead."[16]

Beatrice was a catalyst in Modi's career. Despite or perhaps because of their physical and emotional struggles, the paintings he completed during his two years with her gained in intensity, maturity, even tranquility. After she left him he drank too much, starved himself and caught influenza. He collapsed in his dismal studio in the Bateau Lavoir, where Soutine gradually nursed him back to health.

Nine

INNER EYE,
1915–1916

I

◄੩ AFTER TEN years in Paris, Modi's life had settled into a predictable, if chaotic, routine. Debilitated by tuberculosis, drink and drugs, he could not live within his modest means, sustain a relationship with a woman or control his erratic behavior. Though intent on self-destruction, he worked extremely hard. At night he might be out of control; by day he painted in his studio. His art was the only stable element of his life, his only solace and purpose. He could have said, like T. S. Eliot in *The Waste Land,* "These fragments I have shored against my ruins," and his fragments were exceptionally beautiful. He created thousands of fine drawings, and some of the best portraits and nudes of the twentieth century.

Modi felt compelled to draw and paint despite illness and poverty. The creation of art was his joy and satisfaction (perhaps the only real joy in his life), but his lack of sales and recognition made him bitter. This continuous disappointment caused him to lapse into the ruinous habits that would weaken his creative powers and shorten his life. He painted most of his pictures during the last five years of his life, and completed one every five or six days. He never kept track of these pieces and lost a great many of them. Angry and discouraged, he gave his works away, used them to pay rent and bills, or abandoned them during his frequent moves. Sometimes he deliberately destroyed them, sometimes they were accidentally destroyed. Nevertheless, he went on producing works of art. Twenty-five statues and about

350 paintings have survived, including fifteen portraits of Beatrice, twenty-three of Jeanne Hébuterne and thirty-six nudes.

Modi did not paint still lifes, animals or abstract pictures, and
completed only five landscapes. Instead, he concentrated in both
portraits and nudes on vividly sympathetic images of men,
women and children. He drew or painted as many as 160 subjects, including some of the greatest artists and writers of his
time, and frequently printed their names on the wet paint with
the wooden end of his brush. His characteristically full-face portraits are, like Modi himself, dramatic and confrontational. Most
of them are single figures, confined to a room, with closed doors
behind them. His solitary subjects—elegant or crude, sensual
or cool, brilliant or dull—seem sealed off from the rest of the
world.

Portrait painting reached its peak in the Renaissance, when
images of the great and powerful had political significance and
utility. Traditional portrait painters, concerned with an accurate
likeness of the subject, tried to convey both the visible aspects
of the personality and the psychological interpretation of character. Leonardo da Vinci described the ideal goal of psychological realism when he wrote that the painter can put "before the
lover the very image of the beloved object, and the lover often
engages with it, embracing it and talking with it." Leonardo's
portraits are famous for their mysterious quality, which draws
the viewer into intimate contact with the subject. The art critic
Meyer Schapiro observed that before the nineteenth century,
"the painter of a portrait, especially life-size or nearly life-size,
often aimed to convey the dignity of his subject through en-
nobling, enhancing attributes: costumes, postures, gestures, and
accessories, the indices of rank, role, and achievement." The
finest portraits achieved vivid realism and conveyed the essence
of the sitter's personality.

This was the artistic tradition that Modigliani, like other
modern painters, both imitated and reacted against. In contrast

to a traditional artist, who would spend months on a single work, Modi—temperamentally quick, assertive and impatient—painted with great speed and completed most portraits in a single sitting. He accentuated his natural inclinations with the aid of stimulants and worked himself up to a burst of creative energy that could rarely be sustained or, once spent, revived. The rush of drunken, sometimes violent, inspiration, followed by sudden exhaustion, did not allow him to include the fine details and symbolic attributes that could have added depth and meaning to his pictures. Devoid of context or accoutrements, his isolated actors appear on a bare stage. Yet Modi's genius turned this limitation into a virtue and led him to perfect a refined minimalism. He portrayed, with a frank, unselfconscious vision, the natural appearance of his subjects, and by eliminating characteristic gestures and narrative elements forced viewers to see people differently and work a bit harder to understand them.

By 1914 Modi had abandoned his naturalistic, presculptural portraits, a legacy of his training in nineteenth-century Italy, for a more individualistic style. Influenced by Freudian psychology, he rejected the limitations of the "retinal" tradition and felt free to use, distort or ignore visible reality. John Pope-Hennessy wrote that in the modern age we have become conscious "of the dichotomy between the visible and hidden aspects of the personality, between what can be perceived and what lies concealed within. We may well question the assumption…that external fidelity is the prime criterion of portraiture. [A portrait] in which reality is willfully distorted to reveal the inner man, will seem the most profound."[1]

The invention of the camera seemed to have liberated portraitists from producing exact likenesses, and gave painters like Modi a new freedom to portray their response to the subject as well as the subject itself. Though the model's personality inspired his work, "the facial and psychological traits of the real person," one critic remarked, "were to be the starting point for the creation of forms to be filtered through the screen of stylistic abstraction." As early as 1907, Modi had expressed an ambition worthy of Leonardo: "What I am searching for is neither the real nor the unreal, but the Subconscious, the mystery of what is Instinctive in the human Race."[2] Though the features of his sitters were never exact, he almost always created a recognizable likeness and captured the essence of the character.

When he gave up sculpture and made his dramatic reentry into painting in the summer of 1914, Modi had found an artistic idiom—the simplified forms and distorted features of African sculpture—to augment the traditional forms. In both statues and pictures he depicted a masklike face and oval head with hair piled up on top, small blank eyes, sharp sword-nose, tiny pursed mouth and elongated neck. In the S-shaped *Portrait of a Woman* (1916–17), for example, the primitive-looking head seems to have been severed from the body and then reconnected by a thick swerving column. Like the statues, the paintings exaggerate realistic features. His subjects have heads as heavy and round as cannon balls, or as elongated and concave as African masks.

But Modi also retained the lessons of the Italian masters. As Pope-Hennessy observed of Botticelli, he can "animate the human face, he can apprehend its contours and its planes, he can invest it with a sentient response." Removing the shadows that hid the features he wanted to portray, he reduced his composition to bare essentials and muted colors, but created a "tension between the decorative line that swells and contracts, and the backgrounds scraped and scrubbed and rich in oil." In this way, "the subtle tonal variations emerge or a complementary colour comes through, appearing to adjust the depth of the portrait." Like Giorgione's richly detailed scenes, Modi's glowing nudes "taught educated people that the world could be looked at in a more pleasurable, more subjective way." Despite his "primitive" stylistic mannerisms, his portraits convey the powerful impact of an individual personality. Modi's best portraits concentrate attention on the eyes—even when they are blank—and evoke the mysterious and intriguing character of the sitter. Ehrenburg noted "their sadness, their frozen immobility, their haunted tenderness, their air of doom."[3]

Modi always needed the immediate inspiration of a model and insisted, "To do any work, I must have a living person, I must be able to see him opposite me." Nina Hamnett recalled that he was drawn to unattractive models as well as to beautiful ones. He once "approached a woman with an exceptionally ugly but interesting face. He said, 'Madame, your face interests me enormously. It's the most monstrous mug I've ever seen, but interesting, admirable, from a drawing point of view, and I would love to draw you.' The poor lady was very embarrassed but later, I think, when she found out who he was, she sat for him. Modigliani always said 'Admirrable' when he saw something that pleased him." Like his previous patrons Paul Alexandre and Georges Chéron, the frame maker and art dealer Constant Lepoutre supplied Modi with drink as well as models to fire him up. "He provides the materials, the model too," Modi gratefully exclaimed, using an English word to describe his latest Maecenas, "gives me twenty francs each time, and on the table there's always a quarter-litre of rum. Lepoutre's a *gentleman!*"[4]

Two friends gave detailed accounts of his method. His execution was rapid, but both emphasized his reflection before getting started. The painter Gabriel Fournier mentioned Modi's focus on the sitter's eyes and the way he soothed himself when inspiration took over. He would stare for a while at the eyes, "then the pencil would run in every direction all over the sheet of paper whilst he would keep himself calm by humming tunes to himself....If the first impulse was not satisfactory, Modigliani took on an air of bored indifference; he would look about him quickly before throwing himself on a blank sheet that he would maul violently with his pencil." When it was complete, he would reward himself with a drink—often in exchange for a drawing.

Paul Alexandre described the techniques he used to achieve his subtle effects: "Before painting he would draw in the outline (often in blue) after a long period of thought. Then he would apply his colours diluted with a large quantity of spirit." Like the works of old masters, Modi's paintings have a patina that gives them warmth and depth, and he achieved this effect with deliberate care: "He would varnish the work very carefully spreading a thin layer of wax over it. Then when it was dry he would rub it with a piece of hide or flannel."[5]

II

MODI HAD used stylized African sculpture to simplify and exaggerate the sitter's features, but his sinuous, elongated figures derive from later sources: Byzantine art and the Italian Mannerists. Like El Greco—another Mediterranean transplant who worked in a foreign country—he was influenced by the Byzantine art he'd seen in Venice. These Eastern Orthodox icons (also a major influence on Brancusi) had dark skin, tilted heads, almond-shaped eyes, tiny mouths and sharp noses (like arrows shot onto the face) that merged with the eyebrows. The austere images of the saints also emphasized the serpentine curves of the body. From El Greco himself, whose work he saw in the Salon d'Automne of 1908, Modi adopted the subtle blending of Byzantine stylization and Venetian naturalism, and imitated the attenuated figures placed on a slightly oblique axis.

Always working within his native tradition, Modi was even closer to the Italian Mannerists: Jacopo Pontormo, Agnolo Bronzino and Francesco Parmigianino. Modi was in fact a modern Mannerist who refashioned the sixteenth-century style for the twentieth century. The Mannerists, who also departed from realistic portrayal, combined fine draftsmanship, asymmetrical compositions, exaggerated refinement and graceful sophistication with what Kenneth Clark called "an unnatural length of limb, an impossible slenderness of body, and a self-conscious elegance of bearing." Like the figures in Mannerist art, some of

Modi's subjects (like *Gaston Modot,* 1918) seem to have too many vertebrae in their swanlike, even giraffelike necks, and oval heads that twist like flowers swaying on their stalks.

The subject of Bronzino's *Laura Battiferri* (c.1555) has extremely long fingers, nose and neck, accentuated by her open collar. In Parmigianino's *The Marriage of St. Catherine* (1521), as in Modi's nudes, the curves of the figures (in John Shearman's words) "flow together to climaxes, and then part again—curves filled with their own aesthetic vitality." His *Madonna del Collo Lungo (Madonna of the Long Neck,* 1534–36)—a key picture for Modi—portrays an immensely tall Virgin, with an oval face, extended column of a neck and prehensile fingers. The dome-headed infant Christ, splayed across her lap with drooping arm and head, is also disproportionately long and large, and looks more like a five-year-old than a baby. In Parmigianino's celebrated *Self-Portrait in a Convex Mirror* (c.1524), as in several of Modi's portraits, "the mouth diminishes in disconcerting fashion on the right, and the eyes...appear to rest on two quite different planes."[6]

Modi painted the outline rather than details of the ears, which in his female subjects were often covered by hair. But he paid close attention to the eyes, the most striking aspect of his portraits. Just as he portrayed the inner character as well as the outward form, so his subjects also looked inward and examined themselves. The eyes of his figures—flashing with genius or melting with sadness—wander eerily between the closed or averted eyes of classical nudes and the bold frontal stare of Manet's *Olympia.* In Modi's portraits the eyes are not only open or closed, but can also have one eye open and one closed, and blank eyes that are black, blue, or even crosshatched. His children usually have wide open, innocently inquiring, bright azure eyes that seem to show the sky through their skulls. Modi could have found his idiosyncratic blank eyes in medieval sculpture, like the thirteenth-century Gothic statue of St. John the Baptist in Rheims Cathedral. More significantly, he would have seen blank eyes in Picasso's early paintings, *Bust of a Man* and *Woman with Joined Hands* (both 1907), and a man with one eye open and one shut in Picasso's *Portrait of Pallarés* (1909).

Carol Mann described Modi's various eyes as "blank, yet hypnotic, frequently both; stars, tiny cacti, diamond studs, pools, lakes, whirlpools, metal spheres." Instead of matching the eyes, he emphasized the difference between them by making one light, the other dark. The blank eyes and blank stares — which may have reflected his own drugged state — gave his subjects a distance and aloofness, made them more mysterious and unknowable. The closed eyes suggested an inner meditation and perception of truths denied to those with vision. As Modi told Soutine: "Cézanne's figures, just like the finest statues of antiquity, do not look. Mine, on the contrary, do. They see, even when I have chosen not to draw the pupils." When one of his sitters asked why he'd been portrayed with a single eye, Modi replied: "because you look out at the world with one eye, and into yourself with the other." He may also have meant to suggest his *own* eye penetrating his subject. The heart of his aesthetics reached back to the Neoplatonic doctrine of the eye as the window of the soul and to the contrast between outer and inner vision, both described by the mystic William Blake in "The Everlasting Gospel" (1810):

> This life's five windows of the soul
> Distorts the Heavens from pole to pole,
> And leads you to believe a lie
> When you see with, not thro', the eye.[7]

III

REVIEWING THE major Modigliani show at the Jewish Museum in New York in June 2004, the influential art critic Robert Hughes recycled a clever but superficial judgment of the portraits: "At first glance, Modigliani's art gives the impression of monotony....Yes, and at second glance, too....[His subjects] all look like one another....That is why, if you want to be frank about it, so many of them are so boring." But his subjects, though stylized, are quite distinctive individuals, and it's absurd to claim that his Diego Rivera looks like his Jean Cocteau, that his Soutine resembles his Léon Bakst.

Diego Rivera, a great womanizer, of gargantuan stature and appetites, had a daughter with Marevna and, later on, married the painter Frida Kahlo. Born in 1886 in the silver-mining town of Guanajuato, Mexico, the son of a teacher and school inspector, he went to Spain in 1907 and moved to Paris two years later, where for a time he shared a studio with Modigliani. In 1914 Modi painted the burly, bearded, bearish Rivera in the same stippled, impasto style as his portraits of Picasso and Frank Burty Haviland. Rivera's massive, copper-colored head (tilted to the left), high forehead and large jowly cheeks, encircled by a thick beard, stand out against his dark clothing and the dark swirling background. His huge, lightly sketched arm and bear-paw hand rest on his expansive belly. Below his high eyebrows his eyes are narrow slits and his thick, comically sensual lips meet in a self-satisfied smile. Like the statue of a rotund oriental god or the hearty burger in Edouard Manet's *Le Bon Bock* (*The Good Beer*, 1873), Rivera exudes repletion and contentment, and seems suffused with well-being. His biographer wrote that Modi captured "the savagery, smoldering sensuous fire, fantastic imagination and mighty irony for which Diego was famous. His Rivera is large and heavy, savage and overflowing, mocking and bombastic."

Modi's portraits of two Iberian painters, the Portuguese José Pacheco (1885–1934) and the Spanish Juan Gris (1887–1927), are among his best pictures of 1915. Pacheco wears a gray, flat-topped, broad-banded, wide-brimmed, rakishly tilted Córdoba hat that establishes a dynamic contrast with the angle of his head. He has dark, blank, almond-shaped eyes under thick eyebrows, a long bony nose and cupid's-bow lips. His ocherous skin is clean shaven, but with the suggestion of a heavy beard, and he has a strikingly handsome square jaw and chin. He wears an open tan jacket, and his high-necked gray sweater and blue-striped scarf reflect the colors of the background. Though quite ordinary looking in his photo, Pacheco, in Modi's portrait, becomes a dashing, swaggering, macho personality.

The serious, pensive Juan Gris was born in Madrid, the thirteenth child of a rich Castilian merchant. After abandoning engineering for art, he moved to Paris in 1906 and lived in the Bateau Lavoir. A Cubist follower of Picasso and Braque, he remained in Paris during the war, worked for Diaghilev and the Ballets Russes, and befriended Gertrude Stein and Raymond Radiguet. In 1915 Modi portrayed Gris with thick black hair and eyebrows, downward-sloping eyes with spiky eyelashes, a triangular nose with wide nostrils and soft burgundy lips. His terra-cotta skin, as if burnished by a hot sun, is set against an orange-tinted background; his head, awkwardly supported by a wide un-anatomical neck, swings strangely to the left. The *V* of his white shirt shows between his dark jacket. Modi captured Gris' Spanish gravity as well as the dreamy expression that suggests the contemplation of his next picture.

Modi portrayed the twenty-seven-year-old Jean Cocteau, as he did Max Jacob and Paul Guillaume, as a dandy. John Richardson wrote that the poet, playwright and novelist, screenwriter and balletomane, drug addict and nonstop talker "was undoubtedly charming, decorative, mercurial, witty: a passable poet and *feuilletoniste* [literary essayist] and a dazzling conversationalist.... But he was also...on the make, frivolous, treacherous, snobbish—a poseur whose principal claim to fame was a book of very light verse.... [He had] hollow rouged cheeks, thick, dark curly hair above a high forehead and very large black eyes. Always elegantly dressed, he heightened his complexion with lipstick."[8] Cocteau, defining Modi with a list of contradictory qualities, recalled that he was "handsome, grave and Romantic...

sour-tempered, generous and loyal....A dark fire kindled his entire being, radiating through the fabric of his clothes and confer-
ring on his slovenly figure a certain dandyish air. He was joyful,
witty and charming."

Like Lipchitz, Cocteau tried to pay a little more for the large
40 x 32-inch painting, but graciously accepted it for almost nothing. He also gave a perhaps apocryphal account of how it ended
up in the United States:

> Modigliani wanted to give it to me, but I did not want him to.
> "Won't you sell it to me?" I asked him. So he sold it to me
> for *cent sous*—five francs. But to take away so large a picture
> an open cab was needed, and I didn't have the wherewithal
> to hire one. So it remained a long time in Kisling's studio.
> Kisling owed eleven francs to the owner of the Café Ro-
> tonde; he asked him whether he would take the portrait in-
> stead of the eleven francs, and he did. For a long time it hung
> above the banquette in the Rotonde, and then began that as-
> tonishing voyage that took it to England, where it was sold
> for seven million francs, and then to America, where it was
> sold for seventeen million. It is in America now.

If Cocteau—well off and supported by his mother— could pay
for the portrait, why couldn't he afford a cab? And if he wanted
the portrait, why didn't he arrange to take it home instead of
abandoning it in Kisling's studio? The story illustrates the casual
way people treated Modi's work, leaving it to mildew or subjecting it to the smoke of a café.

Like *The Amazon,* also rejected by its subject, *Jean Cocteau*
(1916) is a masterpiece. Seated in a high-backed red velvet throne,
Cocteau is constricted in a narrow bow tie and a tightly buttoned
black suit, with two points of a handkerchief jutting out of the
breast pocket. He has a thick turban of hair, irregular eyebrows
and eyes: the smaller one closed and black, the larger one showing the white and pupil. His thin wrist and the long elegant

fingers of his skeletal hand rest on his lap; his rouged cheeks and lips highlight his narrow head, pointed triangular chin and jutting nose, sharply angled to his face. The picture's three delicate shades of blue are reprised in the faint patch of blue between his nose and lips. Cocteau's mincing mouth and ossified angularity suggest the pomposity and conceit of this homosexual and poseur: posing and deposed from his throne. Beatrice Hastings said that Modi "loathed Cocteau." In his essay on Modi, Cocteau hinted at his reason for abandoning the painting when he wrote that "his judgement of us, his reaction to us, his liking or antipathy, are distinctly expressed in the drawings." Later on, he spoke of his portrait as being diabolical and said he considered it proof that Modi had detested him.[9]

Léon Bakst created the exuberant décor and costumes of the Ballets Russes, for which Gris and Cocteau provided scenery and scenarios. Born Lev Rosenberg in Russia in 1866, he was fifty-one in 1917, about twenty years older than most of Modi's artist friends. A historian of the Russian ballet described Bakst as having "curly red hair, very carefully brushed, with lively, slightly laughing eyes and clean-shaven cheeks. He was elegantly dressed and smelt of scent"—and, in Modi's portrait, figuratively still does. The French novelist and diplomat Paul Morand commented on Bakst's unusual appearance and odd mannerisms, which appealed to Modi: "Bakst, with his look of a professional soldier, sparse reddish hair, small ridiculously dapper military moustache, nearsighted, glasses, wearing his dinner jacket like a croupier, speaks with a ridiculous lisp."

Unlike Cocteau, Bakst was well pleased with his portrait (now in the National Gallery in Washington). Like many others, he emphasized Modi's aristocratic air, and told a friend: "He's doing my portrait. Here's a line-drawing he's done for it. Look at the care he's taken. All the features in my face are etched as if with a needle, and there's no retouching. I'm sure he must be poor; but he has the air of a *grand seigneur*. He really is 'somebody,' I assure you."[10] Facing the viewer and filling the frame, Bakst has closely cropped red hair, a pale expansive forehead, tiny blue eyes beneath thin eyebrows curving around the sockets, an engagingly crooked smile and a pale drooping unmilitary mustache, much longer and lower on the right side. In contrast to most sitters, he wears a richly colored costume: a luxurious V-shaped indigo scarf below the V of his neck and the even smaller V of his upper lip, and a black jacket decorated with gold medallions and epaulettes. The round face, sloping mustache and exotic robe are vaguely oriental and make Bakst look like an epicene Chinese mandarin.

Modi's 1917 portrait of Madame Georges Van Muyden, related to a family of Swiss artists, once again shows that he could have become a fashionable society painter. Seated in three-quarter view—before a soothing steel blue background that reflects the color of her eyes—she's dressed in a formal black gown, deeply cut and showing slight cleavage, trimmed with gray and with a gray belt around her narrow waist. She holds a fan in her clawlike fingers, wears a bracelet and rests her left hand, cut off at the lower right edge of the picture, on a brown pillow. Her cheeks are red, her chest and arms pale, and her head (like that of Juan Gris) is tilted to the left and almost detached from her neck. Modi portrays her as a gracious and elegant upper-class lady.

The following year Modi did four portraits of Elvira (known as "La Quique," or "La Chica"), who came from the other end of the social scale. Her father was a transient Spanish naval officer, her mother a laundress and prostitute from Marseilles (home of the Garsins). She'd run away to Paris at the age of fifteen, met Modi and, in a glowing testimonial based on extensive experience, said that he "was the best lover she ever had." After living abroad with several different men, she'd been kept by a Dutch aristocrat in Berlin, where she learned to sing.

All four 1918 portraits—two of her seated and dressed, two of her standing and nude—portray the blue-eyed Elvira in front of Modi's characteristic pale grayish blue background. In one seated portrait she wears an elaborate lace collar and folds her hands in her lap; in the other, she leans her left arm on a table, next to a white bowl of fruit, and rests her chin on her hand. In the best standing nude she has bangs and blank almond eyes in a ruddy, masklike face that's darker than her tan, high-breasted body, and modestly holds a thickly painted cloudlike cloth in front of her pelvis. She shows, quite unusually, the collarbone of her soft body, and her arms form an oval that echoes the shape of her face. She has a gentle expression, and looks inward as well as straight out at the viewer. In all the portraits she looks much younger than her actual age of thirty-six (two years older than Modi) and has a melancholy expression that seems to anticipate her tragic fate. Though cocaine soon ruined her voice, she joined a troupe of entertainers during the war and was captured near the front line. The military authorities heard her speaking German, refused to believe she was a singer and shot her as a spy.

Modi rarely did double portraits, like *Bride and Groom* and *Jacques Lipchitz and His Wife,* but two of his finest works are *Gypsy with Baby* (1918) and *Seated Woman with Baby* (1919). "Bohémienne," the French word for a female gypsy, was derived from the mistaken notion that gypsies came from Bohemia, now part of Czechoslovakia; and that word also described artists who led a defiant, nomadic, unconventional life. A historian noted that "attention to gypsies and vagabonds was encouraged by the Romantic fascination for the exotic, the uncivilized, the unclassifiable, the attempt to invoke deeper levels of human nature, which reason could not grasp, nor organized social life satisfy."

The gypsy woman, with an oval face, dark hair parted on her forehead, a little braid dangling down one side, surprisingly bright blue eyes and crimson cheeks, is an attractive Modigliani type. Tidied up for the portrait and dressed in a coral-and-white-striped middy blouse, long knotted gray scarf and billowing aquamarine skirt, she's seated facing the viewer. On her lap and between her clasped hands, she holds a sleeping or perhaps nursing baby, tightly wrapped in a thick navy blue blanket, its face hidden beneath a long pointed woolen wind-sock cap. The stripes of the gypsy's interlaced fingers reprise the stripes on her middy blouse and on the top and bottom of the conical cap. The mother is both gentle with her baby and fiercely protective.

Marc Restellini mentioned the unusual colors in *Seated Woman with Baby:* "aside from black and white, Modigliani adds to his usual palette of brown, russet-red and grey-green, the ultramarine of the child's wrap, the bright green of its bonnet, the pink of the mother's neck-opening and the light blue of her eyes."[11] The expansive background of this late picture is also unusual. Two brown doors open into an empty room, with walls divided into reddish brown panels, easing the characteristic confinement of his subjects.

Though the woman's face is more oval than the round-faced *Peasant Boy Leaning on a Table* that Modi had painted in 1918, they look alike, have the same red hair and blue eyes, and may well belong to the same family. Both the woman and the baby have identical almond-shaped blue eyes. Seated and looking straight out at the viewer, the woman wears a green fringed shawl (matching the baby's hat) over a black velvety jacket and pink blouse, and holds (but doesn't clasp) the baby with her long stiff arm and unusually large right hand. Modi's most notable baby glances to the left, immobile and apparently contented. The baby has a pale round face, puffy cheeks and pudgy hand, and wears a green hat pulled low on the forehead, blue sweater, stiff billowing milky skirt (echoed by the soft bed on the right) and rigid brown boots. In contrast to the gypsy and baby, and to the traditional madonna and child, this woman—nursemaid rather than mother—has no strong, affectionate connection with the doll-like, Russian-looking baby.

Though Modi portrayed very few old people, he was a great painter of the poetic melancholy of children. His children are not cheeky and self-assured like Degas', prettified and soft-focused like Renoir's, perfectly groomed and well behaved like Cassatt's or idealized young tycoons like Sargent's. He shows real compassion for working-class children, who seem orphaned and old for their years, yet trusting and immediately engaging. His children retreat from the harsh adult world into a closely constricted corner. As he paints them, they seem to be enjoying, perhaps for the first time in their lives, the sympathy and absolute attention of an adult.

His three best portraits of children were done in Nice in 1918, when he had trouble finding adult models. They show a great advance on his more conventional and rather wooden portrait, *Alice* (1915), of a little girl in a pale blue dress with a small crucifix pinned to her chest. The austere, bust-length adolescent in *Girl with Blue Eyes* appears before a background of rough gray panels. She has parted russet hair, two uneven braids dangling beside her head, pale blue eyes with no pupils and full ruby lips. She wears a plain, high-necked, dark blue dress. Her expression is pleasant but somewhat blank, as if she'd been surprised by a photographer, and it's difficult to read her sweet but enigmatic character.

The close-up child in *Girl with Braids* is one of Modi's most attractive and popular images. The vertical line in the background, separating the cloudy blue wall and brown door, bisects her head, bangs and braids. She has wide-open, clear blue eyes, with light reflected in the pupils, a button nose and white rabbity teeth between full lips. Her round cheeks curve to a charmingly pointed chin and a reasonably normal neck. Her high-necked red dress, with sloping shoulders, has pleats in front and a hint of maidenly breasts. She seems at once appealing and vulnerable.

The younger girl in *Girl in a Blue Dress* stands on a square-tiled floor and in a corner formed by grayish blue walls. Her bent shadow, unusual in a Modigliani painting, appears on her left like a ghost. The walls, her lace-collared dress and bright eyes are all done in the same shade of blue. With a broad nose and tiny sinuous mouth, she's adorned with a figure-eight ribbon in her dark hair and rivulets of bangs running down her forehead. Clasping her hands in front of her, she shows a bit of her white legs between the hem of her dress and her high black boots. Solitary and winsome, with a graceful gravity, she has the same pose of the figure in *Servant Girl* (also 1918). In contrast to figures in front of the traditional open window and harmonious landscape in Renaissance portraits, she seems trapped by poverty, locked behind closed doors, destined for a life of menial work and domestic service. Modi's children are sweet, sad and sympathetic. Like Blake in his *Songs of Innocence,* he seems to ask:

> Can I see another's woe,
> And not be in sorrow too?
> Can I see another's grief,
> And not seek for kind relief?

Observing the trusting pathos in the portraits of these "hurt" children, Ehrenburg concluded that "the world seemed to Modigliani like an enormous kindergarten run by very unkind adults."[12]

Ten

SIMONE AND JEANNE,
1917–1918

I

⊰ IN JUNE 1916, halfway through the war, Léopold Zborowski succeeded Paul Guillaume as Modi's patron and dealer. Paul Alexandre and Guillaume were well-connected Frenchmen; Zbo, like the artist himself, was a poor foreigner and outsider. Modi's paintings expressed his attitude toward his three patrons: his portrait of Alexandre was formal and respectful; he treated Guillaume with satiric irony and Zbo with affectionate intimacy. Guillaume had been his patron during his liaison with Beatrice Hastings; Modi's connection to Zbo coincided with his friendship with the writer Blaise Cendrars and his affairs with Simone Thiroux and Jeanne Hébuterne. Beatrice had left the scene, taking the intellectual fireworks and domestic comforts with her, and her replacements were young, insecure and emotionally dependent. Modi's new entanglements proved even less sustaining than the old.

Haphazard, generous and idealistic, five years younger than Modi, Zbo had the face of an amiable sheepdog. Like Modi, he was an invalid, and suffered all his life from rheumatism, a weak heart and (according to Cendrars) epilepsy. The son of a jeweler, he was born in March 1889 in the Polish village of Zaleschiki, about 120 miles southeast of Lvov, then under the domination of the Austro-Hungarian empire. After studying literature at the University of Cracow, he came to Paris in 1913 and enrolled in a course on French culture at the Sorbonne. Marevna said that Zbo had originally led a reckless, Modi-like life and called him "a Polish poet who had dragged out a wretched, dissipated, cocaine-saturated existence until an intelligent and sensible Polish woman took him in hand and married him." Anna (called Hanka) Cirowska, the daughter of a rich, aristocratic Polish family, met him soon after his arrival in Paris. When the war broke out, he was interned as an enemy alien for several months.

Zbo lived at 3 rue Joseph Bara, in the same building as his compatriot Moïse Kisling, who called him a poet with his head in the clouds, and introduced him to Modi. Like Theo Van Gogh, Vincent's brother, patron and dealer, Zbo loved Modi, nurtured his genius and tried to sell his work. The two formed a close friendship. Charles Douglas, noting the contrast between artist and patron, wrote that the recently rehabilitated but still sickly Zbo "was sober, patient, long-suffering and gentle in the same degree that Modi was doped, drunken, irritable, and violent." Zbo, who had a passionate love of art and devotion to Modi, believed that he was a "very great artist." But Zbo also lived hand to mouth, did not own a gallery and sold art from his humble flat. He regretted his poverty not for his own sake, but for Modi's, and told a friend: "I'm sorry that I don't have the money to allow him to paint, and to avoid drawing on the terrace of a café."[1] For the remainder of his life, Modi barely managed to exist on the irregular remittances from his mother in Livorno, drawings that he dashed off and sold in cafés, and Zbo's sacrificial yet inadequate patronage — most of which he immediately spent on drink.

When Zbo finally found a studio for Modi, who'd been painting from models as well as on the doors in Zbo's flat, he and Hanka cleaned and furnished it. At first Modi, who slept late in the morning and stayed up till the cafés closed at night, was very punctual and worked from two to six in the afternoon. Zbo deprived himself of tobacco to provide Modi with drink, which released his imagination and stimulated his creative impulse. When he drank in a studio he painted; when he drank in a café he became violent. At the same time Zbo knew he should try to control Modi's alcoholism, which, together with tuberculosis, was destroying his health and ability to work. Cendrars condemned Zbo for exploiting Modi's weakness and for committing a "crime" against an artist to make money. He wrote that Zbo locked Modi in a room with paints, model and drink, and at the end of the day he "opened the door as if it were the cage of a wild beast." This method produced pictures, even if Zbo couldn't sell them.

The novelist Francis Carco — chronicler of Montmartre and lover of Katherine Mansfield — sometimes bought Modi's drawings. He was another ambitious outsider, born on the French Pacific island of New Caledonia. Fernande Olivier said that Carco, "perpetually on the defensive, and jeering with a vicious, observant eye, took in everything." Carco gave a lively account of the perverse way Zbo conducted business and explained why he sold so few of Modi's pictures: "When one went to see Zborowski, he would run down to buy a candle and, setting it in the neck of a bottle, he would take you into a narrow room without furniture, bare, desolate, in a corner of which the painter's canvases were heaped. Lighted by a candle, Zbo showed his treasures, stroking them passionately with his hands and devouring them with his eyes, then, fascinated, he would spit with disgust, talk agitatedly and curse the fate which crushed Modigliani." When Carco finally decided on a purchase, Zbo responded in a strange way:

> I said to him, "sell me that nude, will you?"
> "You love it?"
> "It is very beautiful."...
> "To you," he decided, "I won't sell...I shall give it. Here...I give it to you...because you love it."
> "And the money for Modigliani?"
> "No...Take it, I am so pleased you love it...Forget the money question...Don't bother about that...Tomorrow a

man is coming to buy some clothes...He'll give me twenty francs. That will be enough."

Modi hated intrusions when he was painting and compared them to the violation of a sanctuary. Kiki, who modeled for Kisling in a neighboring studio, reported that Zbo, taking more than a professional interest in the nude models, climbed "the stairs several times in the course of the morning, just to get an eyeful and see how things are coming along."[2] Modi was well aware that his dependence on Zbo's supply of alcohol had turned him into an artistic galley slave. On a rather hasty drawing of *"J"* in 1916, he penitentially wrote (as he had previously written on a drawing of Cocteau), "The artist is drunk. A confession."

Though Modi's unsold paintings piled up in the studio (to be profitably disposed of after his death), between 1916 and 1919 Zbo also commissioned six portraits of himself. The last one (now in São Paulo) is the best. Seated on a gold-framed chair and casting a shadow on the pale blue background, Zbo faces the viewer with legs crossed and hands clasped in his lap. He wears a black tie set against a white collar and a russet suit that matches his thick hair, parted and hanging down the side of his forehead, while his slightly paler beard, trimmed to an elegant point, touches the top of his collar and accentuates his oval face. He has blank blue eyes, a pudgy nose, sensual lips and a divided mustache that slopes down to his beard. His pose is dignified and relaxed, his expression gentle and refined.

During the same period Hanka sat for twelve portraits—the two best completed in 1917. In *Hanka Zborowska with a White Collar,* a bust-length, front-face portrait, she has a long oval head and terra-cotta complexion. One of her eyes is black, the other shows the white. Her hair is elegantly styled, with strands flowing over her ears; and she's dressed in a high, stiff, angel's wing collar, fastened to her V-necked dress with an amber brooch. In this picture, Modi captures Hanka's calm, self-possessed, aristocratic appearance.

In *Hanka Zborowska Seated on a Divan,* she wears a stark black V-necked dress that accentuates her long neck (which echoes the oval shape of her face), and her narrow waist and billowing skirt are set dramatically against a swirling, flame-colored background. She rests her right arm, with hands clasped, on the reddish brown divan, which is streaked with orange and yellow and decorated with wavy lines. Her jet black hair is parted and piled high on her head; her face is pale and masklike; her eyes are tiny black almonds; her nose long and narrow; her lips delicious. In this stunning portrait, Hanka is sensual, yet enigmatic and aloof.

II

BLAISE CENDRARS met Modi just after the artist arrived in Paris in 1906 and was struck by how well dressed he was, how rich he seemed. Since then, Cendrars had traveled the world and fought in the war. Like Soutine and Beatrice, he was a spectacular character, a fascinating liar who created legends about himself. But the facts are colorful enough. Born Frédéric Sauser in La Chaux-de-Fonds, Switzerland, between Neuchâtel and the French border, he came from an Anabaptist family that had fled the French Jura. Soon after his birth, his father, a professor of mathematics, moved the family to Egypt and started a hotel. Cendrars, constantly on the move, was educated in Naples, spent his late teens as a Swiss watch salesman in St. Petersburg, and studied philosophy and medicine at the University of Berne. In 1911 he took the newly completed Trans-Siberian railroad across Russia, which inspired his first major work, *La Prose du Trans-sibérien* (1913). He was in New York in 1912, moved to Paris that year, became a friend of Apollinaire and Chagall, married a Polish woman and had two sons.

When the Great War broke out he joined the French Foreign Legion, like Zadkine and Kisling, and had his right arm blown off by a shell burst. His military citation, testifying to his courage under fire, reported that "although severely wounded at the beginning of the attack on September 28, 1915 and weakened by loss of blood he continued to lead his squadron and remained with them until the end of the battle." Severini, struck by his insouciance, wrote that he took the loss of his arm "in stride with such high spirits, ease, and sense of humor. It was incredible to watch the gestural effects that Cendrars managed to express with that empty sleeve." After the war, the multitalented Cendrars worked for the director Abel Gance on *J'accuse* (1919), a film based on Zola's defense of Captain Dreyfus; wrote the scenario for Darius Milhaud's ballet *The Creation of the World* (1923); and made five trips to South America. During World War II, he saw combat as a correspondent for several French newspapers.

Many English and American artists and writers were impressed by Cendrars' thirst for escape and adventure, his savage melancholy and violent temperament. The English painter Frank Budgen declared that "Cendrars seemed to have been everywhere: Russia. America. New York. St. Petersburg. Forests of the Amazon. He knew them all."[3] John Dos Passos exclaimed of Cendrars, who loved fast cars, that "it was hairraising to spin with him around the mountain roads. He steered with one hand and changed the gears on his little French car with his hook... took every curve on two wheels." Dos Passos' friend Hemingway, who hung out with Cendrars at the Closerie des Lilas, recalled an empty sleeve rather than a hook. In Hemingway's account, he was (like Hemingway himself) an entertaining, heavy drinking fantasist: "[I saw] Blaise Cendrars, with his broken boxer's face and his pinned up empty sleeve, rolling a cigarette with his one good hand. He was a good companion until he drank too much and, at that time, when he was lying, he was more interesting than many men telling a story truly."

Cendrars' disciple and imitator, Henry Miller, was rapturous about his tough guy persona, so irresistible to women. He told Anaïs Nin: "Cendrars looks rough, like a sailor—he is one at bottom—and he speaks rather loudly, but very well. He has only one arm, the empty one, or half-arm slung affectionately around my neck." In Montmartre, there were "whores hanging on to us, and Cendrars hugging them like a sailor, and urging me to take one, take two, take as many as you want." Miller also wrote that Cendrars, passionate about *Les Chants de Maldoror*, looked like the broken-nosed boxer and actor Victor McLaglen and "emanates health, joy, vitality." He praised Cendrars for consorting "with all types, including bandits, murderers, revolutionaries and other varieties of fanatics," and for being a "roustabout, tramp, bum, panhandler, mixer, bruiser, adventurer, sailor, soldier, tough guy." In short, Miller believed that he uniquely "restores to contemporary life the elements of the heroic, the imaginative and the fabulous."4

Like Miller, Modi found much to admire in Cendrars' zest and creativity. Cendrars took his pen name from the French words *braise* and *cendres*, which mean "glowing embers" and "ashes," and saw art as a form of arson. His books, a literary historian has observed, "are attempts to isolate the ego he incessantly contemplated in his multifarious activities—businessman, film-director, jewel-peddler, journalist.... His characters live and move on an epic scale and he has been praised for the resulting 'life-like' quality of his work (in fact due to skillful narrative art), which breaks with the French analytic tradition." Given his energetic volubility in life, it's not surprising that Cendrars conceived "the poem as a Dionysian act, the poet inspired by a [kind of Nietzschean] creative frenzy." "His output became a flood, diffuse in structure, torrential in composition and bewildering in its variety." Cendrars had the same logorrheic and often unreadable cascade of words as Gertrude Stein, Ezra Pound, Hart Crane, Thomas Wolfe, Norman Mailer and Allen Ginsberg.

Capitalizing on Modigliani's notoriety after his death, Cendrars liked to tell a dubious story about their days of drinking. His account, embellished by nostalgia, emphasized their swaggering male friendship and his superiority to Modi. Sitting together on the banks of the Seine with partly emptied bottles of wine and watching the legions of laundresses floating on the real *bateaux lavoir*, they drunkenly toasted the washerwomen, who replied with obscene gestures. Modi offered to give the ugliest old hag the remaining bottle if she allowed him to kiss her on the mouth. She refused, he stripped off his clothes, fished the cooling bottle out of the river and walked toward her barge without the benefit of a plank. Since he couldn't swim, he quickly sank and was hero-ically rescued by his one-armed *copain*. They celebrated the absurd incident by finishing off the last bottle of wine.

Cendrars' very minor poem, "On a Portrait by Modigliani," which compares a beating heart to a ticking watch, vaguely indi-cate the emotional impact of Modi's paintings. It was printed as an introduction to the catalogue of his one-man show at Berthe Weill's gallery in December 1917:

> The interior world
> The human heart with
> its 17 movements
> in the spirit
> And the to and fro of passion.

Modi did a 1917 sketch of Cendrars with his head tilted back and a cigarette dangling from his lips. He also, Cendrars wrote, "painted my portrait as if he were sketching, very quickly. It took him about three hours, and between brush-strokes he recited poetry by Dante and Baudelaire."[5] In this portrait, Modi gave Cendrars a prim little mouth and a broad but not broken nose, and made him look more sensitive than rough.

III

BEATRICE HASTINGS—tough, belligerent and independent— had exhausted him; Modigliani was now attracted to more bour-geois, passive and compliant women. Simone Thiroux, like the children in his paintings, was gentle and vulnerable. Eight years younger than Modi, she was born in Quebec in about 1892, the

daughter of a French-Canadian father and French mother. Orphaned at an early age and brought up by an aunt in Canada, she
was an excellent pianist and a high school graduate. After inher-
iting a legacy from her parents at the age of twenty-one, she
moved to Paris and planned to study medicine. But even more
than Suzanne Valadon, Nina Hamnett and Beatrice Hastings, Simone was an art groupie, a romantic drawn to the bohemian life,
who sought her destiny with an artist.

Charles Douglas described Simone as a pale, blue eyed, "good-
looking blonde; a tallish, elegant figure, very attractive, with a
charm that overcame...[her] careless way of dressing." She liked
to show off her breasts in a low-cut dress. Sad and silent, frail and
rather superficial, she was also stimulated by parties, loved "the
good things of life, [and was] fond of dancing, laughing, and having a merry time....Enchanted with the liberty and fun of the
artistic life, she lent and gave money away right and left." Simone
lived with an aunt in Paris, and by the time she met Modi at Rosalie's restaurant in the summer of 1916, she'd spent most of her
money, had nothing left for university fees, and was supporting
herself by giving English lessons and working as a nurse.

One night at the Rotonde the drunken Modi, upset when
Beatrice turned up with Alfredo Pina, provoked a furious fight
with Simone, cut her with a piece of broken glass and left her
with a permanent scar. This episode gave her a taste of the violent life she'd lead with Modi, and merely whetted her appetite
for more. Like Modi, she was a feverish consumptive who expected an early death, and was reckless about her appearance,
money, health and reputation. She had set out to seduce him,
and as soon as she succeeded he began to lose interest. He preferred to pursue women, and became impatient with the devoted and clinging Simone.

Modi frequently painted Simone, but apart from one stylized
pen-and-ink drawing, inscribed "Simone, 1917," none of her
portraits or nudes have been identified. Since no photograph of
Simone exists, we have to make a calculated guess about which

of his works may portray her. The most likely candidate is the blond, blue-eyed, full-breasted woman in *Lady with a Green Blouse* (1916, National Gallery, Washington, D.C.). Seated in three-quarter view and directly facing the spectator, she appears in front of a tan wall and russet door with two high windows. She has a pale oval face, with slight shading on the left side of her nose, and wears a low, round-necked, pale green blouse, a dark skirt and a pair of dangling earrings. Elegant and attractive, she radiates gentleness and serenity.

The model in *Standing Blond Nude with Lowered Chemise* (1917) has the same pale blue eyes and full breasts as Simone, though her hair, falling to her shoulders, is reddish blond. Standing before the tormented swirls of a bluish green background and next to a divan or bed, she has stippled rather than smooth skin and red cheeks that match her hair. Assuming the classical pose of the Venus de Milo, she submissively drops her white chemise below her faint red pubic hair and seems like a sweet Eve about to lose her innocence.

Another nude, which Osvaldo Patani dates as 1918 but could have been painted the previous year, may also be Simone. This subject, with reddish blond hair, pale blue eyes and ruddy cheeks, has an exquisite mouth. Seated in three-quarter length next to a bed and before a subtle steel blue background, she's luminously naked, with sloping shoulders and full breasts, and crosses her hands above her visible pubic hair. Though she cannot, like the others, hide behind her chemise, she's more withdrawn, meditative and self-possessed.

In August 1916, right after they met, Simone became pregnant, and the following May gave birth to a son, Serge Gérard. But Modi, who'd just met Jeanne Hébuterne, rejected Simone and her baby. He accused her of sleeping around, denied paternity and refused to take responsibility for the child, though people who saw Gérard said he looked exactly like Modi. In any case, neither of them could cope with a baby. Though trained as a nurse, Simone didn't know how to care for Gérard, couldn't even change his diapers, and soon gave him up for adoption. As an adult, Gérard did not want to be known as Modi's son, changed his surname, studied at a religious college and became a priest.

After her scandalous affair with Modi and the birth of her illegitimate child, Simone was rejected by her French relatives and turned out of her aunt's apartment. She continued to support herself by modeling for other artists and by working as a nurse at the Hôpital Cochin, where the boulevard du Montparnasse crosses the rue du Faubourg Saint Jacques. According to the model Kiki, who spent some time in the charity ward, the nurses were rude and insolent, and "in the evening there was only one little lamp to light up that big room where all you could hear were moans and death-rattles." A decade later George Orwell spent two weeks in the same place and described his grim experiences in "How the Poor Die." Though he had a temperature of 103 degrees, he was forced to take a cold bath and, wearing only a thin nightgown, had to walk two hundred yards across open grounds to reach the ward, which had a "foul smell, faecal and yet sweetish." The staff first cupped him with hot glasses and then applied an excruciating mustard poultice to his chest. In this part of the hospital the poor died slow, smelly and painful "natural" deaths.[6]

Weakened by childbirth and by the progress of her disease, Simone worked in the hospital by day and seized what pleasure she could at night. In May 1918 a French writer, noting Simone's lust for celebrities and apparent promiscuity, had reported that "the little Thiroux is running after Scandinavians—read rich Americans—anybody famous will do." In January 1919, twenty months after Gérard was born, Simone, though rejected by Modi, was still deeply in love and hoped to win him back. Her last letter to him (her only surviving words) expressed the same profound misery and pathetic humiliation as Beatrice's last letter to Wyndham Lewis.

In this intelligent, well-written and unbearably poignant valediction—for she knew she was going to die—she hopelessly
begged for reconciliation, consolation, even affection, and swore
she would not hold him responsible for the child:

> My thoughts turn to you on this new year which I so hope
> might be a year of moral reconciliation for us. I put aside all
> sentimentality and ask for only one thing which you will not
> refuse me because you are intelligent and not a coward: that
> is, a reconciliation that will allow me to see you from time to
> time.
>
> I swear on the head of my child, who is for me *everything,*
> that no bad idea passes through my mind. No—but I loved
> you too much, and I suffer so much that I ask this as a final
> plea.
>
> I will be strong. You know my present situation: materi-
> ally I lack nothing and earn my own living.
>
> My health is very bad, the tuberculosis sadly doing its work.
>
> But I can't go on any more—I would just like a little less
> hate from you. I beg you to think well of me. Console me a
> little, I am too unhappy, and I ask just a particle of affection
> that would do me so much good.
>
> I swear again that no hidden thought disturbs me.
>
> I have for you all the tenderness that I must have for you.[7]

But the last thing Modi wanted, two months after the birth of
his daughter with Jeanne, was an emotional entanglement with
another woman and the burden of another child. Horrified by
her disease that reflected his own, he could only harden his heart
against Simone's physical pain and mental anguish.

IV

IN MARCH 1917, when Simone was seven months pregnant,
Modi met the teenaged Jeanne Hébuterne, his last love. She
would take Simone's gentleness and passivity to the extremes of

stupor and paralysis. Fourteen years younger than Modi, she was born in her parents' flat at 8 rue Amyot, near the Panthéon, on April 6, 1898. Her father, Achille Casimir, an inoffensive little man in a frock coat, wore a square white beard and worked as chief cashier in the perfume section of the Bon Marché department store. Her older brother, André, was an academic landscape painter. Jeanne, a talented violinist, studied art at Modi's old school, the Académie Colarossi, on the rue de la Grande Chaumière, off the boulevard du Montparnasse. Here, as André Salmon wrote, "students were admitted without having to take an examination: a regular subscription, instead, gave one the right to draw from a live model and receive a few sketchy lessons and criticisms from a professional artist." Jeanne's talent had no time to develop. Her drawings and paintings, including two sketches of Modi reading (while wearing a hat and coat to keep warm indoors) were strongly influenced by his work.

Jeanne was a Modigliani type—or soon would become one. She appears in a photo with a wide mouth, broad nose and widely spaced eyes. The contrast between her dark hair and pale skin earned her the nickname of *Noix de Coco* (Coconut). Though accounts of her hair color vary, the descriptions agree that she had ashen skin and an odd, otherworldly air. Chana Orloff called her "thin, slender as a Gothic statue, with two long braids, her eyes blue and almond-shaped." To Charles Douglas she was "a pretty girl with china-blue eyes, who wore her nut-brown hair in two loops to the shoulders."[8] Her daughter said "she was small, her hair was chestnut with reddish lights, and against it her complexion was pale."

Anselmo Bucci remembered her peering through an open door, "a tiny transparent waif of a woman with a waxen-white face." Jacques Lipchitz portrayed her as "a strange girl, slender, with a long oval face which seemed almost white rather than flesh colored, and her blond hair was fixed in long braids; she always struck me as looking very Gothic." Gino Severini recalled her most vividly as "very dark-haired, nicely mannered, her features regular, with large orientalish almond-shaped eyes. Also typically oriental, there was a dreamy, absent air about her. She wore a sort of cylindrical turban made of gold-specked damask over two long dark braids that fell down either side of her chest."9 Jeanne was patient, quiet and shy, wraithlike, self-effacing and spectacularly colorless.

Though only nineteen when she met Modi, Jeanne was not an innocent virgin. She'd already had an affair with the Japanese painter Foujita, who ungallantly described her as "vicious and sensual…sickly, pale, thin and mysterious." Chana Orloff, who'd met Jeanne at the Colarossi, introduced her to Modi at an artists' ball—and was later condemned by her family for doing so. The Hébuternes considered him a most unsuitable suitor: a poor, squalid failure; tubercular, alcoholic and addicted to drugs. The fact that he was a foreigner and a Jew made him even worse and provoked additional abuse. Her parents, *croyants* Catholics and complacently bourgeois, were naturally appalled that their well-brought-up daughter had become involved with such a horrible man.

The ill-fated model Elvira had called Modi "the best lover she ever had," but he seems to have raped Jeanne on their first sexual encounter. She told her best friend, Germaine Labaye, that the episode "'was not without a certain horror,' and afterwards she had to sew her underwear back up before going home." Wyndham Lewis' description of Kreisler raping Bertha in *Tarr* suggests what might have happened when Modi assaulted Jeanne: "With the fury of a person violently awakened to some insult he had flung himself upon her: her tardy panting expostulation, defensive prowess, disappeared in the whirlpool towards which they had both with a strange deliberateness and yet aimlessness been steering." Like Kreisler, Modi had switched from tenderness to brutality. He became a strange figure that "had suddenly flung itself upon her and done something disgusting:

and now it was standing idly by the window, becalmed, and completely cut off from its raging self."[10] Despite his brutality, the masochistic Jeanne pretended that nothing traumatic had happened and remained fanatically devoted to him.

Jeanne's parents tried to separate her from Modi and cool her passion by rusticating her to Brittany. In September 1917 she wrote Germaine that she was unmoved by the beautiful Breton scenery and yearned for her lover in Paris: "Despite the [local] atmosphere I am completely empty. I am emptied of all mysticism and calmness. I long for Montparnasse. Nothing doing. All this beauty here bores me and makes me angry. I can look out at the Breton roofs with the little tree growing beside them but all I can think of is going back to Paris."

Osvaldo Patani identified the subject of one of Modi's most stunning portraits as "Germaine Lable," who was probably Germaine Labaye. In *Young Brunette Seated in Front of a Bed* (1919, Los Angeles County Museum of Art) the dark-haired woman sits with her body and head erect before a light orange and gray wall (divided horizontally rather than vertically) on which two framed but blurry pictures hang. Next to her, a gold bedstead, with a puffed-up, cloudlike pillow, rests on a dark wooden floor. She stares at the viewer with eyes like Max Jacob's: one dark blue and hatched, the other pale blue and blank. Her charming oval face is accentuated by parted hair that touches her eyebrows and by sensual cherry-colored lips. She wears a broad choker and black shawl (showing the small *V* of her neck) over a gray blouse with sleeves pushed up almost to her elbows, and rests her large capable hands on her dark gray-flecked skirt. Boldly confronting the spectator, Germaine invites scrutiny but withholds her mystery.

Jeanne posed for Modi, worshipped him and carried him home when drunk. Salmon noted that (like Simone) she had to surrender her own frail ego in order to hold him: "Jeanne was nearly always able to pacify Modigliani, but only by sacrificing her own personality and merging it with his could she subdue him completely. It is possible that she innocently imagined she had to take him or leave him, and that if she could not cherish and admire him as he was, she ran the risk of harming him." The beautiful Swedish woman Thora Klinckowström, who sat for Modi, noted that Jeanne was intensely jealous and fearful that Modi would leave her for another woman. Thora called her a "delicate and fair little creature who looked at me with horror in her eyes and always treated me with the greatest suspicion." Yet Jeanne had to allow Modi to continue to sleep with his models if she wanted to hold him. He had refused Kisling permission to paint Beatrice in the nude, claiming, from personal experience, that "when a woman poses for a painter, she gives herself to him."[11]

Jeanne was more timid and passive than Beatrice Hastings, but her fights with Modi were just as violent. By now his chronic tuberculosis made him cough up blood and he drank to ease the pain. When drunk, he became enraged by Jeanne's passivity, self-sacrifice, domestic bondage and complicity in his self-destruction. His poem of 1918–19 revealed that shattered glass punctuated his combats with Jeanne, provoked by broken promises to marry her, just as it had with Beatrice and Simone:

> a cat scratches his head
> like a poet
> searching for a rhyme
> my wife
> for a priest
> throws a glass at my head.

Salmon witnessed one of Modi's violent public explosions, a bit of street theater for the delectation of his friends: "He was dragging her along by an arm, gripping her frail wrist, tugging at one or other of her long braids of hair, and only letting go of her for a moment to send her crashing against the iron railings of the Luxembourg [Gardens]. He was like a madman, crazy with savage hatred." The worse Modi treated women, the more desperately they clung to him.

Paulette Jourdain, a young girl who worked for Zbo, gave a perceptive analysis of Jeanne's strange, almost catatonic character: "She was incapable of doing anything—always was incapable, disequilibrated, morbid—never *did* anything....Jeanne Hébuterne was defective....[She] was discouraged, somehow, from the first. Incompetent....She had no effect on Modigliani"—who took out his frustrations on her.[12] Maddeningly passive, complicit in his alcoholism and pathetic in her self-sacrifice, desire for respectability and pleas for marriage, Jeanne was inevitably blamed for his disease, his failure and his poverty.

Jeanne, who died young, is mainly known through Modi's twenty-seven portraits. Beatrice seemed quite different in her various portraits; the long necked, blue and almond-eyed Jeanne—kind and submissive—always looked recognizably like herself. The *Head of Jeanne Hébuterne, Facing Front* (1918) is idealized yet realistic. The grayish blue of one background panel echoes the color of her round-necked dress; the yellowish orange panel reflects the tones of her skin. Jeanne's close-up oval face and thick reddish brown hair, falling to her shoulders, fill the frame of the picture. She has widely spaced brown (not blue) eyes, a long narrow (not wide) nose, a sweet smiling mouth, nicely pointed chin and thin neck. In this portrait she looks both calm and contented.

In *Jeanne Hébuterne Seated with Her Arm on a Chair* (1918, Norton Simon Museum, Pasadena) her coconut-shaped red hair is piled high above her extremely oval face, and she has tiny, pale blue blank eyes, a long broad nose and small mouth. Seated sideways on a wooden chair, with one arm leaning on its frame, the other resting openhanded on her lap, she elegantly extends the fingers of both hands as if holding an invisible object. She wears a dark green scoop-necked sweater over long red sleeves and a slightly paler red skirt. Her head tilting to the left and arm reaching to the right form a sinuous S-shape that harmonizes the subtle colors. Her dreamy, languid look suggests her passive character.

Jeanne's appearance becomes increasingly distorted in the portraits. Her head becomes more oval, her neck more elongated, her limbs more extended, her hair ever higher on her head, her nose broader. Her chin becomes double, her breasts heavy, her hips wide, her belly full. The portraits, which show her swelling with unwanted children and becoming less and less attractive, reflect Modi's increasing disillusion with Jeanne and with the constraints of domestic life.

Eleven

BEYOND PLEASURE,
1916–1918

I

⌐ THE CLASSICAL representation of the nude, idealized and remote, chiseled in marble or cast in bronze, achieved perfection at the very beginning of Western art. The Greeks and Romans gave human form to their divinities, and in their statues of Aphrodite and Venus created our ideal of female beauty. The Italian Renaissance masters rediscovered the three-dimensional classical nude and made it the focus of their mythological and biblical paintings. The nude, as Kenneth Clark observed, "remains our chief link with the classic disciplines." And so it was for Modigliani. He had studied in a Florentine academy dedicated to the nude and had an extensive knowledge of the artistic past. He borrowed frequently and systematically from classical and Renaissance art, and painted inventive variants of Old Master nudes. In this respect he represents the last flowering of the Tuscan tradition that began with Giotto.

Just as a Modigliani portrait is instantly recognizable, whatever the subject, so his nudes—all female—bear his distinctive stamp. Unlike such modern masters as Francis Bacon and Lucian Freud, whose nude figures suggest anguish and stir anxiety, Modi sought, like Renoir and Matisse, to convey aesthetic pleasure, and his women are among the most erotic and desirable nudes in the history of painting. He created his characteristic nude in a variety of ways: by imitating the poses of great paintings; by using a sensuous line to define the form of the body; by stripping his nude of virtually all context and attributes in order to focus on the essential female; by following Gauguin, in using a darker, more realistic skin color and frankly showing pubic hair; and by establishing intimacy with, rather than creating distance from, his nudes.

Modi had studied reproductions of the most famous nude in Western art, the marble Venus de Milo (c.100 B.C.), but in Paris he could see her up close in the Louvre. Like artists before him, he recognized the aesthetic value of partial nudity in the Greek statue, where the drapery that both conceals and reveals the shape below adds more curves and swirls to the natural curves of the body. Modi followed the classical, slightly spiral, dignified yet alluring Venus de Milo pose — a standing, armless woman with naked breasts and drapery hanging from her hips — in his standing nude of Simone (1917) and of the ill-fated model Elvira (1918).

Ever since the Renaissance successive artists have recreated earlier images of the nude, and classical poses and settings have been transformed and made new in every age. Modi was enthralled by the voluptuous nudes of Botticelli, Giorgione, Titian, Velázquez, Goya, Ingres, Manet and Gauguin. Like a musician creating variations on classical themes, he used master paintings as models for his pictures, then changed the standing, sitting and reclining poses, the relation of the head to the body, the placement of the arms and legs, the skin tones, the shape and color of the eyes.

Botticelli's *The Birth of Venus* (1482), imitating the classical beauty of the Venus de Milo, used long hair and flowing drapery to accentuate the sensuous form of the body. The head of this goddess leans sideways, her right hand covers a breast and her left hand, holding long protective golden tresses, hides her parts. The face of Botticelli's Venus, however, is a Renaissance face: distinctly individual, rather than idealized and androgynous. She is a Venus with sex appeal. Modi (whom his father had ironically called "Botticelli") reprises this Renaissance Venus in four pictures: *Seated Nude with Necklace, Standing Nude (Venus)* (both 1917) and two others (both 1918) that have the same pose and portray the same model. In *Young Redhead in a Chemise, Half-Length* she's seated against a pale bluish green background with her chemise strap on one shoulder, her left breast exposed and her thick right hand touching it. She has a tilted oval head, reddish blond hair with braids and bangs, tiny blue eyes, delicate red open mouth and an appealing, winsome expression. In *Young Redhead in a Chemise, Seated on a Divan* the woman sits on a couch before an aquamarine background that's painted with visible brushstrokes. Her hair is dark, her face ruddy, her chest pale; her thighs are stippled red; her chemise has slipped below her breasts and she cups one of them with her right hand.

Giorgione's *Sleeping Venus* (c.1510) was an important influence on Modi's reclining nudes. This goddess reclines on richly folded drapery, her body delicately sloping from top left to lower right before a harmonious Veneto landscape. Her eyes are closed, her right arm is folded behind her head and her left hand rests on her crotch. Modi echoes this pose, using the same model and same coral necklace, in *Reclining Nude with Necklace* and *Nude with Eyes Closed and Necklace* (both 1917). In the first, the ruddy-cheeked model, also extended on white drapery, has one blank and one half-closed eye, and wears a colored necklace that precisely matches the medallions at the ends of her breasts. She leans on her right arm and partly covers her pubic hair with her left hand. The second nude complements Giorgione's pose by having the model asleep, with both hands behind her head (which raises her breasts), her nose parallel to the bed, her belly softly sloping and her triangular mound of Venus in full view.

Titian modeled his *Venus of Urbino* (c.1538) on the *Sleeping Venus* by his master, Giorgione, and Modi used the Titian painting as a variation on the theme. Unlike Giorgione's goddess, Titian's long-haired Venus is indoors, not outdoors; awake, not asleep; attended by a maid, not alone. Lying on a luxurious red divan, she leans on her right arm, rests her left hand (with curled fingers) between her legs and modestly faces the spectator. Manet's *Olympia* (1863), a great recreation of Titian, had shocked the mid-nineteenth century public with the model's self-display and arrogant gaze, and Modi also had this picture in mind. Manet's nude challenges and defies the viewer; Modi's *Reclining Nude with Hair on Her Shoulders* (1917) invites and encourages him. This model lies on a thickly painted red velvety couch and a dark green cushion, with the sinuous shape of her body clearly outlined against the distinct colors. The red is reprised in her crimson cheeks, mouth and nipples; the green in the subtly tinted whites of her large asymmetrical eyes: one looking forward, the other slightly to the left. Her oval, masklike face, at a right angle to her body, looks intently at the viewer. With long torso, high waist and slightly sloping belly, she rests on her right arm. One breast is frontal, like her face; the other in profile, like her body; one leg is extended, the other invitingly raised. Distinctly modern, self-absorbed but openly seductive, almost unaware of what she's doing, she seems to be pleasuring herself, and deliciously balances the angelic with the decadent, subtle contentment with erotic abandon.

Velázquez's *The Toilet of Venus* (c.1645–48) recreates the image of a winged Cupid holding up a mirror to a nude woman in Titian's *Woman with a Mirror* (1555), just as Titian's picture recreated Botticelli's pose of protective hands on the breast and between the legs. Modi, in turn, used Velázquez's Venus as a pattern for his *Nude Reclining on Her Left Side* (1917). His model reclines languidly on a white bed, with back and buttocks facing the viewer and one leg beneath the other. The face of the Spanish Venus is reflected in the mirror held by Cupid; Modi's Venus swivels her head backward and shifts her eyes to face the viewer. She has stylish brown hair and the most exquisite features of all his nudes: large dark almond-shaped eyes, high cheekbones, a retroussé nose, inviting lips. A graceful S-shaped line runs from her head, neck and shoulders, through the grooves in her back and bottom (showing a patch of pubic hair from behind), along her bent leg and down to her feet (the latter rarely seen in Modi's work). The triangular shape between her extended legs hints at the pubic hair that's hidden in front. The delicately stroked, velvety skin tones vary from pale tan and slightly rouged to ripe apricot. In contrast to Velázquez's unattainable goddess, this luscious lady, flourishing in her uninhibited nakedness, has no secrets and offers a body that glows with incandescent sexuality.

Goya's high-breasted *Maja Desnuda* (c.1800), with hair falling to her soft shoulders, lies on a couch with arms folded behind her head. In a similar pose, the woman in Modi's *Reclining Nude with Her Arm on Her Forehead* (1917) squarely frames her cushioned head with her long arms. Her huge, wide-open eyes, staring at the viewer, extend to the very edge of her face. One nipple turns to the viewer, the other rises upward; and her waist gracefully narrows before the ample swelling of her hips. The curlicues on the red divan echo the curls of her pubic hair which, characteristically in his nudes, has a bare patch on the left side of the triangle. Not quite as self-possessed as Goya's *Maja,* Modi's model, with startled doelike eyes, seems slightly alarmed by the proximity of the viewer and the exposure of her body.

In his *Grande Odalisque* (1814) Ingres recreates the back-to-front pose of Velázquez's *Toilet of Venus.* A variant figure in Ingres' *Odalisque with Slave* (1839–40) twists on her side, with arms behind her head. Her face looks upward, and her breasts, dipping waist, full belly and high thighs face the viewer. In Modi's version of this picture, *Reclining Nude with Joined Hands* (1917), the model's unusually pale body, seen from above, is flattened against a heavily brushed red background and floats above some swirling black, gray and pale blue patterns in front. The effect is slightly vertiginous. Her dark brown hair forms a high cone cut off by the frame, her eyes are blank blue, her lips a cupid's bow that shows her teeth. Her generous hips swell into a mound, her

sensual languor suggests the Turkish baths of Ingres and the for-
bidden harems of Delacroix.

In their nudes Ingres, Delacroix and Manet followed the Renaissance masters in smoothing out their brushstrokes to create
ivory, milky skin, and omitted pubic hair. Though Modi used the
classical poses to structure his paintings, he transformed the traditionally cool, marmoreal nude into a far more earthy figure.
His models seem as warm, carnal and accessible to the viewer as
they were in real life to the artist himself.

Paul Gauguin had already made the transition in nude painting from smooth sexual parts and pearly complexion to realistic
pubic hair and dark skin, like a suntanned body on the beach.
He painted these nudes just before tanned skin first became
fashionable on the French Riviera in the 1920s. Modi had seen
the great Tahitian paintings at Gauguin's major retrospective in
the Salon d'Automne in 1906. The dark exotic face, paler than the
body, of Modi's emaciated *Seated Nude* showed the influence of
Gauguin as early as 1909. Gauguin's *The Delightful Land* (1892)
portrays a nude with a triangle of pubic hair with a bare patch
on one side. *The Noble Woman* (1898), which shows a reclining
nude holding a fan behind her head and placing her hand between her legs, echoes Giorgione and anticipates Modi's nudes
with coral necklaces. In *Where Do We Come From? What Are We?
Where Are We Going?* (1897–98) the crouching nude figure on the
left, with legs folded beneath her, foreshadows the pose of
Modi's voluptuous *Crouching Nude* (1917), which Kisling portrayed in *Modigliani's Studio.* The main figure in *Two Tahitian Women*
(1899)—standing, facing front, with stylized features and bare
breasts—prefigures Modi's *Standing Nude (Elvira)* (1918).

Gauguin's sculpture and paintings led Modi back to primitive
art. The nudes of both artists have the heavy thighs, pneumatic
breasts and serpentine postures of Indian erotic sculpture from
Ajanta and Ellora. Modi's primitivistic art celebrates life; his
women are sensual, fleshy and eternal. D. H. Lawrence praised

these qualities in the art of the ancient Etruscans: "To the Etruscan all was alive, the whole universe lived; and the business of
man was himself to live amid it all. He had to draw life into himself, out of the wandering huge vitalities of the world." Though
Gauguin took his inspiration from Pacific Islanders and Modi
painted pale Parisian models, both artists took the sun-ripened
bodies of their nudes from the warm terra-cotta colors of the
lively, dancing, erotic figures in Etruscan frescoes.

A French critic — alluding to Modi's sculptural solidity, linear
rhythm and lyrical color — called him "a species of Negro Botticelli."[1] Modi deprived his nudes of all myth, history and social
context, and even placed the masked heads of his statues on
their voluptuous bodies. Despite his apprenticeship to the Old
Masters, he deliberately sacrificed Botticelli's watery background
and flowing hair, Giorgione's harmonious landscape, Titian's
servant and palace, Velázquez's cupid and mirror, Goya's lavish
cushions and drapery, Ingres' turban and peacock, Manet's choker
and cat. Manet and Degas had thrown out the classical or mythological contexts of traditional artists and had painted modern
women — barmaids, dancers, performers, washerwomen — going
about their daily business. Modi went one step further and offered a series of direct confrontations with alluring women. He
portrayed the psychological character of the face but, as in the
sculpted Venus de Milo, concentrated on the essential form of
the body. The artistic tradition that Modi had absorbed, and that
underpins his modern versions of the Venus theme, enhances
their intellectual interest and aesthetic value.

II

MODI'S HARD-EDGED nudes show that he considered the
outline the most essential aspect of painting. He followed the
tradition of sensuous draftsmanship that ran from Ingres
through Degas to Lautrec, and his line is swift, certain, sponta-
neous and elegant. The shape of his ideal body surges and flows

in languorous undulations: breasts are full, waists narrow, hips ample. His nudes have a direct and immediate appeal, and possess the tactile values that Bernard Berenson had praised in Italian Renaissance art. Like the nudes of Matisse, Modi's are "attractive, abundant and available...detached and contemplative; as if removed from [their] own seductiveness." Janet Hobhouse observed that "the characteristic of a Modigliani nude is to hold a tension between the abstract and the real. The abstract qualities of his nudes, which tell us that they are not of this world, include non-naturalistic colouring, distortions and simplifications of form, vagueness of setting." The nude's stylization contrasts with her blatant sexuality, and our intellectual contemplation is invaded by her sensual appeal.

Lacking divine attributes and unrelated to any profession or dramatic situation, Modi's nudes have a classical repose and exist solely for our contemplation. With no other context but their femaleness, they can variously be enigmatic or erotic, dormant or alert. Kenneth Clark persuasively argued that "no nude, however abstract, should fail to arouse in the spectator some vestige of erotic feeling, even though it be only the faintest shadow—and if it does not do so, it is bad art and false morals." In Modi, as in Renoir, "the female body, with all its sensuous weight, is offered in isolation, as an end in itself." Unlike Degas, Forain, Picasso and Pascin, Modi never did erotic drawings, but his nudes—raising their arms to show off their breasts—are always sexy. Eager for sex or sexually satisfied, Modi's models seem to have slipped out of their clothes as easily as they'd slipped into his bed. They not only arouse our emotions, but seem to respond to them with the promise of erotic compliance. They represent, in Blake's words, the "lineaments of gratified desire."

Modi's nudes celebrate the modern fascination with the human body, from Molly Bloom's sexual affirmation to Connie Chatterley's sexual surrender. When Hans Castorp falls in love with Clavdia Chauchat in Thomas Mann's *The Magic Mountain*

(1924), he exalts both the divine and the sensual aspects of the female figure. The body, Hans exclaims, is "a miraculous image
of organic life, a holy marvel of form and beauty, and the love of
the human body is an extremely humanitarian interest and more
powerfully educational than all the pedagogy in the world....
Look at the marvelous symmetry of the human edifice, the shoulders and the thighs and the breasts flowing on the chest, and the
sides arranged in pairs, and the navel in the middle of the softness
of the belly, and the hidden sex between the folds!"[2]

Modi's more unusual nudes, not directly connected to classical models, achieve a stylized but completely individual distinction. His first postwar nude, and one of his greatest, *Seated Nude*
(Courtauld Galleries, London), has the same face as the dressed
model in *Margherita* (both 1916). Margherita, seated in a straight
wooden chair, wearing a gray belted dress, faces to the right and
turns her head and large brown eyes toward the viewer. Her long
wavy hair is parted on her forehead and frames her face. The
delicate curves of her high cheekbones, pertly pointed chin and
amused upper lip are repeated in the slight protrusion of the
belly between her flat chest and tightly bound waist.

Modi transplanted Margherita's dark-skinned, stylized face to
the realistically painted high pale breasts and slightly tilted torso
of *Seated Nude*. The primitive face heightens the sensuality of the
radiant nude body, sharply outlined against a cobalt and crimson
background. Her eyes are closed, her cheek rests on her raised
shoulder, and her long dark hair flows along her arm and down
to her nipple. Her breasts (unlike Margherita's) are full, firm and
inviting; her waist is narrow and her navel nicely notched. Her
pubic hair, accented by curlicues and arabesques, rises above
thighs divided by a thick curvy line. She leans back, supports
herself on her hands and willingly exposes her delicious body to
a gaze she cannot see.

Modi portrayed the Algerian Almaisa, as he did Margherita,
both dressed and nude. Most of his nudes are read from left to

right, but Almaisa's head appears on the right side of the picture and her body flows downward to the left. When dressed, she has an alert and dignified expression; when nude, she seems languid and sensual. In *Nude on a Divan (Almaisa)* (1916), she wears the same amber necklace and wraparound serpentine bracelet as in the dressed portraits, but her nakedness emphasizes the difference between her head and torso, mind and body, ego and id. She is enveloped, almost embraced, by the warm red folds of the velvety couch that set off the enticing tones of her body: terracotta head, neck and arm; ruby lips and bull's-eye nipples; polished tan and ocher skin. Lifting her right arm to the top of the divan, she places her left hand, holding a cigarette, against her cheek. She has thick parted hair, heavy eyebrows and mysterious jet black eyes, and a triangular flat-bottomed nose and wavy upper lip that extends beyond the lower one. The deep indentation between her heavy pendulous breasts and high rounded hip suggests open legs, while the deep groove between crotch and hip hints at buttocks. Her face and torso are frontal; her legs, crossed over a thatch of pubic hair, give her body an alluring flow and torsion.

The woman in *Reclining Nude with Open Arms (Red Nude)* (1917) is seen close-up and from above, as if the viewer were gazing down at her before joining her in bed. Clearly outlined, she lies on a background of distinctly separated colors: a lush red divan with yellow curlicues, two azure and ebony cushions, and a white cloth on a streaked and spotted russet backdrop. Her face is exceptionally glamorous and appealing. She has thick curly hair, large dark eyes, charming nose and full sensual lips. Her budding nipples, warm radiant skin and slightly open legs, above a pubic patch that's bare (as usual) on the left side, suggest pleasures just realized or soon to come.

The *Long Nude* (1917, Museum of Modern Art, New York) takes the pose of the *Red Nude* to grotesque extremes. The sleeping figure reclines, with the right hand on her cheek and the left behind her head, on a red divan with a black saddle of blanket crossing it. She has high ballooning breasts and an abnormally stretched cylindrical torso that meets, below her pubic triangle, her ruddier hips and thighs. Asleep, she appears to defy the laws of gravity—suspended over and about to fall into a dark chasm.

The head of the model in *Nude Reclining on Her Back* (1917)—appearing in profile, with firm chin, tiny lips, straight bladelike nose and closed eyes—seems to be approaching the moment of pleasure. Her fist is clenched, her breasts are ripe, her body twisted into a *contrapposto* form. She lies on a divan whose colors suggest flaming sunsets and fiery passions. Falling into a pre-ecstatic or post-orgasmic swoon, like Bernini's Baroque statue of St. Teresa, she unashamedly arouses desire and makes the spectator imagine what it would be like to make love to this warm, submissive woman. The attitude of Modi's models toward the spectator varies intriguingly from dreamy oblivion to erotic attraction.

There's a clear evolution of Modi's mature paintings after he gave up sculpture in 1914. He created his best portraits in 1915–16, his best nudes in 1917, his best pictures of children in 1918. His nudes declined in 1919 as his health deteriorated. During the last year of his life, he painted three comparatively rough, unfinished sleeping nudes, with arms behind their heads and rudimentary, atavistic feet, like mermaids' tails, that lack his usual delicacy.

In a 1919 review in a Swiss art journal, Francis Carco noted Modi's eagerness to depict "the sometimes soft, animal-like stillness, with its erotic abandon and subtle contentment," of the female body. The Canadian realist painter Alex Colville has recently explained why we continue to be fascinated by Modi's nudes. "I have always responded to his images. I attribute this largely to sex—they are very much female animals. But also they have some of the qualities of ancient Egyptian sculpture (and painting) which give them a kind of simple power that much expressionist work lacks. So the result might be called monumental sexuality."[3]

III

MODI'S NUDES figured prominently in his first and only one-man exhibition. Arranged by Zbo, it took place at Berthe Weill's new gallery at 50 rue Taitbout (a few streets east of the Gare St. Lazare) from December 3 to 30, 1917. She'd opened her gallery in 1901, showed many avant-garde artists, and had exhibited revolutionary works by Matisse and the Fauves in 1907. Matisse's biographer described her appearance and character: "Tiny, inconspicuous, bespectacled, Mlle. Weill moved with little trotting steps like a mouse or a mole until something excited her, when… the molehill erupted into a volcano. For all her meek air and drab getup, she was as combative as she was stubborn and quixotic."

As early as the fifteenth century an artist from the school of Hans Memling had showed in a *vanitas* not only pubic hair but also the cleft of the vulva. Such realism was acceptable in Old Masters and a moralistic context. Contemporary artists who depicted the nude for its own sake were not granted the same license. Paris boasted thousands of officially sanctioned if discreetly situated whorehouses, yet the bourgeois were easily shocked. In 1912, for example, the police had sanitized Jacob Epstein's memorial to Oscar Wilde in Père-Lachaise Cemetery by affixing a piece of bronze to cover up an angel's private parts. Artistic scandals continued to reverberate in the sexually sophisticated but hypocritical city.

To advertise the exhibition, Weill placed one of Modi's striking nudes in her shop window, and the ploy succeeded only too well. A curious crowd gathered, complaints were made and the hard-nosed police, pretending to be outraged by the appearance of pubic hair, ordered her to remove the offensive pictures from the windows and walls. Weill recalled that when she complied— there was no question of opposing the police—the show

remained open: "I shut the shop at once and the guests imprisoned inside helped me to take down the [nude] paintings....
Once they are all down, the exhibition continues: only two
drawings are sold...30 francs each. In order to compensate
Zborowski...I buy five paintings."4 The intervention of the police merely excited the interest of the public, and the notoriety
of the exhibition strengthened the artist's maudit legend and
guaranteed his success—though not in his lifetime. After waiting his whole professional life for a one-man show, Modi was
devastated by the personal scandal and financial failure.

Twelve

The Light in Nice,

1918−1919

I

⊰ THE GREAT WAR continued for four harrowing years, and
in the west was mostly fought on French soil. The front was only
a few hours away by train, and the people of Paris were subjected
to terrifying air and artillery attacks. In January 1918 fifty German planes bombed Paris and caused tremendous damage. In
March the Germans made their last great offensive of the war
and final attempt to break through the front at Amiens. Until
August the loud, ominous German super-cannon, Big Bertha,
firing every eighteen minutes from an extraordinary range of
sixty miles, blasted the city and bit huge chunks out of the
houses. Civilians, forced to descend into icy bomb shelters, ner-
vously smoked and trembled in the fetid underground air. In
April almost half a million people fled the endless bombardment
and the epidemic of Spanish influenza to the safety of the south.

That month, when the art market collapsed along with
Modi's health, Zbo also decided to move to the French Riviera
in search of a safe refuge, salubrious climate and prosperous
clients in the expensive hotels. On this risky journey he took his
wife, Hanka, the ailing Modi, the pregnant Jeanne Hébuterne,
and Jeanne's mother, Eudoxie, who had finally accepted her
daughter's condition and chose to accompany her. Zbo also
brought two other artists in his stable: Soutine and Foujita, the
latter accompanied by his wife, Fernande Barrey. Hanka hated
Soutine (who was crude and weird as ever); Modi loathed and
quarreled violently with the moralistic and hostile Eudoxie. He

had previously suspected Beatrice and Simone of infidelity, and was none too pleased by the close proximity of Foujita, who'd deflowered Jeanne and been her lover. Zbo had to escort this combustible crowd, house them in different villas, pay all the bills, force the artists to work, sell their paintings, and keep the peace. Clinging to the last shreds of propriety, Eudoxie insisted on a separate residence for Jeanne and kept her hidden away from Modi. Angry, and cut off from consoling drugs and spirits, he was desperate as always for funds.

They settled at first in Haut-de-Cagnes, a Provençal fortress village in the heights above Nice. This one-time feudal residence of the powerful Grimaldi family was perched on a hilltop and dominated by a medieval château, with ramparts, gateways and ancient houses that overlooked the Bay of Angels. Twisted olive trees, citrus groves and cultivated carnations covered the perfumed landscape. The weather was almost perfect, the vegetation luxuriant; the fragrances were exotic, the sea and sky azure, the light dazzling and the colors brilliant.

It was almost like going back to Italy, whose frontier was only thirty miles away (Nice had belonged to Italy until 1860). Despite the war that raged in the north, they were able to lead a normal life in Provence. Soon after Modi arrived, he wrote a reassuring letter to his beloved mother, whom he hadn't seen since 1913, and connected his anguish to his creativity: "My dear Mama— Too much time passes without writing, but I never forget you! Don't worry about me. Everything is all right. I work and I'm tormented sometimes, but I'm no worse than I was before. I wanted to send you some photos but they haven't turned out very well. Send me your news. I kiss you heartily.—Dédo."

When he first came to Paris, Modi had complained to Louis Latourettes about the difficulty of adjusting to a northern climate: "My damned Italian eye can't recreate the light of Paris... a light so enveloping. I'll never be able to get it. You can't imagine how I've conceived new expressions of themes in violet, in orange, in deep ochre. There's no way of expressing all that." If his Italian eyes couldn't get used to the Parisian light, he should have felt quite at home in the luminous clarity of Mediterranean Cagnes. But after years in Paris he was disturbed by the glaring southern light that distorted his perception of reality.

A social historian observed that during the war artists had "escaped some of the economic hardships of the city, for life in the country was cheaper and easier....Nevertheless most felt at home in the city and feared a loss of creativity through detachment from urban artistic life." Juan Gris, for example, exclaimed that "isolation turns one into a ridiculous and provincial imbecile....What stagnation!"[1] Modi, who'd always lived in cities, found it difficult to adjust to the constricted life of a village.

He took small comfort from his companions. Tsuguharu Foujita (1886–1968), an outsider among outsiders, belonged to Modi's circle of friends. Born in Tokyo, the son of an army medical officer, he'd studied at the Imperial School of Fine Arts, traveled extensively in China and Korea, lived in London and settled in Paris in 1913, where he soon became quite frenchified. Synthesizing the Japanese and Western traditions, he painted cats, nudes and solemn little girls with precise draftsmanship, harmonious colors and smooth, lacquerlike surfaces. His first wife, Fernande, had been a whore before she became a model and model wife. Foujita returned to Tokyo in 1933, after Japan had invaded Manchuria, and became a war artist. He came back to France in 1950, converted to Catholicism and took the baptismal name of Leonard.

With charming manners and exotic looks, Foujita was affectionately called the Eskimo. He had pale gray skin, long gray bangs, thick owlish spectacles and a brush mustache. He liked to smoke cigars, made his own clothes and dressed in a singlet and baggy pajama trousers, a leather belt and Japanese sandals. A French critic described his engaging appearance: "He always wore his hair Papuan-style, and sported earrings; and his shirts he made for himself out of the oddest materials, such as sacking, curtain material and corset fabrics....He was always the same small figure, with his thatch of hair pressed down on his head like the straw roof of a Hottentot hut, the spectacles that made him look like an Oriental philosopher, and an impeccably white silk blouse." He and Modi stepped warily in a friendly armed truce.

Foujita called Soutine the Lizard, for he spent most of his time sleeping in the sun. When Zbo came back from visiting the hotels, he'd stir from his torpor to see if he'd managed to sell anything. Marc Restellini wrote that there was considerable tension between Zbo and Soutine, whom Modi had persuaded the dealer to support: "The two men heartily disliked each other. Soutine was not congenial company; he is described as neurasthenic, sickly and hypersensitive. He terrorized those around him, since, shy as he was, he was subject to outbursts of temper and unbearable fits of obstinacy. Moreover, Zborowski had little faith in his talent, frequently humiliated him, and rarely paid his monthly allowance on time." In an awkwardly written letter, Soutine told Zbo how wretched he felt in Provence and how he missed urban life: "I am in a bad state of mind and I am demoralized....I want to leave Cagnes, this landscape that I cannot endure....I am in Cagnes against my will, where, instead of landscapes, I shall be forced to do some miserable still lifes. You will understand in what a state of indecision I am. Can't you suggest some place for me? Because, several times I have had the intention of returning to Paris."[2]

Equally unhappy in the spring of 1918, Modi looked up his artist friends Léopold Survage and Alexander Archipenko, who were then living in Nice. Survage, born Sturzwage in Moscow in 1879, had a Finnish father and Danish mother. A Cubist painter and engraver, he'd come to Paris in 1908, met Modi four years later and since 1914 had been spending the winters in Nice. Modi often drank with him, borrowed money from him and painted in his studio. His affectionate bust-length portrait of Survage, painted in 1917, resembles the pictures of his carefully dressed patrons, Paul Alexandre and Léopold Zborowski. Outlined against a roughly stroked bluish green background and looking to the left, Survage has brown wavy hair, a broad forehead, one blank and one blue eye, ruddy cheeks, a bold aquiline nose and elegant brown mustache that almost hides his upper lip. Dressed in a dark suit and tie, with a long scarf draped around his sloping shoulders, he looks both forceful and dignified.

Feeling trapped, Modi complained about his miserable domestic life to the Russian-Cubist sculptor, Archipenko. Three years younger than Modi, he had lived in Paris since 1908. Archipenko recalled that Modi "sounded like a henpecked husband." The sculptor and his wife listened patiently to his outbursts, letting him drink and talk himself out. When it came time to go, he gave Modi a bag and let him help himself to the vegetables and fruit in his garden. "Modi arrived like a man who had escaped from the clutches of rapacious women," he said, "and left like an escaped convict voluntarily returning to prison."

Weary of life in the villa and his quarrels with Eudoxie, Modi (always a difficult guest) moved down to Cagnes, to lodge with some friends of Zbo: the Swedish painter Anders Osterlind and his wife Rachel. Their house was right next to the villa Les Collettes, where Auguste Renoir had lived since 1907. With Monet and Cassatt, he was one of the last surviving Impressionists. The seventy-seven-year-old painter was now deformed by arthritis and confined to a wheelchair. René Gimpel, who visited Renoir in March 1918, just before Modi met him, gave a vivid account of the crippled artist in the last year of his life:

The garden resembles a poverty-stricken farmyard....Seated, he is a frightful spectacle, elbows clamped to his sides, forearms raised; he was shaking two sinister stumps dangling with threads and very narrow ribbons [used to tie the paint brushes to his arthritic hands]. His fingers are cut almost to the quick: the bones jut out, with barely some skin on them....

His head was sunk on a curved, humped back. He was wearing a large, tall English traveling cap. His face is pale and thin; his white beard, stiff as gorse, hangs sideways as if windblown.

Modi's friends expected him to appreciate Renoir's paintings, especially his warm, sumptuous nudes, and admire his courage in continuing to work under such difficult circumstances. But, in a perverse mood, he was rude to the sweet-tempered old man. Osterlind described their clash of temperaments:

> The master lay crumpled in an armchair, shriveled up, a little shawl over his shoulders, wearing a cap, his whole face covered with a mosquito net, two piercing eyes behind the veil.
>
> It was a delicate thing putting these two face to face: Renoir with his past, the other with his youth and confidence; on the one side joy, light, pleasure and a work without peer; on the other, Modigliani and all his suffering....
>
> A grim, sombre Modigliani listened to him speak.
>
> "So you're a painter too then, eh, young man?" he said to Modigliani, who was looking at the paintings.
>
> "_____"
>
> "Paint with joy, with the same joy with which you make love."
>
> "_____"
>
> "Do you caress your canvases a long time?"
>
> "_____"
>
> "I stroke the buttocks for days and days before finishing a painting."
>
> It seemed to me that Modigliani was suffering and that a catastrophe was imminent. It happened. Modigliani got up

brusquely and, his hand on the doorknob, said brutally, "I don't like buttocks, monsieur."³

Modi felt no great fondness for the Impressionists or for Renoir's late bovine beauties and preferred linear to painterly art. He thought Renoir had had his day and continued long past his time. Renoir had never heard of him, and Modi resented the well-meaning but condescending tone of the great artist. Though he *did* like buttocks, and spent a great deal of time studying and painting them, he thought Renoir's remark reduced painting to physical touch. Finally, he was irritated by what he considered the desperate eroticism of a pathetic old wreck.

II

IN JULY, when Paris seemed safer and Cagnes became very hot, Soutine and the Foujitas returned to the capital. The Zborow-skis, Modi, Jeanne and Eudoxie then moved to the Hotel Tarelli in Nice. Prodded by Zbo and gradually adjusting to the southern light, Modi had been fitfully painting. His very first picture, twenty years earlier, had been a Tuscan landscape. He now told Zbo, "I'm trying to paint landscapes. The first canvases will perhaps be a bit amateurish." Instead of capturing the brilliant light and colors of Provence, he used muted tones and portrayed rather stark scenes.

Midi Landscape, the best of Modi's four scenes (all finished in 1919), was strongly influenced by Cézanne, who'd spent his whole adult life painting this locale. The coral red strip of road in the foreground balances five tall conical cypress trees. They jut into a typical hillside village with cultivated terraces in various shades of green that rise to the top of the picture. The closely packed houses have tan walls, green shutters and red-tiled roofs. The harmonious painting, with no people in sight, captures the spirit of the place.

Modi, as usual, concentrated on portraits. The anguished expression in his 1919 portrayal of the thirty-eight-year-old Belgian

writer Frans Hellens shows the late influence of the German Expressionists, who'd also been important at the beginning of his
career. Outlined against a somber hunter green background,
Hellens' head seems enormous compared to his thin, frail body.
His thick wavy hair falls over his broad forehead and his long,
narrow, hollow-cheeked face bulges on one side; his heavy-
lidded brown eyes tilt downward, his nose is straight and firm,
his mouth half open as if to utter an Edvard Munch-like cry of
despair. Sensing Modi's torment, Hellens called him "a charming and a strong-minded man but 'completely out of his element
in this world.' Modigliani's penetrating artistic judgement and his
talent for graphology made him 'a sort of magician.' Hellens did
not like the portrait…but later came to recognize its prophetic
qualities. His youngest son looked exactly like the portrait. And
Hellens said he sensed a terrible mystery at the heart of the
man."4

While in Nice Modi also painted some charming portraits of
the young, anonymous farmers and servants who were willing to
pose for a modest fee. The figure in *Young Peasant* (1918, Tate
Gallery, London) is seated on a wooden chair, directly facing the
viewer, with a bluish green wall and closed gray door behind
him. He has a round tanned face, ruddy cheeks, small blank blue
eyes, tiny red mouth and bump on his chin. He wears a brown
velour hat (unusual in Modi), a white, collarless, too-tight, hand-
me-down shirt pulled open on his chest, and an olive green suit
with a too-small vest drawn open on his belly. His working
trousers have patched knees and his large farmer's hands lie
stiffly on his lap, above his open legs. Grateful for a rest, and
blending beautifully with the backdrop, he seems calmly resigned to a life of arduous toil.

The girl in *The Beautiful Grocer* (1918) has the same pose as the
young peasant, and is not particularly beautiful. She sits outdoors
(again rare in Modi) in a stark, grayish green setting, in front of
three pollarded, leafless trees that recede into the background,

standing across a bare street and next to the green-shuttered store where she works. Seated rather stiffly in a wooden chair below the middle tree, she wears a billowing bluish green dress, adorned with a round white collar above her sloping shoulders and covered by a large white apron in front of her wide hips. She has red hair with curly bangs, characteristically expressionless blue eyes and a mouth twisted to the left of (rather than under) her broad nose. She seems at once placid and exhausted.

The figure in *Servant Girl* (1918) stands full length, clasping her hands in front of her, on hexagonal red tiles and in a corner with a steel gray wall and bluish gray door brushed with white. The drabness of her long blue belted dress and black boots (one placed in front of the other) is slightly relieved by her white collar. Her extended neck and large oval head, tilted to the left and with long strands hanging from her parted dark brown hair, seem out of proportion to her small body. She has a sweet face with broad forehead, wondering blank blue eyes and delightful mouth. Cornered both literally and figuratively, she seems, like most of Modi's young subjects, both vulnerable and sympathetic.

In 1919 Modi painted Zbo's servant, the fifteen-year-old Paulette Jourdain. She had come to Paris from Brittany at the age of fourteen and worked in Zbo's household while studying part-time at a commercial college. (Of sturdy peasant stock, she lived until 1997.) According to William Fifield (who gives no evidence), she later became Zbo's mistress and the mother of his child. Paulette was attractive, with the fresh look of a country girl, and had greenish eyes, straight teeth and short dark hair sloping down the left side of her forehead. Though Modi was fond of Paulette, he failed to capture her good looks. In the portrait she's seated frontally on the familiar wooden chair, with bare forearms and hands clasped on her lap. Her face is outlined by an orange wall and placed next to a slanted russet door. Her dark hair curves over her forehead, with strands jutting out behind her ears, and her drab black dress is unadorned. Her eyes are blank, her nose and mouth twisted, her chin notched, her expression sullen and resentful.

III

REFERRING TO the notable braids of the rather fey Jeanne Hébuterne, the Spanish avant-garde writer Ramón Gómez de la Serna said that "the young blonde of Pre-Raphaelite type who accompanied Modigliani had hair combed in *tortillons* [spiral twists of braid] on her temples like two sunflowers or earpieces, the better to hear the discussion." Modi painted two portraits of the pregnant Jeanne, her hair unbraided, in 1919. In *Jeanne Hébuterne* (Metropolitan Museum of Art, New York), a three-quarter-length portrait, she's resting on a tan sofa. Her red hair, parted along the line that divides the olive and sky blue colors of the background, falls below her shoulders. Her pale blue eyes match the back panel that seems visible through her apparently transparent sockets. Jeanne wears a low-cut, square-necked, white-strapped maternity dress over heavy breasts and broad hips. Her right index finger extends on her lap; her left one curves against her cheek in a reflective gesture that tilts her sharply angled head and suggests complete absorption with her unborn baby.

Modi's last portrait of his doomed lover, *Jeanne Hébuterne Seated in Front of a Door,* shows the familiar russet glass-paneled door separating an unusually chromatic pink, orange and tan background and violet floor. The S-shaped Jeanne is seated on a wooden chair, with one hand on the edge of the seat, the other stretching across her full-bellied blue maternity dress. Her red shawl, crossed over a white blouse with long sleeves and white cuffs, is tucked into her skirt. She's set back from the frame of the picture and framed by the door, with a small head in relation to her body and huge nose in relation to her tiny eyes and mouth. In this picture she once again seems withdrawn into the mysterious world she shares with her unborn infant. By 1919

Modi's mannerisms had become exaggerated, even self-parodic. He compressed the faces of Jeanne and Hanka, as if in a vise, into an extremely narrow oval, and extended the columns of the neck (always, for him, an awkward bridge between head and body) to an unnatural length.

On November 29, 1918, two weeks after the end of the war, Modi's daughter Jeanne (or Giovanna) was born at the Ternier maternity clinic on the rue d'Assas in Nice. Irresponsible as ever, he got happily drunk on the way to register the birth and never reached the town hall. Legally, his illegitimate child did not exist. In early 1919, about five weeks after the birth, Modi wrote his mother about the irregular situation, promised to send a photo (which probably never arrived) and referred to yet another new residence where he was living with Jeanne, but did not mention his father or Jeanne: "Darling Mother, A million thanks for your loving letter. The baby is well and so am I. You have always been so much of a mother that I am not surprised at your feeling like a grandmother, even outside the bonds of matrimony. I'll send you a photograph. I have changed my address again; write to me, 13 Rue de France, Nice."[5]

Just twenty years old, Jeanne was not particularly interested in her first child. According to Lunia Czechowska, a Polish friend of the Zborowskis, the birth had been difficult and she "had bad memories of that time." She also suffered from physical exhaustion and postnatal depression, compounded by lack of money and the continuing disapproval of her mother. Blaise Cendrars' wife, Félicie, then living in Nice, told Modi's mother that the Hébuternes found it impossible to care for the infant in a cramped hotel room and were "going to look for a wet-nurse, because neither she nor her mother could do anything with the child. The baby was only three weeks old, and Jeanne was still very tired." The remoteness of the seated woman, who seems to be holding the baby at arm's length in Modi's painting of 1919, reveals Jeanne's ambivalent feelings about their infant.

Lunia also reported, too optimistically, that Modi "was terribly happy, and adored the child.... He never tired of describing
her beauty and her charm."[6] But these paternal feelings were
short-lived. Félicie believed that Modi (who couldn't even take
care of himself) was terrified of this new responsibility. He had
the typical Italian love for small children—except his own. He'd
renounced his first child, by Simone, gave away his second and
virtually killed himself while Jeanne Hébuterne was pregnant
with his third. (All this would be pitifully described by his daughter Jeanne in a book about the father she never knew.)

In late December 1918, a month after the baby was born, Eudoxie and the Zborowskis returned to Paris. During the next two
months Modi sent his absent patron a series of letters—his
most substantial correspondence since writing to Oscar Ghiglia
in 1901—which contained several cunning and desperate pleas
for cash. On the stroke of midnight, December 31, 1918, drunk
and living it up with Survage at a nightclub in Nice, Modi fanta-
sized about his success, confessed that he was spending freely
and asked for more money. He ended (in faulty Latin) with allusions to John 11:25—"I am the resurrection, and the life"—
and to Dante's *La Vita Nuova,* hoping for a renewal of his own
life at the start of the new year:

> Dear Friend; I embrace you as I would have done if I could
> the day you left.
> I am hitting it up with Survage at the Coq d'Or. I have
> sold all my pictures. Send me some money soon.
> Champagne is flowing like water.
> We send you and your dear wife our best wishes for the
> New Year.
> Resurectio Vitae.
> Hic incipit vita nova. The New Year.

The next, more sober letter, disabused the gullible Zbo about
the sale of the pictures and announced the latest disaster to be-

fall him. He'd been robbed by the Corsican thieves who preyed on the honest folk of Nice:

> Dear Friend. You are naïve and can't take a joke. I haven't sold a thing. Tomorrow or the next day I'll send you the stuff.
>
> Now for something that is *true* and very serious. My wallet with 600 francs has been stolen. This seems to be a specialty of Nice. You can imagine how upset I am....
>
> Naturally I am broke, or almost. It is all too stupid....
>
> That was all that was needed...and now, of all times, just when I thought I had finally found a little peace.

Though Modi probably *was* robbed while drunk, it's unlikely that he was carrying such a large sum of money. In any case, the theft gave him an excellent opportunity to extract more cash from Zbo. His identity card had been stolen, so that he could once again put off the long-promised marriage to Jeanne.

Fortifying his plea with scraps of Shakespeare, and wavering incoherently between a begging and threatening tone, Modi accepted some responsibility for the robbery, but also resorted to emotional blackmail. He held out the bait of four supposedly completed pictures, and warned that if Zbo did not send more money, he would stop painting:

> Here is the question: or: *that is the question.* (See *Hamlet*) that is, *To be or not to be.*
>
> I am the sinner or the fool, we agree: I recognize my blame (if there is a blame) and my debt (if there will be a debt) but the question is now this: if I'm not completely broke, I am at least in serious difficulty. Understand. You sent 200 francs, of which 100 naturally went to Survage, to whose help I owe the fact that I'm not completely broke...but now...
>
> If you free me, I'll recognize my debt and go ahead.
>
> If not, I shall remain immobilized at my place, hands and

feet tied....To whose interest would that be....There are presently four canvases.

I have seen [Paul] Guillaume. I hope that he can help me with the documents. He gave me some good news. Everything would be going well if it were not for this damnable piece of bad luck. Why can't you help me—and quickly—so as not to stop something that is going well? I have said enough. Do what you will—and can—but answer me...it's urgent. Time presses.

At the end of January, when the baby was still with them, Modi compared himself to a black slave (oppressed by both Jeanne and Zbo) and said the unseasonably cold weather had prevented him from painting: "Dear Zbo. Thank you for the money....I am like the Negro, just going on. I don't think I can send more than four or five canvases at a time, because of the cold. My daughter is wonderfully healthy."

Writing to Zbo on February 27, and mentioning the various factors that got on his nerves and impeded his work, Modi proudly announced that he was finally beginning to paint—though he'd supposedly been painting all this time. He was, however, thinking seriously about his future pictures, so he'd be able to paint when inspiration came. Through the efficient intervention of his politician-brother, Emanuele, he'd nearly managed to replace his travel document and would soon be free to return to Paris.

I am going to start work at 13 Rue de France. All these changes, changes of circumstance and the change of season, make me fear a change of rhythm and atmosphere. We must give things time to grow and flower.

I have been loafing for the past few days. Fertile laziness is the only real work.

Thanks to my brother, the business of the papers is almost

finished. Now, as far as that goes, we can leave when we want
to. I am tempted to stay here and go back only in July.[7]

Jeanne had given birth in November 1918, and by April 1919
the woman who couldn't care for one child was now pregnant
with her second. In May, still in Nice and bitter about the ab-
surdity of his situation, Modi wrote Marevna: "I'm getting fat
and becoming a respectable citizen.... I'm going to have two
kids. It's unbelievable, it's sickening." Shortly before leaving, he
wrote Survage: "Thanks for being a good friend. *Au revoir, peut-
être* [Goodbye, perhaps]. This is a good place to recuperate. But
now back to the hell of Paris, that stimulates my work."[8] He now
associated Nice, provincial and remote from Paris, with the birth
of his baby and domestic entrapment. Though Paris was "hell,"
Nice was worse, and he was especially eager to leave.

On May 31 he returned to Paris to prepare the way for Jeanne.
On June 24, Jeanne, still languishing alone in Nice and wondering what Modi was up to, sent him an urgent telegram, in care
of the inexhaustibly patient Zbo, who was, as always, expected
to provide the funds: "Need money for trip. Wire hundred sev-
enty francs plus thirty for nurse. Letter follows. Arriving Saturday morning [June 28] at eight by fast train. Let nurse know."
His daughter Jeanne Modigliani later recounted Modi's pathetic
efforts to be a good father: "The correspondence with the
nurse, a good honest girl from near Paris, to whom little Jeanne
was handed over, is a graph of Modigliani's ups and downs; tele-
grams, presents and baby caps alternate with long silences."

Jeanne, back in Paris, must have pressured Modi to sign a
strange agreement, witnessed by Jeanne, Zbo and Lunia: "Today,
7 July 1919, I pledge myself to marry Mlle. Jane [*sic*] Hébuterne
as soon as the documents arrive."[9] The misspelling of her name,
deliberate or drunken, was like the misspelling of *Madam Pompadour* on the portrait of Beatrice Hastings. But the documents,
whatever they were, never arrived or were intentionally misplaced,

and his promise was as worthless as his previous vow—that he wouldn't get drunk till the end of the war.

Modi left one piece of unfinished business in Nice. According to a book and article on Jeanne, Modi had a third illegitimate child "by a local woman who modeled for him…Madame Jacobelli, a farmer's wife and mother of a brood of barefoot children." His putative daughter, Lina Jacobelli, was born in Haut-de-Cagnes in 1919. She later married the film director Roger Lebon in Nice and had a son who died. She wound up selling perfume in a shop.

Jeanne's letter to Germaine Labaye, written in 1919 after her mother had left Nice and she'd slept with Modi in a shabby hotel room, recalled the unhappy letter she'd sent from Brittany. It revealed her isolation, disappointments and failures, and was filled with foreboding about the future: "I am here completely alone. So alone that I've got no more reason to be. Forgive me but I suffocate and I do not regret that I went to bed or admitted it.… All the time lately I've been very bored. I have a headache. I can't even do any more work."[10]

IV

WHILE JEANNE was in Nice and Modi was back in Paris, he became involved with Lunia Czechowska, a beautiful Polish woman whose husband, Casimir, had been a childhood friend of Zbo. When Modi first met her in 1916 her husband, a poet and revolutionary, had been present. Modi had made a powerful impression on Lunia, as he did on most women, and she was strongly attracted to him. "I was struck by his distinction," she said, "by his radiance and the beauty of his eyes. He was at once very unassuming and very noble. How different he was in his every gesture, even the way he shook hands.…He had superb hands, they were very sure hands."

Sensing Lunia's feelings, Modi had tried a bold seductive maneuver. Completely ignoring her husband, he imperiously insisted that Lunia come with him: "Modigliani asked, after a few minutes and in the presence of my husband, that I leave with him that evening. For Modigliani, I was alone. He felt such a strong feeling for me that he wanted me to abandon everything and follow him." Though she didn't follow him that evening, they became close friends. Lunia must have awakened memories of another exotic Slavic beauty, Anna Akhmatova, for Lunia's lyrical description of wandering through the Luxembourg Gardens with Modi recalls Anna's account of reading the poems of Verlaine in that romantic place: "We walked and walked, often stopping by the little wall along the Luxembourg Gardens. He had so many things to talk about that we were never able to say goodnight."

When the Russian Revolution broke out in October 1917, Casimir joined the Red Army to fight for the liberation of Poland. During the civil war he was wounded, captured and executed. In the summer of 1919 Modi had Lunia to himself and confided his anxieties to her. As always during a crisis, he mentioned his longing for his distant and unattainable loved ones. He spoke "about his mother, Livorno and his darling daughter. His dream was simple and touching: to live near his mother in Italy where he thought he could recover his health." In darker moods, and prophetically, "he spoke of Italy, which he would never see again, and of his child, whom he would never see grow up, but he never breathed a word about his art."

Idealizing Modi after his death and emphasizing his generosity, Lunia wrote that the artist "saw only that which was beautiful and pure. He was never jealous of anyone or made malicious remarks." He declared his love (as he often did with women) and urged her once again to run off with him. But she felt loyal to the pregnant Jeanne and managed—rare in the history of his amorous relations—to resist his advances: "He was charming, fine and sensitive. I knew that he loved me, but I felt for him only a profound friendship." When she became strongly attracted to another man, Modi did become jealous and forced her to stop seeing his rival. Later on, she married a Baron Chorosco and ran a perfume shop (like Jeanne's father and Modi's illegitimate daughter) near Nice.

Modi painted ten portraits of Lunia—four in 1917, six in 1919—and the last two were the best. She gave a perceptive account of how he drank and sang while painting and what it was like to sit for him:

> I'll never forget the first time I posed for him. As the hours gradually went by, I was no longer afraid of him. I can see him now, in his shirtsleeves, his hair tousled, trying to put my features down on canvas. From time to time his hand would extend towards a bottle of cheap brandy. I could see that the alcohol was having its effect, he was getting increasingly excited; I no longer existed, he only saw his painting. He was so absorbed in it that he spoke to me in Italian. He painted with such violence that the painting fell on his head as he leaned forward to look at it more closely. I was terrified; he was genuinely sorry to have scared me and began to sing Italian songs, to make me forget the incident.

While posing, she felt he'd plumbed the depths of her character. She "had the impression of having the soul laid bare and of being in the strange position of being able to do nothing to disguise her feelings."[11]

In *Lunia Czechowska with a Fan,* she's seated in a three-quarter-length, frontal view before a chest of drawers and near the edge of an indistinct framed picture. She wears a canary yellow dress over a silky short-sleeved white blouse that contrasts with the thick brushstrokes of the cherry red background. Her left hand is draped across her lap; her raised right hand, adorned with a white ring, holds a white fan whose pleats echo the lines between her closed fingers. Her ramrod neck, with clavicle showing, rises unnaturally out of a pyramidal base. Her pale, extremely elongated face is topped by a cone of parted brown hair. She has a long wide nose, and tiny Japanese-style eyes and mouth that recede into her face between her pointed hair and pointed chin.

In the starker yet more appealing *Lunia Czechowska in Profile* she's sharply outlined in *profil perdu* against a swirling grayish blue background. She has high, streaked red hair, tied in a bun, which rises from her forehead and drops down the back of her exceptionally long, cranelike neck. She has almond-shaped eyes (the same color as the background), a ski-jump nose and delicate expressive mouth. Her open white blouse plunges down her chest to the bottom of the picture before reaching her breasts. In both portraits Lunia is withdrawn and reflective. Modi's portrayals of the elegant and attractive Hanka and Lunia provide a notable contrast to the swollen and sometimes sullen Jeanne.

In August 1919, two months after returning from Nice and while courting Lunia, Modi took part in an exhibition of "French Art, 1914–1919." The show, organized by the foppish and literary Sitwell brothers, was held at the Mansard Gallery on the fourth floor of Heal's department store, on Tottenham Court Road in London. England had been cut off from French art during the war, and the show had a powerful impact. With nine paintings and fifty drawings, Modi had more works than any other artist. "It was the newcomers," wrote Osbert Sitwell, "such artists as Modigliani and Utrillo, who made the sensation in this show. And my brother [Sacheverell] and I can claim the honor of having been the first to introduce Modigliani's pictures to the English public."

Osbert, who met Zbo when planning the show in Paris, described him as an apparently disinterested but quite shrewd merchant, who made a fortune out of Modi's work after his death: "With flat, Slavonic features, brown almond-shaped eyes, and a beard which might have been shaped out of a beaver's fur, ostensibly he was a kind, soft businessman, and a poet as well. He had an air of melancholy." The French dealers, realizing that

Modi's prices would shoot up after his demise, sent an opportunistic message to Zbo in London. During the exhibition, wrote Osbert, "when Modigliani, recovering from a serious crisis of his disease, suffered a grave relapse, a telegram came for Zborowski from his Parisian colleagues to inform him; the message ended with a suggestion that he should hold up all sales until the outcome of the painter's illness was known."

Osbert acquired one picture, whose subject he described as "monumental, posed forever in her misty blue world...a wry-necked peasant girl of northern France, with her fair hair, sharp, slanting nose, and narrow eyes...hands clasped, resting stoutly on a wooden chair in a transparency of vaporous blue."[12] This sounds like *The Servant Girl* (1918), which he bought for £4 ($20). Five years later he sold it for £80; a week later that buyer sold it for £2,000; and only three months after that, the price in Paris had risen to £4,000. At the Mansard exhibition Modi's drawings, available in a huge wicker basket, could be picked up for a shilling (25 cents) apiece.

The English novelist Arnold Bennett, in his preface to the catalogue, enthusiastically exclaimed: "I am determined to say that the four figure subjects of Modigliani seem to me to have a suspicious resemblance to masterpieces." For 1,000 francs ($250) Bennett bought a portrait of Lunia, who reminded him of the heroines of his novels—though the attenuated and highly stylized Slav was entirely different from Bennett's robust Midlands characters. In his journal of August 1929, Bennett (like Osbert) noted the sharp rise in Modi's prices: "Eight [i.e., ten] years ago I bought a portrait of a woman by Modigliani—certainly one of the greatest painters of this century—for £50. So that when I received an invitation to a private view of Modiglianis in a West End Gallery, I accepted at once. There were no £50 items in this show. I halted before a picture which pleased me most, and asked the price of it. The Manager replied, 'A Paris dealer offered me £6,000, but I refused it.' " Osbert added that "Arnold himself, in the great slump, parted shortly afterwards with his own Modigliani at a huge profit."[13]

Unlike Bennett, the London *Times* reviewer was hostile. Mocking what he failed to understand, he claimed to have "tottered from one 'ghastly' picture to another until he found a sign reading 'No Escape By Way of Roof.' " The distinguished art critic Roger Fry was more perceptive, though slightly condescending, and connected Modi's work to the Renaissance tradition: "the large nude where he has taken over the theme of Giorgione's *Venus* is sensitive throughout and of great beauty. Modigliani is still, I think, a finer draughtsman than he is a painter, but there is no denying his aptitude for developing a kind of pictorial-sculptural idea of form—a method, by the bye, which was common enough among the painters of the Renaissance."

Modi still sought his mother's approval and tried to show that he'd finally achieved success as an artist. In a letter of August 17, 1919 to Eugenia, he enclosed Carco's article in the Swiss art journal: "Dear Mama, thanks for your nice card. I am sending you a review, *l'Éventail* [*The Fan*], with an article about me. I am having a show with others in London. I have told them to forward you press cuttings....My little daughter, who had to be brought from Nice and whom I have placed near [Paris] in the country, is very well. I am sorry that I can't have some photos of her. I kiss you.—Dédo." On December 27, 1919, Eugenia sent what would be her last letter to her son: "I hope, my very dear Dédo, that this will arrive in time for the first morning of the New Year, as if it were a hearty kiss from your old Mama, bringing you all the blessings and good wishes possible. If telepathy is any good you will feel me near you and yours. A thousand kisses— Mama."[14] In less than a month he'd be dead.

Modi painted three major portraits at the very end of his life. At the Rotonde in October 1919 he met a beautiful twenty-year-old Swedish woman, Thora Klinckowström. Though ruined by disease, drink and drugs, he was still irresistibly attractive and hazardous to women. Thora found him "quite small, with a weather-beaten complexion, black untidy hair and the most wonderful hot dark eyes....In he marched wearing a black velvet suit with a red scarf knotted carelessly around his neck.... You had only to look at him to see that he was dangerous."[15] In her portrait Thora, wearing a high-crowned black hat, is seated in a frontal, three-quarter view before the familiar russet door with paneled window. Her arms show through the transparent sleeves of her blouse, worn under her round-collared and billowing black dress, and her hands are placidly clasped in her lap. She has red hair that sets off her pale skin and ruddy cheeks, a Byzantine nose that runs into her eyebrow and a slightly open mouth. One of his most attractive models, Thora looks innocent and vulnerable.

On his preparatory drawing of the Greek musician Mario Varvogli, made on January 1, 1920, Modi used the same sadly optimistic Latin-Italian tags—"*Il Novo Anno. Hic Incipit Vita Nova*"—that had appeared in his previous New Year's letter to Zbo. He painted the portrait of the musician in three sittings at the beginning of 1920. Varvogli is seated facing front, his legs crossed and cut off at the feet, with tan and green walls and a glass-windowed door, tilted downward, behind him. One hand lies on his lap; the other, unusually large, hangs down above it. His head angles to the left and, dressed entirely in funereal black, he wears a hat, drooping bow tie, jacket and coat hanging down to the floor. Like José Pacheco, he's clean shaven, but with the suggestion of a heavy Mediterranean beard around his indented, dimpled chin. His expression, characteristic of Modi's subjects, is reflective and rather sad.

Despite his impressive good looks and charismatic personality, none of his many artist friends ever painted Modi's portrait. His drawing of himself in 1918 was more lifelike and flattering than his *Self-Portrait* the following year, painted realistically but not a close likeness. He gives himself a brush and palette with a clearly marked range of colors: pale green, gray, black, blue, white, red, tan and orange (a contrast to the muted tones of the portrait), which he awards to no other artist. Seated erect and sideways in a thin wooden chair that scarcely supports him, he tilts his head back and looks to the left. Bundled up against the wintry cold of his studio, he wears a heavy gray shawl, velvety russet jacket and brown trousers. He has thick brown hair, a long straight nose and handsome mouth. His brown eyes, as if he couldn't bear to look at them, are blank. In his last testament, the old swagger is gone. He appears pale and sickly, and seems to accept his tragic fate. In his more revealing last photo, with deep lines on his face and deep pouches under his eyes, Modi looks a decade older than thirty-five. Shabby, ravaged and sad, he seems to be in pain and aware of his impending death.

Thirteen

THE SOUL'S MIDNIGHT,
1920

I

⚏ IN DECEMBER 1919 Modi was still hoping to take Jeanne and the farmed-out baby to Italy. He'd escaped the postwar epidemic of Spanish influenza but was a physical wreck. His blackened teeth had been giving him a great deal of pain since 1908. In a prosperous moment he'd replaced two that were missing, and later had to wear false teeth. In the past he had made some attempt to preserve his looks and health, but it was now clear he'd given up, and was fatalistically drifting downward. When Marie Wassilief met him shortly before he died, she "couldn't believe the change in him. He had lost his teeth; his hair was flat, straight, he had lost all beauty. 'I'm for it, Marie,' he said." He knew he was dying and did nothing to save himself.

Modi had had weak lungs since childhood; now the tuberculosis he had neglected during his Bohemian lifetime had reached a critical stage. Considered a romantic disease and associated with creative agony, it had afflicted artists like Edvard Munch and Aubrey Beardsley in the nineteenth century, and killed many young people in the first half of the twentieth. His brother Emanuele remarked that Modi had only a lung and a half. When he found it hard to breathe, he smoked heavily to induce a cough and clear his lungs, but would then bring up blood. Inured to these frequent episodes, which would terrify most people, he adopted a defiant attitude and refused to face reality. When Zbo urged him to take care of himself, get medical treatment and

224

enter a Swiss sanatorium, Modi became angry, treated him like an enemy and told him: "Don't give me lectures." Driven by the need for alcohol and the desire to create, Modigliani felt most alive when drinking and painting, when the "high" of drink and the elation of art became one. His haste to complete a picture showed that he cared more about the act of painting than the finished work. When Severini asked how he'd dealt with his serious illness, he acknowledged, "Most of all I didn't take it seriously."[1]

By now, Modi's addictions and artistic obsessions had led to delusional mental illness. Like his Nietzschean heroes, he deliberately took risks. He defied the severe cold of winter, rarely wore an overcoat, and tried to prove that he was still strong and fit. This stubborn self-testing, a kind of suicidal perversity, undermined his always precarious health. An Italian friend who saw him at the end of 1919 thought his recklessness had led to the delirium tremens and hallucinations described in by Lautréamont's *Maldoror* and Rimbaud's *Bateau ivre:* "He wanted to 'get' everybody. He had no friends; never had any; they were all traitors, mountebanks, and far worse. He wanted them all to sit in the cold and wet on a seat on the boulevard, raving that it was the quay of some imaginary, miraculous sea. Nothing would shift him." He said he was waiting for a boat to take him to a miraculous country, but it was more like Charon ferrying him across the Styx to the land of the dead. His foaming mouth, his shouts and curses, made him seem like a madman.

His mental state was compounded by the painful physical illness that destroyed his ability to breathe. In pulmonary tuberculosis the lungs are damaged by the multiplication of bacilli in infected tissues. Small rounded nodules, or tubercules, form, which contain bacteria and white blood cells. The bacteria cause lesions in the lungs and enter the sputum. The wasting disease slowly progresses from tuberculous lesions, necrosis and formation of cavities, to the erosion of blood vessels and bleeding into the lungs. If massive, this can cause the victim to drown in his own blood. In *The Magic Mountain,* which takes place in a Swiss sanatorium before the Great War, Thomas Mann described this pathological process, and its usually fatal resolution, as "the formation of nodules, the manifestation of soluble toxins and their narcotic effect upon the system; the breaking-down of the tissues, caseation, and the question of whether the disease…would create still larger cavities, and destroy the organ."

Highly contagious, and incurable until streptomycin was discovered in 1944, Modi's disease was too dangerous to ignore. The only hope for the patient was to have rest, careful nursing and a nourishing diet in the hygienic environment of a sanatorium. This was the last thing Modi could afford or would accept, and in any case it was too late. His physical suffering must have been acute. In August 1920, Katherine Mansfield, dying of tuberculosis, recorded the effect of this disease on the half-asphyxiated victim: "I cough and cough and at each breath a dragging, boiling, bubbling sound is heard. I feel that my whole chest is boiling. I sip water, spit, sip, spit. I feel I must break my heart. And I can't expand my chest; it's as though the chest had collapsed."[2]

Toward the end of his life Modi wrote four obscure, untitled poems in French, which expressed his feelings about art and his struggle with mortality. Influenced by the poetry of his friend Max Jacob, he used what Jacob called "the data of the unconscious: liberated words, free association of ideas, day and night dreams, hallucinations." They begin with two fragments. One suggests his guilt about not working: "My fairest mistress / Is laziness." The other reveals his expectation of death and the paranoia he'd shown during his delirium tremens: "In the hallway / There's a man bearing me / a deadly grudge."

The first poem is full of grief about the failure of Modi's artistic ambitions. The artist, a king among men like Jesus, King of the Jews, weeps tears of frustration. His great work (the "pearls," by implication, cast before swine), inspired by his suffering, rain down and are swallowed up in the heat of the night:

> from up on the black mountain, the king,
> the chosen to rule, to command
> weeps the tears of a man who could not reach the stars
> and from the dark crown of clouds
> fall drops, pearls
> on the extravagant night heat.

The next poem suggests Modi's own dark night of the soul as he meditates on what he has lost. He yearns for, but cannot reach, the creative power of the sun:

> Evoke...hubbub
> great silent hubbub
> in the soul's midnight
> o silent cries!
> bayings, calls, melodies
> high, high toward the sun.

The third poem clearly contemplates death as an escape from the pain of illness, and like D. H. Lawrence's "Ship of Death," uses the image of a ship to suggest the passage to extinction. Its form was influenced by Apollinaire, who dispensed with punctuation and constructed calligrams, poems with pictorial typography. The thematic words "voluptuous rhythms," slant down the printed page from upper left to lower right, "rip. [rest in peace] numbing lacerations" rise up from lower left to upper right, both forming a large *X* on the page. The poem itself portrays Modi as a wanderer and exile, listening to the paradoxical "bugles of silence" (as he had to the "silent cries"), which lead him to the longed-for peaceful death and promise of a better life:

the goddess
calling all nomads
calling all far-off nomads
bugles of silence
    ship of tranquility
    lull me to sleep
    rock me to sleep
until the new day breaks.

The final poem, dreamlike and surrealistic, is a more direct
farewell. It uses repetitive imagery—"nocturnal," "alert fairy
palaces," "avalanches of light" and "pillars of light,"—and begins with the Roman salutation from Catullus (*ave atque vale*) of
those who are about to leave, or die. After troubling and hope-
ful dreams, or sexual pains and pleasures, the poet experiences a
celestial illumination that he equates with death:

hail and farewell
    recognition
muffled nocturnal dramas
and nocturnal ruby fairylands
until there gush from
alert fairy palaces
avalanches of light
in alert fairy palaces
on pillars of light.

Michelangelo, painter and poet, had expressed the same longing
for oblivion in the sixteenth century:

Welcome to me is sleep, and dearer still,
While wrong and shame endure, my stony death.[3]

II

MODI ALSO warned his friends about his sense of doom and
expectation of death. He told Paulette Jourdain, "I'll die at the

same age as Christ." Charles Douglas recounted that "he was obsessed by the desire to achieve fame quickly, knowing subconsciously that he had not much time....He would thump his chest, saying, 'Oh, I know I'm done!'" He also exclaimed that he adored cemeteries and asked: "wouldn't it be magnificent... if we could only contemplate our own cadavers?"[4] In his last weeks he seemed to be rehearsing, anticipating, even hastening his own death.

He had recited over himself a prayer for the dead. Echoing the syphilitic Gauguin's despairing lament, "No more brain, no more work, and without hope," he told Ortiz de Zarate, just before his death: "You know, I've only a tiny bit of brain left. I can't help feeling it's the end." In his last lucid moments he whispered to Zbo: "I am leaving the mud behind. I now know all there is to know, and soon I'll be no more than a handful of dust. I've kissed my wife. Please take her back to her parents. This is the right moment. Anyhow we're sure of eternal happiness, she and I, whatever happens."[5] Abandoning the earthly mud of human life, he left his dusty remains to the earth. He called Jeanne his "wife," and fatally instructed Zbo to return her to her family, hinting at a death pact that would reunite them in the afterlife.

On January 14, 1920, Modi was attacked by severe kidney pains that a doctor mistook for nephritis, or inflammation of the kidneys, but he was not taken to a hospital. The doctor later said that he had tubercular meningitis, though this diagnosis could not be confirmed without an autopsy, which was not performed. Meningitis could have spread from his lungs to his brain through the discharge of the bacilli into the cerebrospinal fluid. The initial symptoms of meningitis are lassitude, headaches, low-grade fever and personality change. These are followed, in the next stage of the illness, by severe headaches, vomiting, acute fever and palsy. The final phase causes stupor, seizures, partial paralysis and coma. If untreated, the disease progresses rapidly and the victim dies in a matter of weeks.

Modi's depression would have deepened every time he looked around him. His tuberculosis was aggravated by his use of hashish, ether and alcohol, and hastened by lack of heat and food. He'd spent fourteen years as a professional painter, yet his careless disregard for his own work and his financial failure forced him to live with Jeanne in an austere flat on the top floor of 8 rue de la Grande Chaumière. It was on the same street as the Académie Colarossi, where both of them had once studied. The large, L-shaped flat—a horrible contrast to his first, nicely decorated room in Montmartre—was fiery in summer, frigid in winter. There was no coal to feed the stove, and the walls dripped with damp. Water had to be carried up from a single tap in the courtyard; there was only one toilet on the landing for the entire building; the only light was from candles and oil lamps. When the crisis came, Modi and Jeanne were completely alone. Ortiz de Zarate was away for a week, and Zbo was sick in bed with influenza. Adoring and completely passive, too stupefied and grief-stricken to call a doctor, Jeanne sat next to him and watched him die. She might have saved him (this time, at least) if she had heated the flat, fed him properly and sent for medical help.

When Zarate returned, he found Jeanne silently observing Modi in the freezing and incredibly squalid flat, littered with drained bottles and slimy cans: "He was in a bad way [Zarate said]. Lying with his wife on a repulsively dirty pallet-bed....I worried about him. 'Are you eating at least?' I asked him....I noticed that the two mattresses, the floor as well, were covered with greasy oily markings...with more empty tins and lids all about....Modigliani, already at the point of death, had been eating sardines for eight days!"

In a letter to Emanuele the guilt-ridden Zbo tried to soften the blow and give the impression that he'd done "everything possible" to save his friend:

> The doctor came every day. The sixth day of his illness I became sick and my wife went to visit him in the morning.

Upon her return I learned that Modigliani was spitting blood. We hurried to find the doctor who said that he had to be taken to a hospital but that it would be necessary to wait two days for the bleeding to stop. Two days later he was taken to the hospital; he was already unconscious. His friends and I did everything possible. We called several doctors but tubercular meningitis began to set in; it had been weakening him for a long time without the doctor recognizing it.[6]

Zbo's account is suspect in a number of ways. Modi's disease was chronic, and he'd been spitting blood for years; now he was hemorrhaging and his life was clearly in danger. Why would the doctor assume the bleeding would stop? And why did he allow Modi's condition to deteriorate by waiting two more days before sending him to a hospital? Zbo suggests he was too sick to visit Modi but went to find the doctor, or doctors. If in fact he had been on the scene and the doctor, however incompetent, had been seeing Modi every day, they surely would have recognized the gravity of his illness.

On January 22 the unconscious Modi was brought to the Hôpital de la Charité, the clinic for the poverty stricken and the homeless, at the corner of the rue Jacob and the rue des Saints Pères. In one of his late poems, written in Italian, he'd nostalgically evoked his birthplace with an agonizing cry:

> titter and chitter of swallows
>   over the Mediterranean
>   O Livorno!
> this crown of cries this crown of shrieks
>   I offer thee,
>   poet of the goat-head.

His last, semi-delirious words were *"Italia! Cara, cara Italia!"* (Italy! Dear, dear Italy), which echoed *"Cara Livorno,"* the way his townsfolk traditionally referred to their town.

He died on Saturday, January 24 at 8:50 P.M., at the age of

thirty-five. One last mishap mangled the once-beautiful Modigliani. In a desperate effort to save a remnant of his physical appearance before he was gone forever, Kisling and a friend tried
to make a death mask. But they botched the job, and tore off
strips of his face and eyebrows. The sculptor Jacques Lipchitz
recalled that "they did it very badly and came to me for help with
a lot of broken pieces of plaster full of adhering bits of skin and
hair. Patiently, I put the fragments together, and since many
pieces were missing, I had to restore these missing parts as well
as I could."[7]

III

CHARLES DOUGLAS wrote that when Modi's lover saw his
dead body in the hospital, "poor blue-eyed Jeanne, so little given
to speech and who so rarely laughed…was nearly insane with
grief" and let out "the most piercing cry that ever a woman ut-
tered when confronted by the corpse of her man." Jeanne, the
passive, long-suffering mistress who'd burdened him with a child
he didn't want and couldn't support, fell into deep despair. She
was grief stricken about his horrific death, her precarious future,
and the rage and rejection of her family who (like Simone Thiroux's) condemned her without pity. Afraid to sleep alone in the
old flat, she spent the night in a cheap hotel with Paulette Jourdain, profoundly depressed and obviously suicidal. She had once
made a drawing of herself stabbing a knife into her own chest,
and her only surviving painting shows a view of a deep courtyard, with a spiky, sinister tree, vertiginously seen from the top
of a tall building. Nine months pregnant and waddling as she
walked, she seemed calm, though the hotel chambermaid found
a dagger under her pillow.

The next day, January 25, Jeanne's parents and brother came
to Zbo's flat, where Paulette had taken her, and brought her back
to the rue Amyot. She had told Zarate, "I know very well that
he is dead, but I know too that he will soon live again for me,"

and there was a romantic, even operatic element in her sacrificial desire to fulfill their pact and join him in death. Influenced by literary models, Modi and Jeanne must have thought of Shakespeare's Juliet, who awakens to find Romeo dead in the tomb and kills herself; or of Coleridge's poem "Kubla Khan," where a woman wails, like Jeanne, for her demon lover. One of the greatest Italian operatic heroines, Puccini's Tosca, realizing that Scarpia has deceived her, and that her lover, Cavaradossi, is dead, throws herself over the parapet. On January 26 at 4 A.M., just thirty-one hours after Modi's death, Jeanne stepped backward through the window of her fifth floor room, so that she would not have to look down before she jumped. She fell for a few seconds and, with a crashing thud, splattered her skull on the stone street and killed the living child within her.

Jeanne's parents, appalled by the suicide (to which they had no doubt contributed), refused to take their daughter's shattered corpse into the house. Jacob Epstein recalled that when Modi died, the café owner Rosalie Tobias had "naturally turned to her cupboard for his drawings, as dealers were after them, but, alas! for Rosalie's hopes, the drawings, mixed with sausages and grease, had been eaten by rats."[8] Now Jeanne was brought back to the flat she had shared with Modi, and two friends had to sit up with her to prevent the rats from gnawing at her corpse. Her parents, fearing more scandal, banned Modi's friends from her funeral. She was quietly buried in a remote cemetery at Bagneux, in the southern suburbs of Paris.

Emanuele wired Kisling, who took charge of Modi's funeral: "bury him like a prince." They did so in the cemetery of Père-Lachaise, which Mark Twain had described as "a solemn city of winding streets and of miniature marble temples and mansions of the dead gleaming white from out of a wilderness of foliage and fresh flowers." Bouquets, wreaths and a cortège of artists on foot followed the hearse through the streets of the city while policemen, who'd so often had to arrest Modi, respectfully saluted the procession.[9] There was a religious ceremony at the graveside and Modi was buried as a Jew: "a rabbi in the traditional tri-cornered hat and robes of the French synagogue officiated at the burial of one who had been a freethinker since boyhood."[10] The substantial bill from the funeral home came to 1,340 francs. Five years later, in May 1925, Modi's family and friends finally persuaded the Hébuternes to let Jeanne's body be moved and buried next to Modi in Père-Lachaise. Her tombstone, in Italian, reads: "Devoted companion unto the ultimate sacrifice."

Modi was not only *maudit* himself, but also seems to have cursed the women and friends who were closest to him.[11] The sweet, pathetic Simone Thiroux remained devoted till the very end. When Jeanne came to the hospital morgue to see Modi for the last time, she met a weeping Simone at the door. Sad, silent and lost in the crowd, Simone also walked in his funeral procession. In 1921, still in her twenties, she died of tuberculosis in the Hôpital Cochin.

Beatrice Hastings, having survived the cancer ward, moved to Worthing, Sussex, at the beginning of World War II and started her third, short-lived magazine (price: two pence), which printed her increasingly loony and otherwise unpublishable work. She was solitary and poor, embittered and paranoid, ravaged by age and drink, sick and hemorrhaging. In 1943, suffering from cancer, she committed suicide, along with her pet mouse, by gas. There were no obituaries. She left an estate of £314 and papers, including precious drawings by Modi and confessional letters from Katherine Mansfield, which the British Museum refused to accept and have not survived. In a letter about her death she asked to be cremated and casually noted that if her friend "Miss Green will kindly throw the ashes down a hill or in a field, I shall be obliged."

Zbo prospered in the 1920s by selling Modi's work and was seen about town in a smart suit and expensive fur coat, but he'd always had cardiac troubles and died of a heart attack, aged forty-three, in March 1932. Paul Guillaume, a shrewd businessman, profited from the strong dollar in postwar France and also became rich, but on October 1, 1934, at the age of forty-three, he shot himself.

Of Modi's Jewish friends, Pascin hanged himself in 1930, and during World War II Chagall, Lipchitz and Kisling escaped to America. Soutine was not so fortunate. During the German occupation of France he acquired false papers and managed to hide in the countryside, but in August 1943 he had a severe attack of bleeding ulcers. It took him more than twenty-four hours to get to a doctor in Paris, and he died on the operating table.

Max Jacob had the saddest story. The last photo of him shows a stooped, shabby and self-effacing figure. Though a Catholic convert, he was forced to wear the yellow star that stigmatized the Jews. He lived in an abbey with monks, but they were unable to hide or protect him. In February 1944, only six months before the liberation of France, he was arrested and sent to the prison camp at Drancy (north of Paris) to await transport to Auschwitz. Picasso, now world famous, was asked to help Max, but refused and disingenuously insisted: "There's no point in doing anything. Max is an angel. He doesn't need our help to escape his prison." What accounted for Picasso's inhumanity and evasion of moral responsibility? Though friends, like Cocteau, tried to intercede for him, Picasso believed that Max was probably doomed. Living precariously in German-occupied Paris, Picasso did not want to associate himself publicly with a notorious homosexual and Jew with whom he'd once shared a room, and even a bed, in the Bateau Lavoir. Ultimately, he cared more about his own reputation than about the life of his old comrade. At Drancy, poor Max apologized to the other Jewish prisoners for offering prayers to a Christian God, and died of pneumonia before he could be sent to certain death in the gas chambers of Poland.

Little Jeanne was adopted at the age of fourteen months by Modi's unmarried older sister, Margherita, and brought up by her in Livorno. She met her future husband, Victor Nechtschein, in Toulouse during the German occupation of France, when they supposedly worked for the Resistance. They married in Paris and had two daughters, Anne and Laure, one of them handicapped. Jeanne taught at the University of Lille, took up painting and had several shows. A photo of her shows a rather plain woman, with short dark hair and thin lips, standing in front of her abysmal pictures. Her last years were unhappy. She began to drink heavily and became mentally ill; she was divorced in 1980 and died (during her father's centenary year) in 1984.

IV

MODI HAD received no recognition during his lifetime, but he would surely have become successful if he'd lived through the 1920s, when American buyers came to postwar Paris and the booming art market was fueled by wealthy speculators. In 1923, Dr. Albert Barnes, the patent-medicine millionaire from Philadelphia, bought some works by Soutine and several of Modi's portraits and nudes. Lipchitz clearly remembered that day, "which caused a lot of noise in Montparnasse and will remain forever in the annals of art history. It was at this point that the two friends, Modigliani and Soutine, began to win international recognition."[12] Toward the end of his life Modi's pictures sold for about 150 francs. A decade later, when eager collectors were attracted by his tragic legend and unique vision, his prices shot up astronomically to about 500,000 francs.

Modi had no followers, but his posthumous success provoked an industrious school of forgers. After selling his painter's palette for a substantial price, his friends began to collect other palettes and fobbed them off as his. Zbo added to the confusion by supposedly paying Kisling to complete Modi's unfinished works. Since Modi kept no formal record of his substantial oeuvre, forgeries could not be checked against an authentic list. A large number of fake paintings and drawings, imitating his easily recognizable style, were placed on the market and snatched up by eager buyers. One museum curator observed that Modi was "more faked than any other artist of the century. Once the limited supply of Modigliani's works ran out and demand continued to grow, those fakes multiplied."

Entirely unknown in Italy during his lifetime, Modi's art was first exhibited in the Venice Biennale in 1922, and his reputation continued to grow in his own country. On July 12, 1959, the seventy-fifth anniversary of his birth, the city of Livorno belatedly recognized his achievement by placing a plaque on the house where he was born, with the elegiac inscription: "One who lived the life of genius and courage, the painter Amedeo Modigliani." On the seafront in southwest Livorno there's now a Piazza Modigliani, possibly named for both Amedeo and the anti-fascist politician, Emanuele, who was driven into exile by Mussolini in the 1920s.

Inspired by the story of the lost sculptures that Modi had thrown into the Fosso Reale in 1913, officials of the town dragged the canal after World War II, but found nothing. In 1984, a hundred years after his birth, the director of the Contemporary Art Museum in Livorno raised the money to once again dredge the canal—and discovered three twelve-by-eighteen-inch sculpted heads. The excitement lasted for a month, and the hoax ended when three students demonstrated their technique by sculpting a fourth head on national television. The cunning forgers, "motivated by the media frenzy over the proposed dredging of the Fosso Reale, claimed they had carved the heads with hammers, chisels, a screwdriver, and a Black & Decker electric drill, fashioning them after images of the artist's paintings and few surviving sculptures, and then sunk them in the canal." The museum director, who watched this event on television, collapsed and was rushed to a hospital. Local bakers, capitalizing on the incident, made large loaves shaped like the newfound heads. The tool company publicized the event with an advertisement that boasted: "It's easy to be talented with a Black & Decker."

Arguments about the authenticity of Modi's works continued into the twenty-first century, when two rival scholars were drawn into heated controversies. In the fall of 2002, Jeanne Hébuterne's nephew said that works supposedly by her, and exhibited in Segovia by Christian Parisot, were fakes and the show was closed by the police. Marc Restellini, then co-director of the Musée du Luxembourg in Paris, had identified a number of fake drawings and reduced their value to a negligible amount. But in the fall of 2001 death threats to him and his family forced him to cancel his projected catalogue raisonné.

In our time Modi's reputation as well as his prices have continued to soar. In the early 1960s a curator at the Fogg Art Museum at Harvard declared that Modi's late drawings "descend directly from the greatest master of the line, Leonardo da Vinci."[13] Between 2002 and 2004 there were major exhibitions of his work, with lavish catalogues, in Paris; in Los Angeles, Buffalo and Fort Worth; and in New York, Toronto and Washington. In November 2003 his gorgeous *Nude Reclining on Her Left Side* (1917), modeled on Velázquez, sold at Christie's for $26.9 million. A year later, in November 2004, the portrait of the pregnant *Jeanne Hébuterne Seated in Front of a Door* (1919) sold at Sotheby's for $31.3 million.

Gauguin, living in the South Seas, had prophesized that "a time will come when they will believe me to be a myth, or perhaps an invention of the newspapers," and the same was true of Modi.[14] Three of his closest writer-friends, André Salmon, Blaise Cendrars and Francis Carco, circulated fantastic stories about him. Ordinary people were drawn to an artist who was free from all conventional restraints and could indulge in drink, drugs and endlessly available women. Modi's life, legend and astonishing posthumous career have inspired many mediocre imaginative works: nine novels, a play and five poems, as well as a documentary and three feature films.[15]

Modi belongs with the major painters—from Giorgione and Raphael to Van Gogh, Seurat and Lautrec—who died in their thirties. Their work, achieved but not completed, suggested the alluring possibility of future masterpieces. But it's not at all clear that Modi would have gone on to create greater works if he'd survived his fatal struggle with tuberculosis. Toward the end, drink and disease had caused a noticeable decline of his artistic power. If he'd recovered his health, he might have continued his career, but this is unlikely. If he stopped drinking he could not paint; and if he drank he became violent and self-destructive. He might not have been able to arrest the downward spiral, even if he gave up alcohol, and may have been too far gone to regain his creative impulse.

Modi's survivors, shattered by his death, felt guilty that they had not done enough to help him while he was alive. The melancholy angel lived on in the memories of the friends who admired him and of the women, like Anna Akhmatova and Lunia Czechowska, who loved him. His physical beauty, glamour and charm, his great talent and frenzied work, his self-destruction and early death made him a legend. Modigliani's life was tragic, but he had great courage as an artist. He did not try for easy success by joining the Cubists and Futurists and becoming another imitator of Picasso or Marinetti, and had the strength of character to forge his own individual style. He could not entirely fulfill his artistic destiny, but he left us some of the most beautiful and original paintings of the twentieth century.

One: Livorno Childhood

1. Christopher Hibbert, *The House of Medici: Its Rise and Fall* (New York, 1975), p. 279; Montgomery Carmichael, "Leghorn," *Pall Mall Gazette,* 16 (November 1898), 392; Leghorn came from Legorno, the old name of the town; Cecil Roth, *The History of the Jews in Italy* (Philadelphia, 1946), pp. 399, 348–349.

2. Lewis Knapp, *Tobias Smollett: Doctor of Men and Manners* (Princeton, 1949), p. 287; Newman Ivey White, *Shelley,* (New York, 1940), 2.15; Mary Wollstonecraft Shelley, *Letters,* ed. Betty Bennett (Baltimore, 1980), 1.102; Quoted in Carmichael, "Leghorn," p. 392.

3. David Vital, *A People Apart: The Jews in Europe, 1789–1939* (New York, 1999), pp. 61–62. Roth, *History of the Jews in Italy,* p. 348; Mario Toscano, in *Gardens and Ghettos: The Art of Jewish Life in Italy,* ed. Vivian Mann (Berkeley, 1989), p. 30 (this book includes a photo of the magnificent interior of the Livorno synagogue); Arnoldo Momigliano, "The Jews of Italy," *New York Review of Books,* October 24, 1985, p. 22.

4. Carmichael, "Leghorn," p. 392; Henry James, *Italian Hours* (Boston, 1909), pp. 309–310; Alan Mallach, *Pietro Mascagni and His Operas* (Boston, 2002), pp. 4–5; Dana Facaros and Michael Pauls, *Tuscany, Umbria and the Marches* (London: Cadogan, 1990), p. 262; Charles Baudelaire, *Flowers of Evil,* ed. Jackson Mathews (New York, 1955), p. 55.

5. Ilya Ehrenburg, *People and Life, 1891–1917,* trans. Anna Bostock and Yvonne Kapp (New York, 1962), p. 153; Benedict de Spinoza, *A Spinoza Reader: The "Ethics" and Other Works,* trans. and ed. Edwin Curley

(Princeton, 1994), p. 197; Modigliani and Eugenia, in Jeanne Modigliani, *Modigliani: Man and Myth,* trans. Esther Clifford (New York, 1958), pp. 107–108; 11. This book, by Modigliani's daughter, is a valuable repository of family documents.

6. Donatella Cherubini, *Giuseppe Emanuele Modigliani: Un riformista nell' Italia liberale* (Milano, 1990), pp. 30n; 32n; Eugenia, in Marc Restellini, *Modigliani: The Melancholy Angel,* trans. Chris Miller (New York, 2002), p. 417; Eugenia, in Jeanne Modigliani, *Man and Myth,* p. 20.

7. Nicholas Murray, *Kafka* (New Haven, 2004), p. 30; Renato Natali, in William Fifield, *Modigliani: The Biography* (New York, 1976), p. 36; Eugenia, in Jeanne Modigliani, *Man and Myth,* p. 19.

8. Norma Broude, *The Macchiaioli: The Italian Painters of the Nineteenth Century* (New Haven, 1987), p. 202; Eugenia and Silvano Filippelli, in Jeanne Modigliani, *Man and Myth,* pp. 20–21; 24; *Georg Trakl: A Profile,* ed. Frank Graziano (Manchester, 1984), p. 24; Kimberly Smith, *Between Ruin and Renewal: Egon Schiele's Landscapes* (New Haven, 2004), p. 155.

9. Theda Shapiro, *Painters and Politics: The European Avant-Garde and Society, 1900–1925* (New York, 1976), p. 104; Cherubini, *Emanuele Modigliani,* pp. 37; 143.

Two: Italian Journey

1. Eugenia, in Restellini, *Melancholy Angel,* p. 417; Frieda Lawrence, *Not I, But the Wind* (New York, 1934), p. 195; Roy McMullen, *Degas: His Life, Times and Work* (London, 1985), pp. 50–51; Jeffrey Meyers, *Somerset Maugham: A Life* (New York, 2004), p. 32.

2. Modigliani, in Pierre Sichel, *Modigliani: A Biography* (New York, 1967), pp. 51–52; 53–55.

3. Broude, "Giovanni Fattori," *The Macchiaioli,* pp. 185; 196; 242; 248.

4. Gino Severini, *The Life of a Painter,* trans. Jennifer Franchini (Princeton, 1995), p. 15; McMullen, *Degas,* pp. 75–76; Thomas Mann, *Death in Venice and Seven Other Stories,* trans. H. T. Lowe-Porter (1912; New York: Vintage, 1954), p. 20.

5. Ardengo Soffici, in Gaston Diehl, *Modigliani,* trans. Eileen Hennessy (New York, 1969), p. 18; Jean-Paul Crespelle, in Sichel, *Modigliani,*

p. 227; Gaspar Galaz y Milan Ivelic, *La Pintura en Chile desde la colonia hasta 1981* (Valparaíso: Universidad Católica, 1981), p. 207 (Ortiz de Zarate's *Notre Dame de Paris,* executed in thick, mud-colored paint, is reproduced on p. 206 of this book; three other paintings appear in Christian Parisot, *Modigliani e i suoi: Jeanne Hébuterne, André Hébuterne, Georges Dorignac, Amedeo Modigliani* [Torino, 2000], pp. 244–246); Giorgio De Chirico, in Werner Schmalenbach, *Amedeo Modigliani: Paintings, Sculptures, Drawings* (Munich, 1990), p. 189.

    I have used Osvaldo Patani's handsomely produced *Amedeo Modigliani: Catalogo Generale / Depinti* (Milano: Leonardo, 1991), as the source, with dates, of Modigliani's paintings. He conservatively includes 349 works painted between 1898 and January 1920.

6. Adolphe Basler, in Schmalenbach, *Modigliani,* p. 185; Ehrenburg, *People and Life,* p. 154; Dante Aligheri, *Inferno,* trans. John Sinclair (London, 1939).

7. *The Portable Oscar Wilde,* ed. Richard Aldington (New York, 1946), pp. 610; 102; "The Albatross," *Baudelaire,* ed. Francis Scarfe (London: Penguin, 1961), p. 9; Arthur Rimbaud, letter of May 15, 1871, *Complete Works,* ed. Paul Schmidt (New York, 1975), pp. 102–103; Modigliani, in Corrado Pavolini, *Modigliani,* (New York: Mentor, 1966), p. 24.

8. André Gide, *Journals,* trans. Justin O'Brien (New York, 1948), 1.156; Joyce Reid, ed., *The Concise Oxford Dictionary of French Literature* (Oxford, 1976), p. 338; W. Anderson, in *The Penguin Companion to Literature. Vol. 2: European,* ed. Anthony Thorlby (London, 1969), p. 463.

9. Comte de Lautréamont, *Les Chants de Maldoror,* trans. Guy Wernham (New York, 1943), pp. 112; 181; Beatrice Hastings, in Sichel, *Modigliani,* p. 278; Modigliani, in Nina Hamnett, *Laughing Torso* (1932; London: Virago, 1984), p. 78; Lautréamont, *Chants de Maldoror,* p. 165.

10. Severini, *Life of a Painter,* p. 41; Friedrich Nietzsche, *The Case of Wagner,* trans. Walter Kaufmann (New York, 1967), p. 165; Friedrich Nietzsche, *The Will to Power,* trans. Walter Kaufmann (New York, 1968), pp. 491; 493; Friedrich Nietzsche, *Ecce Homo,* trans. Walter Kaufmann (New York, 1967), p. 303.

11. Friedrich Nietzsche, *Thus Spake Zarathustra,* in *The Portable Nietzsche,* trans. Walter Kaufmann (New York, 1954), pp. 153, 135; 300; 143, 216; 312, 129, 363.

12. Modigliani, in Sichel, *Modigliani,* pp. 55–56; Denis Mack Smith, *Italy: A Modern History* (Ann Arbor, 1959), p. 252; Gabriele D'Annunzio, *Il Trionfo della morte* (Milano, 1894), p. 375.

13. Jeffrey Meyers, "Gabriele D'Annunzio," *A Fever at the Core: The Idealist in Politics* (London, 1976), p. 91; Modigliani, in Alfred Werner, "Unhappy Genius," *Commentary,* 15 (May 1953), 482; Franco Russoli, *Modigliani: Drawings and Sketches,* trans. John Shepley (New York, 1969), pp. 84 and XXXI; 91 and XXXI.

   Part of the Italian quotation, "di coloro che sanno," comes from Dante's description of Aristotle in *Inferno,* IV.131: "maestro di color che sanno." James Joyce also quoted this Dantean phrase in the first paragraph of the "Proteus" chapter of *Ulysses* (1922).

14. Nietzsche, *Ecce Homo,* p. 248; Smith, *Italy,* p. 239.

Three: Down and Out in Paris

1. Louis Latourettes, "Modigliani à Montmartre," in Arthur Pfannsteil, *Modigliani* (Paris, 1929), p. III; Charles-Albert Cingria, in Schmalenbach, *Amedeo Modigliani,* p. 189; David Sweetman, *Paul Gauguin: A Life* (New York, 1995), p. 258.

2. Beatrice Hastings, in Carol Mann, *Modigliani* (New York, 1980), p. 91; Marevna, *Life with the Painters of La Ruche,* trans. Natalie Haseltine (London, 1972), p. 32; Severini, *Life of a Painter,* p. 40; Sweetman, *Paul Gauguin,* pp. 258–259.

3. Enzo Maiolino, ed., *Modigliani Vivo: Testimonianze inedite e rare* (Torino: Fògola, 1981), p. 132; Wyndham Lewis, *Tarr* (1918; London: Jupiter, 1968), pp. 9; 78; 117; 69; 215.

4. Fernande Olivier, *Picasso and His Friends,* trans. Jane Miller (New York, 1965), p. 101; Michel Georges-Michel, *From Renoir to Picasso: Artists in Action,* trans. Dorothy and Randolph Weaver (Boston, 1957), p. 143; Zadkine, in André Salmon, *Modigliani: A Memoir,* trans. Dorothy and Randolph Weaver (New York, 1961), p. 2; Ossip Zadkine, "Recollections of Modigliani," *Adam International Review,* 300 (1965), 72.

5. Christian Parisot, *Modigliani,* trans. Carole Fahy (Paris, 1992), p. 26; Musée d'Art Moderne de la Ville de Paris, *Amedeo Modigliani, 1884–1920*

(Paris, 1981), p. 212; Salmon, *Memoir,* p. 46; Noël Alexandre, *The Unknown Modigliani: Drawings from the Collection of Dr. Paul Alexandre* (New York, 1993), pp. 84; 76.

6. Ludwig Meidner, "The Young Modigliani: Some Memories," *Burlington Magazine,* 82 (April 1943), 87; André Salmon, *Modigliani: sa vie et son oeuvre* (Paris, 1926), p. 13; Adolphe Basler, in Schmalenbach, *Amedeo Modigliani,* p. 186; Francis Carco, *From Montmartre to the Latin Quarter,* trans. Madeleine Boyd (New York, 1928), p. 228.

7. Shapiro, *Painters and Politics,* p. 73; Salmon, *Modigliani: Memoir,* p. 45; Olivier, *Picasso and His Friends,* p. 27; Louis Latourettes, in Sichel, *Modigliani,* p. 98.

8. Meidner, "Young Modigliani," p. 88. Meidner's last sentence recalls Alexander Gilchrist's description of another struggling artist in his *Life of William Blake,* ed. Graham Robertson (New York, 1922), p. 322: "He ennobled poverty, and, by his conversation and the influence of his genius, made two small rooms in Fountain Court more attractive than the threshold of princes"; Adolphe Basler, in Schmalenbach, *Amedeo Modigliani,* p. 185; Florent Fels, in Parisot, *Modigliani,* p. 91.

9. Meidner, "Young Modigliani," p. 88; Giovanni Scheiwiller, ed., *Omaggio a Modigliani nel decimo anniversario della sua morte* (Homage to Modigliani on the Tenth Anniversary of his Death), (Milano: Giovanni Scheiwiller, 1930), n. p.; Meidner, "Young Modigliani," p. 88.

10. Modigliani, in Latourettes, "Modigliani à Montmartre," p. VII; Modigliani, in Charles Douglas [pseud. of Douglas Goldring], *Artist Quarter: Reminiscences of Montmartre and Montparnasse in the First Two Decades of the Twentieth Century* (London, 1941), p. 111.

11. Alexandre, *Unknown Modigliani,* p. 54; Jean Cocteau, *Opium,* trans. Margaret Crosland and Sinclair Road (1929; London, 1967), pp. 12, 14; Restellini, *Melancholy Angel,* p. 114; Alexandre, *Unknown Modigliani,* pp. 92–93.

12. F. T. Marinetti, "Initial Manifesto of Futurism" (1909), in *Futurismo, 1909–1919: Exhibition of Italian Futurism* (Newcastle upon Tyne: Hatton Gallery, 1972), pp. 25–26; Severini, *Life of a Painter,* p. 81; Ehrenburg, *People and Life,* p. 155.

13. Pablo Picasso and Juan Gris, in Kenneth Silver, *Esprit de Corps: The Art of the Parisian Avant-Garde and the First World War, 1914–1925* (Princeton, 1989), pp. 349; 251; Alexandre, *Unknown Modigliani,* p. 89.

Four: Aristocrat in Rags

1. Henry Certigny, in Maiolino, *Modigliani Vivo,* p. 142; Frederick Wight, ed., "Recollections of Modigliani By Those Who Knew Him," *Italian Quarterly,* 2 (1958), 50.

2. Daniel-Henry Kahnweiler, in Jeanine Warnod, *Washboat Days,* trans. Carol Green (New York, 1972), p. 158; Restellini, *Melancholy Angel,* p. 225; Neal Oxenhandler, *Looking for Heroes in Postwar France: Albert Camus, Max Jacob, Simone Weil* (Hanover, New Hampshire, 1996), p. 104.

3. Gerald Kember, *Max Jacob and the Poetics of Cubism* (Baltimore, 1971), p. xxiii; Olivier, *Picasso and His Friends,* p. 33; Douglas, *Artist Quarter,* p. 53.

4. Francis Carco, in Kember, *Max Jacob,* p. xxvii, and Carco, *From Montmartre to the Latin Quarter,* p. 18; Liane de Pougy, in John Richardson, *A Life of Picasso. Volume I, 1881–1906* (New York, 1991), p. 206 and John Richardson, *A Life of Picasso. Volume II, 1907–1917* (New York, 1996), p. 4.

5. Richardson, *Life of Picasso,* 1.205, 203; Severini, *Life of a Painter,* pp. 101–102.

6. Max Jacob, in Kember, *Max Jacob,* pp. xvii; xviii; Jean Cocteau, in Oxenhandler, *Looking for Heroes,* p. 146; Marevna, *Life with Painters,* p. 69.

7. S. I. J. Lockerbie, in *Penguin Companion to Literature: European,* p. 395; Max Jacob, Préface à *Le cornet à dés* (1917; Paris, 1964), p. 14.

8. Max Jacob, in Maiolino, *Modigliani Vivo,* p. 163; Max Jacob, in Doris Krystof, *Amedeo Modigliani, 1884–1920: The Poetry of Seeing,* trans. Christina Rathgeber (New York, 1996), p. 52; Max Jacob, in Scheiwiller, *Omaggio a Modigliani,* n.p.

9. Malcolm Cowley, "André Salmon and His Generation," *Bookman* (New York), 56 (February 1923), 714; Olivier, *Picasso and His Friends,* p. 75; Richardson, *Life of Picasso,* 1.24.

10. Olivier, *Picasso and His Friends,* pp. 26–27; Fernande Olivier, *Loving Picasso: Private Journal,* trans. Christine Baker and Michael Raeburn (New York, 2001), p. 195.

11. Severini, *Life of a Painter,* p. 72; Modigliani, in Douglas, *Artist Quarter,* p. 76; Picasso, in June Rose, *Modigliani: The Pure Bohemian* (New York, 1991), p. 69; Picasso, in Alfred Werner, *Modigliani* (New York, 1966), p. 96.

12. Picasso, in Ariana Huffington, *Picasso: Creator and Destroyer* (1988; New York: Avon, 1989), p. 129; Roland Penrose, *Picasso: His Life and Work,* revised edition (New York, 1973), p. 226; Anselmo Bucci, in Sichel, *Modigliani,* p. 109.

13. Modigliani, in Salmon, *Memoir,* p. 95; Modigliani, in Janet Hobhouse, *The Bride Stripped Bare: The Artist and the Female Nude in the Twentieth Century* (New York, 1988), p. 148; Modigliani, in Latourettes, "Modigliani à Montmartre," p. VI.

14. Cyril Beaumont, in Denys Sutton, *André Derain* (London, 1959), p. 33; René Gimpel, *Diary of an Art Dealer,* trans. John Rosenberg (New York, 1956), p. 346; Richardson, *Life of Picasso,* II.70, 74; André Derain, in Gaston Diehl, *Derain,* trans. A. P. H. Hamilton (New York, n.d.), p. 33. In August 1954 Derain's car broke down, he was hit by another vehicle and died in hospital a week later, aged seventy-four.

15. Jean Selz, *Vlaminck,* trans. Graham Snell (New York, 1963), p. 5; Olivier, *Picasso and His Friends,* pp. 103–104; Maurice de Vlaminck, *Dangerous Corner,* trans. Michael Ross, intro. by Denys Sutton (London, 1961), pp. 140–141.

16. Douglas, *Artist Quarter,* pp. 40–41; [No author], *Utrillo and the Painters of Montmartre* (New York, 1970), p. 13; Rosalie Tobias, in Sichel, *Modigliani,* p. 189; Maurice Utrillo and Modigliani, in Georges-Michel, *From Renoir to Picasso,* pp. 254; 143. Picpus is a district on the eastern edge of Paris; Fontenay is an eastern suburb.

Five: Carving Direct

1. Alexandre, *Unknown Modigliani,* p. 95; Constantin Brancusi, in Edward Lucie-Smith, *Lives of the Great Twentieth Century Artists* (New York, 1986), p. 103; Brancusi, in Anna Chave, *Constantin Brancusi: Shifting the*

Bases of Art (New Haven, 1993), p. 11; Henri Rousseau, in Pontus Hulten, *Brancusi* (London, 1988), p. 84.

2. Brancusi, in Sanda Miller, *Constantin Brancusi: A Survey of His Work* (Oxford, 1995), p. 61; William Carlos Williams, *Autobiography* (New York, 1951), p. 188; David Lewis, *Constantin Brancusi* (London, 1957), p. 8; Brancusi, in Hulten, *Brancusi,* pp. 129–130.

3. Jeffrey Meyers, *The Enemy: A Biography of Wyndham Lewis* (London, 1980), p. 206; Brancusi, in Hobhouse, *Bride Stripped Bare,* p. 137; Sidney Geist, *Brancusi: A Study of the Sculpture* (New York, 1968), p. 28; Lewis, *Constantin Brancusi,* p. 14.

4. Franz Marc, in Shapiro, *Painters and Politics,* p. 97; Robert Goldwater, *Primitivism in Modern Art,* revised edition (New York: Vintage, 1967), p. 236; Geist, *Brancusi,* p. 140.

5. William Rubin, "Picasso," *"Primitivism" in Twentieth-Century Art* (New York, 1984), 1.17; Pablo Picasso, in André Malraux, *Picasso's Mask,* trans. June and Jacques Guicharnaud (New York, 1976), pp. 10–11; Goldwater, *Primitivism in Modern Art,* p. 238.

6. Modigliani, in Jacques Lipchitz, *Modigliani* (New York, 1953), p. 2; Curt Stoermer, in Alfred Werner, *Modigliani the Sculptor* (New York, 1962), p. XXI; Severini, *Life of a Painter,* p. 101; Miller, *Constantin Brancusi,* p. 127.

7. Ossip Zadkine, in Salmon, *Memoir,* p. 147; Lipchitz, *Modigliani,* p. 2; Jacob Epstein, *Epstein: An Autobiography,* 2nd edition (London, 1963), p. 46.

8. Augustus John, *Chiaroscuro* (1952; London: Readers Union, 1954), p. 96; Hamnett, *Laughing Torso,* p. 59; Malcom Easton and Michael Holroyd, *The Art of Augustus John* (London, 1974), p. 173; Douglas, *Artist Quarter,* pp. 249–250; Zadkine, in Wight, "Recollections of Modigliani," p. 73.

9. Meyers, *The Enemy,* p. 68; Ezra Pound, *Gaudier-Brzeska* (1916; New York, 1970), p. 44.

10. Evelyn Silber and David Finn, *Gaudier-Brzeska: Life and Art* (London, 1996), pp. 37; 51; Hamnett, *Laughing Torso,* pp. 78–79; Denise Hacker, *Nina Hamnett: Queen of Bohemia* (London, 1986), p. 72.

11. Silber, *Gaudier-Brzeska,* p. 62; Alan Wilkinson, "Paris and London: Modigliani, Lipchitz, Epstein and Gaudier-Brzeska," in *"Primitivism"*

in Twentieth-Century Art, pp. 443–444; Henri Gaudier-Brzeska, in Mervyn Levy, *Gaudier-Brzeska: Drawings and Sculpture* (London, 1965), p. 14.

12. [Henri] Gaudier-Brzeska, "Vortex," *BLAST,* 1 (June 20, 1914), 158; Ezra Pound, in Roger Cardinal, review of Paul O'Keeffe's *Gaudier-Brzeska, Times Literary Supplement,* April 9, 2004, p. 18; Silber, *Gaudier-Brzeska,* pp. 48; 51.

Six: Artificial Paradise

1. Kenneth Silver and Romy Golan, *The Circle of Montparnasse: Jewish Artists in Paris, 1905–1945* (New York, 1985), p. 18; Alexandre, *Unknown Modigliani,* p. 99; Modigliani, in Jeanne Modigliani, *Man and Myth,* p. 56.

2. Isaiah Berlin, ["Anna Akhmatova"], *Personal Impressions,* ed. Henry Hardy (1980; London: Penguin, 1981), p. 190; Joseph Brodsky, "The Keening Muse," *Less Than One: Selected Essays* (New York, 1986), p. 36; Orlando Figis, *Natasha's Dance* (New York, 2002), pp. 435; 442. Her name is stressed on the second syllable: Akhmátova.

3. Anna Akhmatova, in Restellini, *Melancholy Angel,* p. 148; Amanda Haight, *Anna Akhmatova: A Poetic Pilgrimage* (Oxford, 1976), p. 16; Anna Akhmatova, "Amedeo Modigliani," *My Half-Century,* ed. Ronald Meyer (Ann Arbor, 1992), pp. 76–78; Paul Verlaine, in *An Anthology of French Poetry from Nerval to Valéry,* ed. Angel Flores (Garden City, New York: Anchor, 1958), pp. 85; 89; 92.

4. Akhmatova, "Amedeo Modigliani," p. 79; 80; See the illustrations in Roberta Reeder, *Anna Akhmatova: Poet and Prophet* (New York, 1994) and Mason Klein, ed., *Modigliani: Beyond the Myth* (New York, 2004), pp. 172–173; Reeder, *Akhmatova,* p. 342; Akhmatova in Restellini, *Melancholy Angel,* p. 148.

5. Michael Ignatieff, *Isaiah Berlin: A Life* (New York, 1998), p. 153; Berlin, "Anna Akhmatova," pp. 200, 207; Akhmatova, "Amedeo Modigliani," p. 76; Laura Garsin, in Jeanne Modigliani, *Man and Myth,* p. 50.

George Orwell, another tubercular, also tried to prove he was healthy by taking reckless chances. In December 1933, while riding his motorbike without an overcoat, he got completely soaked in a freezing rainstorm, caught pneumonia and landed in a hospital.

6. Vlaminck, *Dangerous Corner,* p. 9; Monroe Wheeler, *Soutine* (New York, 1950), p. 31; Modigliani, in Sichel, *Modigliani,* p. 293.

7. Giovanni Scheiwiller, ed., *Amedeo Modigliani—Selbstzeugnisse, Photos, Zeichungen* (Zürich, 1958), p. 76; Adolphe Basler, in Parisot, *Modigliani,* p. 91; Hans Arp, in Richardson, *Life of Picasso,* II.368; Douglas, *Artist Quarter,* p. 206.

8. Marevna, *Life with Painters,* p. 61 (Marevna also described how Modi's old friend Ortiz de Zarate would, under the influence of drink and drugs, strip off his clothes and pursue women like a satyr); Lipchitz, *Modigliani,* pp. 1–2; William James, *The Varieties of Religious Experience* (1902; New York, Mentor, 1958), p. 297; William Styron, *Darkness Visible* (New York, 1990), p. 40.

9. Charles Baudelaire, "The Poem of Hashish," *The Essence of Laughter and Other Essays, Journals and Letters,* ed. and intro. Peter Quennell, trans. Norman Cameron (New York: Meridian, 1956), pp. 71, 93; Severini, *Life of a Painter,* pp. 47–48; Maurice Vlaminck, in Mann, *Modigliani,* p. 92; Douglas, *Artist Quarter,* p. 229.

10. Baudelaire, "The Poem of Hashish," pp. 71–72; 101, 83; 99; 95; 80–81, 102, 105.

11. Anselmo Bucci, in Sichel, *Modigliani,* p. 193; Ardengo Soffici, *Ricordi di vita artistica e litteraria* (Firenze, 1942), p. 219; Carlo Carrà, in Schmalenbach, *Amedeo Modigliani,* p. 188. This photo appears in an exhibition catalogue of the Musée d'Art Moderne, *Amedeo Modigliani,* p. 17.

12. Lipchitz, *Modigliani,* p. 6; Modigliani, in Alexandre, *Unknown Modigliani,* p. 32 (no date).

13. Gastone Razzaguta, in Jeanne Modigliani, *Man and Myth,* p. 62; Alexandre, *Unknown Modigliani,* p. 104; Modigliani, in Rose, *Modigliani,* p. 92.

14. Alexandre, *Unknown Modigliani,* p. 106; Modigliani, in Restellini, *Melancholy Angel,* p. 21.

Seven: Jews in Paris

1. Modi came from the same Jewish-Italian culture that produced many distinguished modern novelists: Italo Svevo, Carlo Levi, Alberto Moravia, Giorgio Bassani, Natalia Ginzburg and Primo Levi.

2. Epstein, *Autobiography,* p. 195; Ehrenburg, *People and Life,* p. 153 (the story of the Jewish runner is confirmed by Albert Boime, *Art in the Age of Counterrevolution, 1815–1848* [Chicago, 2004], p. 129); John, *Chiaroscuro,* p. 96.

3. Anselmo Bucci, in Klein, *Beyond the Myth,* p. 217; Akhmatova, "Amedeo Modigliani," p. 81; Hamnett, *Laughing Torso,* pp. 48–49; Paul Guillaume, in Maiolino, *Modigliani Vivo,* p. 173.

4. Douglas, *Artist Quarter,* pp. 292–293; Léon Indenbaum, in Maiolino, *Modigliani Vivo,* p. 115 (the newspaper was probably *Machmadim* [*Delights*], which Indenbaum founded at La Ruche. Mark Schwarz, a contributor, published *Modigliani* [Paris, 1927] in Yiddish); Modigliani, in Latourettes, "Modigliani à Montmartre," p. IX; Douglas, *Artist Quarter,* p. 76.

5. Paul Guillaume, in Maiolino, *Modigliani Vivo,* p. 169; Emily Braun, in Klein, *Beyond the Myth,* p. 34; Mason Klein, in *Beyond the Myth,* p. 8.

6. For the caryatid, see Werner, *Modigliani the Sculptor,* p. 14; for the drawings, see Mann, *Modigliani,* pp. 130–131 and Musée d'Art Moderne, *Amedeo Modigliani,* pp. 200–202. Robert Alter translated the Hebrew.

7. Marc Chagall, in Sidney Alexander, *Marc Chagall: An Intimate Life* (New York, 1978), p. 36; Silver and Golan, *Jewish Artists in Paris,* p. 60; Marc Chagall, in Alexander, *Marc Chagall,* p. 42.

8. Gimpel, *Diary,* p. 411; Douglas, *Artist Quarter,* p. 208; Ossip Zadkine, in Wight, "Recollections of Modigliani," p. 41.

9. Lipchitz, "Amedeo Modigliani," pp. 2; 4; Kenneth Clark, *Rembrandt and the Italian Renaissance* (1966; New York, 1968), p. 144; George Szabo, "A Study in Jealousy," *Drawing* (New York), 10 (January-February 1989), 106.

10. Horace Brodzky, *Jules Pascin* (London, 1946), p. 11; Robert McAlmon and Kay Boyle, *Being Geniuses Together, 1920–1930* (New York, 1968), p. 300; Ernest Hemingway, *Islands in the Stream* (New York, 1970), pp. 72–73; Ernest Hemingway, *A Moveable Feast* (1964; New York: Bantam, 1965), pp. 104; 103.

11. George Grosz, in Alfred Werner, *Pascin: 10 Drawings* (New York, 1972), p. xi; Alfred Werner, *Jules Pascin* (New York, 1962), p. 22; Pascin, in Paolo D'Ancona, *Modigliani, Chagall, Soutine, Pascin,* trans.

Lucia Krasnik (Milano, 1953), p. 79; Pascin, in Douglas, *Artist Quarter,* p. 168.

12. Lewis, *Tarr,* p. 265; McAlmon, *Being Geniuses Together,* p. 342; Joseph Kessel, *Kisling* (New York, 1971), p. 32; Douglas, *Artist Quarter,* pp. 176–177.

13. Marevna, *Life with Painters,* pp. 20–21; Gimpel, *Diary,* p. 399.

14. Marevna, *Life with Painters,* p. 21; Chana Orloff, in Wight, "Recollections of Modigliani," p. 45; Francis Steegmuller, *Cocteau: A Biography* (Boston, 1970), p. 150n; Moïse Kisling, in Scheiwiller, *Amedeo Modigliani,* p. 66.

15. Chaim Soutine, in Irene Patai, *Encounters: The Life of Jacques Lipchitz* (New York, 1961), p. 192; Chaim Soutine, in Wheeler, *Soutine,* p. 37; Arbit Blatas, in Alfred Werner, *Soutine* (New York, 1977), p. 58.

16. Gimpel, *Diary,* p. 373; Marevna, *Life with Painters,* p. 19; André Salmon, in Lucie-Smith, *Lives of Artists,* p. 95.

17. Henry Miller, *My Life and Times* (Chicago, 1971), p. 18; Léon Indenbaum, in Sichel, *Modigliani,* p. 340; Léopold and Hanka Zborowski, in Norman Kleeblatt and Kenneth Silver, *An Expressionist in Paris: The Paintings of Chaim Soutine* (New York, 1998), p. 101.

18. Soutine, in Gimpel, *Diary,* p. 377; Lucie-Smith, *Lives of Artists,* p. 97.

19. Waldemar George, in Wheeler, *Soutine,* p. 48; Modigliani, in David Irwin, "Current Exhibitions," *Burlington Magazine,* 105 (October 1963), 462; Modigliani, in Jeanne Modigliani, *Man and Myth,* p. 78.

Eight: Wild Colonial Girl

1. Albert Guerard, *France: A Modern History* (Ann Arbor, 1959), p. 377; Alfred Cobban, *A History of Modern France. Volume 3: 1871–1962* (London, 1965), p. 119.

2. Jay Bochner, *Blaise Cendrars: Discovery and Recreations* (Toronto, 1978), p. 56; Modigliani, in Dario Durbe, *Due pietre ritrovate di Amedeo Modigliani* ([Livorno,] 1984), p. 52 and Jeanne Modigliani, *Man and Myth,* p. 108; Juan Gris, in Silver, *Esprit de Corps,* p.165; Modigliani, in Sichel, *Modigliani,* p. 446.

3. Henri Certigny, in Maiolino, *Modigliani Vivo,* p. 144; Ehrenburg, *People and Life,* pp. 156; 199.

4. Paul Guillaume, in Colette Giraudon, *Paul Guillaume et les peintres du XXᵉ siècle* (Paris, 1993), p. 30; Paul Guillaume, in Marevna, *Life with Painters,* p. 18.

5. John Carswell, *Lives and Letters* (New York, 1978), p. 28; Edgar Jepson, *Memories of an Edwardian and Neo-Georgian* (London, 1937), p. 105; Alice Marks, in Miron Grindea, "300," *Adam International Review,* 300 (1965), 12.

6. James Moore, *Gurdjieff and Mansfield* (London, 1980), p. 84; Gorham Munson, in Sichel, *Modigliani,* p. 271; Max Jacob, in Restellini, *Melancholy Angel,* p. 68.

7. Carswell, *Lives and Letters,* p. 63; [Ida Baker], *LM: The Memories of Katherine Mansfield* (New York, 1972), p. 65; Katherine Mansfield, *Collected Letters. Volume One, 1903–1917,* ed. Vincent O'Sullivan and Margaret Scott (Oxford, 1984), pp. 159–160; 164–165; 180.

8. Ruth Pitter, in Carswell, *Lives and Letters,* p. 74; Katherine Mansfield, *Notebooks,* ed. Margaret Scott (Minneapolis, 2002), 2.242; Katherine Mansfield, *Journal,* ed. John Middleton Murry (London, 1954), p. 285; Beatrice Hastings, *The Old "New Age," Orage—and Others* (London, 1936), p. 28.

9. Hastings, in Meyers, *The Enemy,* p. 72.

10. Hastings, in Mann, *Modigliani,* p. 106; Lewis, *Tarr,* p. 93; Hastings, in Mann, *Modigliani,* pp. 93; 96; 114.

11. Ehrenburg, *People and Life,* pp. 155–156; Fernande Barrey, in Sichel, *Modigliani,* p. 282; Hastings, *New Age,* 15 (July 16, 1914), 259.

12. Hastings, in Carswell, *Lives and Letters,* pp. 121–122; Marevna, *Life with Painters,* pp. 117, 119; Frieda Lawrence, *Not I, But the Wind,* p. 34; Thora Klinckowström, in Fifield, *Modigliani,* p. 250.

13. Hastings, in *New Age,* 15 (July 9, 1914), 236; February 11, 1915, p. 401 (Werner, *Modigliani the Sculptor,* p. 22, shows a head with a chip near the right eye, now in the Philadelphia Museum of Art); February 18, 1915, pp. 425–426; Grindea, *Adam International Review,* p. 13.

14. Kenneth Wayne, *Modigliani and the Artists of Montparnasse* (New York, 2002), pp. 204, 208, 210; 207.

15. Hastings, in Carswell, *Lives and Letters,* p. 168. See Russoli, *Modigliani,* p. 36, for the "beatific" drawing; José Maria Faerna, *Modigliani,* trans.

Alberto Curotto (New York, 1997), p. 6, for the standing nude; and Rose, *Modigliani,* p. 131, for *Les Pampas.*

16. Hastings, in Carswell, *Lives and Letters,* p. 134; Marie Wassilief, in Wight, "Recollections of Modigliani," p. 42; Hastings, in Margaret Crosland, *Raymond Radiguet: A Biographical Study* (London, 1976), pp. 101–102.

Nine: Inner Eye

1. Jean Paul Richter, ed., *The Literary Works of Leonardo da Vinci* (Oxford, 1939), 1.64; Meyer Schapiro, *Impressionism* (New York, 1997), p. 254; John Pope-Hennessy, *The Portrait in the Renaissance* (Princeton, 1966), p. 300.

2. Russoli, *Drawings and Sketches,* p. xvii; Modigliani, in Alexandre, *Unknown Modigliani,* p. 91.

3. Pope-Hennessy, *Portrait in the Renaissance,* p. 23; Jacqueline Munck, in Restellini, *Melancholy Angel,* p. 60; Pope-Hennessy, *Portrait in the Renaissance,* p. 132; Ehrenburg, *People and Life,* p. 157.

4. Modigliani, in Werner, *Modigliani,* p. 144; Hamnett, *Laughing Torso,* p. 60; Modigliani, in *Melancholy Angel,* p. 310.

5. Gabriel Fournier, in Mann, *Modigliani,* pp. 91–92; Alexandre, *Unknown Modigliani,* p. 65.

6. Kenneth Clark, *The Nude: A Study in Ideal Form* (1956; New York, 1959), p. 192; John Shearman, *Mannerism* (London, 1967), p. 65; Pope-Hennessy, *Portrait in the Renaissance,* p. 126.

7. Mann, *Modigliani,* p. 100; Modigliani, in D'Ancona, *Modigliani, Chagall, Soutine, Pascin,* p. 20; Léopold Survage, in Restellini, *Melancholy Angel,* p. 29; William Blake, *Poetical Works,* ed. John Sampson (London, 1958), pp. 152–153.

8. Robert Hughes, *Guardian* (London), June 10, 2004; Bertram Wolfe, *Diego Rivera: His Life and Times* (New York, 1939), pp. 74–75; Richardson, *Life of Picasso,* 2.38.

9. Jean Cocteau, *Modigliani,* trans. F. A. McFarland (London, 1950), pp. [2–3]; Cocteau, in Faerna, *Modigliani,* p. 6; Steegmuller, *Cocteau,* p. 150n; Cocteau, *Modigliani,* p. [5]; Steegmuller, *Cocteau,* p. 150n.

10. S. L. Grigoriev, *The Diaghilev Ballet, 1909–1929*, trans. Vera Brown (London, 1953), pp. 5–6; Paul Morand, in Steegmuller, *Cocteau*, p. 170; Léon Bakst, in Michel, *From Renoir to Picasso*, p. 142.

11. Elvira's daughter, in Patrice Chaplin, *Into the Darkness Laughing: The Story of Modigliani's Last Mistress, Jeanne Hébuterne* (London, 1990), p. 12; Jerrold Seigel, *Bohemian Paris: Culture, Politics, and the Boundaries of Bourgeois Life, 1830–1930* (New York, 1986), p. 24; Restellini, *Melancholy Angel*, p. 394.

12. Blake, "On Another's Sorrow" (1798), *Poetical Works*, p. 78; Ehrenburg, *People and Life*, p. 155.

Ten: Simone and Jeanne

1. Marevna, *Life with Painters*, p. 18; Douglas, *Artist Quarter*, p. 309; Lunia Czechowska, "Souvenirs," in Ambrogio Ceroni, *Amedeo Modigliani, Peintre* (Milano, 1958), p. 20.

2. Blaise Cendrars, "Modigliani," *Bourlinguer* (*The Knockabout*), (Paris, 1948), p. 199; Olivier, *Picasso and His Friends*, p. 77; Carco, *From Montmartre to the Latin Quarter*, pp. 232; 234; *Memoirs of Kiki: The Education of a French Model*, introduction by Ernest Hemingway, trans. Samuel Putnam (1929; London: Tandem, 1964), p. 43.

3. Bochner, *Blaise Cendrars*, p. 58; Severini, *Life of a Painter*, p. 174; Frank Budgen, *Myselves When Young* (London, 1970), p. 133.

4. John Dos Passos, *The Best Times* (New York, 1966), p. 204; Hemingway, *Moveable Feast*, p. 81; Henry Miller, *Letters to Anaïs Nin*, ed. Gunther Stuhlmann (New York, 1965), p. 143; Henry Miller, "Blaise Cendrars," *Books in My Life* (New York, 1969), pp. 65; 62; 66; 60.

5. J. N. J. Palmer, in *Penguin Companion to Literature: European*, p. 175; Walter Albert, "Introduction," to Blaise Cendrars, *Selected Writings* (New York, 1966), pp. 22; 29; Cendrars, in Wayne, *Modigliani and Montparnasse*, p. 70; Cendrars, in Schmalenbach, *Amedeo Modigliani*, p. 189.

6. Douglas, *Artist Quarter*, pp. 246; 326, 247; *Memoirs of Kiki*, pp. 39–40; George Orwell, "How the Poor Die," *Decline of the English Murder* (London, 1965), p. 33.

7. André Delhay, in Fifield, *Modigliani*, p. 224; Simone Thiroux, in Jeanne Modigliani, *Man and Myth*, pp. 115–116.

8. Salmon, *Memoir,* p. 179; Chana Orloff, in Wight, "Recollections of Modigliani," p. 45; Douglas, *Artist Quarter,* p. 264.

9. Jeanne Modigliani, *Man and Myth,* p. 87; Anselmo Bucci, in Chaplin, *Into the Dark,* p. 117; Lipchitz, *Amedeo Modigliani,* p. 5; Severini, *Life of a Painter,* p. 183.

10. Tsuguharu Foujita, in Frederick Wight, *Modigliani: Paintings and Drawings* (Los Angeles, 1961), p. 26; Jeanne Hébuterne, in Linda Lappin, "Missing Person in Montparnasse: The Case of Jeanne Hébuterne," *Literary Review,* 45 (2002), 795; Lewis, *Tarr,* p. 178.

11. Jeanne Hébuterne, in Chaplin, *Into the Dark,* p. 65; Salmon, *Memoir,* p. 200; Thora Klinckowström, in Rose, *Modigliani,* p. 205; Modigliani, in Hobhouse, *Bride Stripped Bare,* p. 164.

12. Modigliani, in Sichel, *Modigliani,* pp. 484–485; Salmon, *Memoir,* p. 203; Paulette Jourdain, in Fifield, *Modigliani,* pp. 277–278.

Eleven: Beyond Pleasure

1. Kenneth Clark, *The Nude,* p. 24; D. H. Lawrence, *Etruscan Places,* in *D. H. Lawrence and Italy,* intro. by Anthony Burgess (1932; New York, 1972), p. 49; Adolphe Basler, in Restellini, *Melancholy Angel,* p. 54.

2. Hobhouse, *Bride Stripped Bare,* pp. 75, 95; 140; Clark, *The Nude,* pp. 29; 183; Thomas Mann, *The Magic Mountain* (1924; London, 1957), pp. 342–343, my translation from a passage in French.

3. Francis Carco, in Faerna, *Modigliani,* p. 44; Letter from Alex Colville to Jeffrey Meyers, August 4, 2004.

4. Hilary Spurling, *The Unknown Matisse* (New York, 1999), p. 231; Berthe Weill, *Pan! Dans l'oeil* (*Smack in the Eye!*), (Paris, 1933), p. 227.

Twelve: The Light in Nice

1. Modigliani, in Douglas, *Artist Quarter,* p. 272; Modigliani, in Latourettes, "Modigliani à Montparnasse," pp. 41–42; Shapiro, *Painters and Politics,* p. 62.

2. Georges-Michel, *From Renoir to Picasso,* pp. 164; 168; Restellini, *Melancholy Angel,* p. 279; Soutine, in Wheeler, *Soutine,* p. 61.

3. Sichel, *Modigliani,* p. 416; Gimpel, *Diary,* pp. 11–12; Anders Osterlind, in Hobhouse, *Bride Stripped Bare,* p. 135.

4. Modigliani, in Liège, *Modigliani* (Liège, Belgium: Musée Saint-Georges, 1980), p. 42; Hellens, in Rose, *Modigliani,* p. 178.

5. Ramón Gómez de la Serna, in Wolfe, *Diego Rivera,* p. 77; Modigliani, in Jeanne Modigliani, *Man and Myth,* pp. 91–92.

6. Czechowska, "Souvenirs," p. 33; Félicie Cendrars, in Jeanne Modigliani, *Man and Myth,* p. 89; Czechowska, "Souvenirs," p. 26.

7. Modigliani, in Jeanne Modigliani, *Man and Myth,* pp. 108; 90; 109; 92.

8. Modigliani, in Fifield, *Modigliani,* p. 260. Fifield, offering no evidence, states that while in Nice (April 1918 through May 1919) Modi spent time with the Russian terrorist and assassin, Boris Savinkov. Though Savinkov had met Modi in Paris in 1910, he was in Russia from April 1917 to December 1918, when he returned to Paris. For a description of Savinkov's career, see Meyers, *Somerset Maugham,* pp. 126–128.

9. Modigliani, in Marevna, *Life with Painters,* p. 149; Jeanne Hébuterne and Modigliani, in Jeanne Modigliani, *Man and Myth,* p. 95.

10. Lappin, "Missing Person in Montparnasse," p. 802 and Jeanne Hébuterne, in Chaplin, *Into the Dark,* p. 88.

11. Czechowska, "Souvenirs," pp. 20–21; 28–29; 24; 21; Werner, *Modigliani,* p. 156.

12. Osbert Sitwell, *Laughter in the Next Room* (Boston, 1948), pp. 166; 164; 177; 182, 184, 186.

13. Arnold Bennett, in Wayne, *Modigliani and Montparnasse,* p. 69; Osbert Sitwell, *Noble Essences* (Boston, 1950), p. 333.

14. *Times* review, in Valerie Grove, *Dear Dodie: The Life of Dodie Smith* (London, 1996), p. 60; Roger Fry, "Modern French Painting at the Mansard Gallery II," *Athenaeum,* August 15, 1919, p. 755; Modigliani and Eugenia, in Douglas, *Artist Quarter,* pp. 286–287; 291.

15. Thora Klinckowström, in Rose, *Modigliani,* p. 204.

Thirteen: The Soul's Midnight

1. Marie Wassilief, in Wight, "Recollections," p. 43; Léopold Zborowski, in Jeanne Modigliani, *Man and Myth,* p. 114; Modigliani, in Severini, *Life of a Painter,* p. 242.

2. Lascano Tegui, in Sichel, *Modigliani,* pp. 496–497; Mann, *Magic Mountain,* p. 432; Mansfield, *Journal,* p. 207.

3. Max Jacob, Préface à *Le Cornet à dés*, p. 5; Modigliani, in Sichel, *Modigliani*, pp. 478–481; Michelangelo, in Clark, *The Nude*, p. 333.

4. Paulette Jourdain, in Maiolino, *Modigliani Vivo*, p. 82; Modigliani, in Douglas, *Artist Quarter*, pp. 203; 231–232.

5. Paul Gauguin, *Letters from the South Seas*, trans. Ruth Pielkovo (New York, 1992), p. 53; Modigliani, in Claude Roy, *Modigliani*, trans. James Emmons and Stuart Gilbert (New York, 1958), p. 116; Modigliani, in Helen Hubbard, *Modigliani and the Painters of Montparnasse* (New York, 1970), pp. 6–7.

6. See John Leonard and Roger Des Prez, "Tuberculosis of the Central Nervous System," *Neurology and General Medicine*, ed. Michael Aminoff, 3rd edition (New York: Churchill Livingstone, 2004), pp. 697–702; Ortiz de Zarate, in Sichel, *Modigliani*, p. 499; Léopold Zborowski, in Jeanne Modigliani, *Man and Myth*, p. 114.

7. Modigliani, in Sichel, *Modigliani*, p. 478; Lipchitz, *Modigliani*, pp. 5–6.

8. Douglas, *Artist Quarter*, p. 299; Ortiz de Zarate, in Schmalenbach, *Amedeo Modigliani*, p. 198; Epstein, *Autobiography*, p. 47.

9. Mark Twain, *The Innocents Abroad* (1869; New York, 1966), p. 106.
    Zarate, Severini, Jacob, Salmon, Picasso, Derain, Vlaminck, Valadon, Brancusi, Lipchitz, Kisling, Soutine, Zborowski, Carco, Foujita, Survage, Indenbaum, Léger and van Dongen attended the funeral.

10. Werner, *Pascin*, p. 28.

11. The same was true of Picasso. On the day of Picasso's funeral in 1970, his grandson Pablito, who was excluded from the ceremony, took poison from which he later died. Picasso's former mistress, Marie-Thérèse Walter, hanged herself four years later. His widow Jacqueline shot herself in 1986.

12. Beatrice Hastings, in Carswell, *Lives and Letters*, p. 227; Picasso, in Oxenhandler, *Looking for Heroes*, p. 88n; Jacques Lipchitz, in Howard Greenfield, *The Devil and Dr. Barnes: Portrait of an American Art Collector* (1987; New York, 1989), p. 81.

13. William Lieberman, in David D'Arcy, "The Unknown Modigliani," *Art and Antiques*, 16 (January 1994), 50; Maurice Berger, in Klein, *Be-*

yond the Myth, p. 76; Agnes Mongan, in John Russell, *Modigliani* (London: Arts Council, 1963), p. 8.

14. Paul Gauguin, in George Shackelford and Claire Frèches-Thory, *Gauguin: Tahiti* (Boston, 2004), p. 299.

15. There are novels: Michel Georges-Michel, *Les Montparnos* (Paris, 1924), André Salmon, *La Vie passionnée de Modigliani* (Paris, 1957), Frederick Wight, *Verge of Glory* (New York, 1957), Thaddeus Wittlin, *Modigliani: Prince of Montparnasse* (Indianapolis, 1964), Stephen Longstreet, *The Young Men of Paris* (New York, 1967), Anthony Wilmot, *The Last Bohemian: A Novel about Modigliani* (London, 1975), Ken Follett, *The Modigliani Scandal* (New York, 1976), Jon Kite, *The Modigliani Caper* (San Francisco, 1995), Gonzalo Millán del Pozo, *Maldito: novela basada en la vida de Modigliani* (*Accursed: A Novel Based on the Life of Modigliani*) (Madrid, 1995); a play, Dennis McIntyre, *Modigliani* (New York, 2002); and five poems: Barbara Holender, "Portrait by Modigliani," *New York Times,* October 16, 1960, Hugo Manning, *Modigliani* (London, 1976), Michael Lawrence, *Modigliani in Fluorescent* (Los Angeles, 1978), Martin Grey, *Modigliani* (Victoria, British Columbia, 1997), Stephen Kessler, "Modigliani's Garage Sale," *After Modigliani: Poems* (Berkeley, 2000).

In Anthony Powell's twelve-volume *A Dance to the Music of Time* (1951–75) Modi's drawing of a nude survives many vicissitudes, passes through the hands of several characters (one of whom rescues it from the flames) and finally ends up in the possession of an art dealer.

A forty-four-minute video, *Who Was Modigliani?,* with many previously recorded interviews, came out in 1991; and there have been three sensationalized films: *Modigliani,* (1958), with Gérard Philipe, Lili Palmer and Anouk Aimée; *Modigliani* (1988), with Richard Berry and Elide Melli; and *Modigliani* (2005), with a convincing look-alike, Andy Garcia.

Akhmatova, Anna. "Amedeo Modigliani." *My Half Century*. Ed. and trans. Ronald Meyer. Ann Arbor: Ardis, 1992. Pp. 76–83.

Alexandre, Noel. *The Unknown Modigliani: Drawings from the Collection of Paul Alexandre*. Trans. Christine Baker and Michael Raeburn. New York: Abrams, 1993.

Augias, Corrado. *Il Viaggatore Alato: Vita Breve e Ribelle di Amedeo Modigliani*. Milano: Mondadori, 1998.

Chaplin, Patrice. *Into the Darkness Laughing: The Story of Modigliani's Last Mistress, Jeanne Hébuterne*. London: Virago, 1990.

Cocteau, Jean. *Modigliani*. Trans. F. A. McFarland. London: Zwemmer, 1950.

Czechowska, Lunia. "Souvenirs." in Ambrogio Ceroni. *Amedeo Modigliani, Peintre*. Milano: Edizione del Milione, 1958. Pp. 19–34.

Douglas, Charles [pseudonym of Douglas Goldring]. *Artist Quarter: Reminiscences of Montmartre and Montparnasse in the First Two Decades of the Twentieth Century*. London: Faber and Faber, 1941.

Ehrenburg, Ilya. *People and Life, 1891–1921*. Trans. Anna Bostock and Yvonne Kapp. New York: Knopf, 1962. Pp. 149–158, 199.

Fifield, William. *Modigliani: The Biography*. New York: Morrow, 1976.

Gray, Stephen. "Beatrice Hastings." *Free-Lancers and Literary Biography in South Africa*. Amsterdam: Rodopi, 1999. Pp. 59–76, 179.

Grindea, Miron, "300," *Adam International Review*, 300 (1965), 7–17 (on Beatrice Hastings).

Hall, Douglas. *Modigliani*. Oxford: Phaidon, 1984.

Hamnett, Nina. *Laughing Torso*. 1932; London: Virago, 1984.

Hobhouse, Janet. "Amedeo Modigliani." *The Bride Stripped Bare: The Artist and the Nude in the Twentieth Century.* London: Cape, 1988. Pp. 135–166.

Klein, Mason, ed. *Modigliani: Beyond the Myth.* New Haven: Yale University Press, 2004.

Kruszynski, Anette. *Amedeo Modigliani: Portraits and Nudes.* Trans. John Brownjohn. New York: Prestel, 2000.

Krystof, Doris. *Amedeo Modigliani, 1884–1920: The Poetry of Seeing.* Trans. Christina Rathgeber. New York: Taschen, 1996.

Latourettes, Louis. "Modigliani à Montmartre," in Arthur Pfannstiel, *Modigliani.* Paris: Scheur, 1929. Pp. I-XVI.

Lipchitz, Jacques. *Modigliani.* New York: Abrams, 1953. Pp. 1–6.

Maiolino, Enzo, ed. *Modigliani Vivo: Testimonianze inedite e rare.* Torino: Fògola, 1981.

Mann, Carol. *Modigliani.* New York: Oxford University Press, 1980.

Meidner, Ludwig, "The Young Modigliani: Some Memories," *Burlington Magazine,* 82 (April 1943), 87–91.

Modigliani, Jeanne. *Modigliani: Man and Myth.* Trans. Esther Clifford. New York: Orion, 1958.

Musée d'Art Moderne de la Ville de Paris. *Amedeo Modigliani, 1884–1920.* Paris, 1981.

Note e Ricordi su Amedeo Modigliani. Genova: Officine della S.A.I.G.A., 1945.

Olivier, Fernande. *Picasso and His Friends.* Trans. Jane Miller. 1933; New York: Appleton-Century, 1965.

Omaggio a Modigliani nel decimo anniversario della sua morte. Ed. Giovanni Scheiwiller. Milano: Giovanni Scheiwiller, 1930.

Parisot, Christian. *Modigliani.* Trans. Carole Fahy. Paris: Terrail, 1992.

Parisot, Christian. *Amedeo Modigliani: Biographie.* Torino: Canale Arte, 2000.

Parisot, Christian. *Modigliani e i suoi: Jeanne Hébuterne, André Hébuterne, Georges Dorignac, Amedeo Modigliani.* Torino: Canale Arte. 2000.

Patani, Osvaldo. *Amedeo Modigliani: Catalogo Generale / Dipinti.* Milano: Leonardo, 1991.

Perl, Jed, "The Court Painter of Montparnasse," *New Republic,* 227 (November 11, 2002), 23–28.

Restellini, Marc. *Modigliani: The Melancholy Angel.* Trans. Chris Miller. New York: Skira, 2002.

Richardson, John. *A Life of Picasso. Volume II: 1907–1917.* New York: Random House, 1996.

Rose, June. *Modigliani: The Pure Bohemian.* London: Constable, 1990.

Roy, Claude. *Modigliani.* Trans. James Emmons and Stuart Gilbert. Paris: Skira, 1958.

Russell, John. *Modigliani.* London: Arts Council, 1963.

Russoli, Franco. *Modigliani: Drawings and Sketches.* Trans. John Shepley. New York: Abrams, 1969.

Scheiwiller, Giovanni, ed. *Amedeo Modigliani—Selbstzeugnisse, Photos, Zeichungen.* Zürich: Der Arche, 1958.

Schmalenbach, Werner. *Amedeo Modigliani: Paintings, Sculptures, Drawings.* Munich: Prestel, 1990.

Shapiro, Theda. *Painters and Politics: The European Avant-Garde and Society, 1900–1925.* New York: Elsevier, 1976.

Sichel, Pierre. *Modigliani: A Biography.* New York: Dutton, 1967.

Silver, Kenneth and Romy Golan. *The Circle of Montparnasse: Jewish Artists in Paris, 1905–1945.* New York: Universe, 1985.

Soby, James Thrall. *Modigliani.* New York: Museum of Modern Art, 1951.

Stoermer, Curt, "Erinnerungen an Modigliani," *Der Querschnitt,* 11 (Juni 1931), 387–390.

Wayne, Kenneth. *Modigliani and the Artists of Montparnasse.* New York: Abrams, 2002.

Werner, Alfred. *Modigliani the Sculptor.* New York: Arts, Inc., 1962.

Werner, Alfred. *Modigliani.* New York: Abrams, 1966.

Wight, Frederick, "Recollections of Modigliani by Those Who Knew Him," *Italian Quarterly,* 2 (Spring 1958), 33–51.

Zadkine, Ossip, "Recollections of Modigliani," *Adam International Review,* 300 (1965), 72–74.

Index

Hemingway, Ernest, 118, 175; *Islands in the Stream,* 119, *A Moveable Feast,* 119
Hobhouse, Janet, 195
Hughes, Robert, 160–161

Ibsen, Henrik, *The Wild Duck,* 9
Indenbaum, Léon, 109, 112, 126–127, 251n4
Ingres, J. A. D., 193; *Grande Odalisque,* 192; *Odalisque with Slave,* 192

Jacob, Max, 33, 43, 49, 53, 54–59, 63, 101, 113, 134, 143; and Beatrice Hastings, 138, 139, 140, 141, 144, 147, 148; death, 235; influence on Modi, 98, 226; *Le cornet à dés,* 58
Jacobelli, Lina, 216
James, Henry, *Italian Hours,* 4–5
James, William, 97–98
Jepson, Edgar, 137
John, Augustus, 77, 78, 107; *In Memoriam: Amedeo Modigliani,* 79
Jourdain, Paulette, 186, 209, 232

Kafka, Franz, 11
Kahnweiler, Daniel-Henry, 54, 113
Kiki, 173, 180
Kisling, Moïse, 38, 57, 112, 131, 163, 235; and Modi, 54, 120–122, 171, 233, 236; *Modigliani's Studio,* 123
Kitrosser, Berthe, 115
Klein, Mason, 110
Klinckowström, Thora, 145, 185, 221–222
Kremegne, Pincus, 112

Labaye, Germaine, 183
Lapin Agile, 36–37, 85
Latourettes, Louis, 43, 62–63, 107
Lautréamont, Comte de [Isidore Ducasse], 33, 60; *Les Chants de Maldoror,* 27–29, 102, 176
Lautrec, Henri de Toulouse, 34

Lawrence, D. H., 16–17, 145, 193–194
Lawrence, Frieda, 16–17, 145
Le Fauconnier, Henri, 69
Lepoutre, Constant, 157
Lewis, Wyndham, 72, 81, 142; *Tarr,* 38, 119–120, 143, 183–184
Lipchitz, Jacques, 49, 53, 54, 112, 114–117, 124, 131, 235; and Modi, 75, 97, 102, 182, 236
Livorno, 1–6

Macchiaoli, 12, 21
Mallarmé, Stéphane, *Un coup de dés,* 58
Manet, Edouard, 33, 61, 193, 194; *Le Bon Bock,* 161; *Lola de Valence,* 150; *Olympia,* 159, 191
Mann, Carol, 160
Mann, Thomas, *Death in Venice,* 22, *The Magic Mountain,* 195–196, 226
Mansfield, Katherine, 139–142, 226
Marc, Franz, 73, 131
Marinetti, F. T., "Initial Manifesto of Futurism," 49
Matisse, Henri, 34
McAlmon, Robert, 118, 120
McMullen, Roy, 21
Meidner, Ludwig, 40, 44, 45, 46
Micheli, Guglielmo, 12, 18
Milhaud, Darius, *The Creation of the World,* 175
Miller, Henry, 126, 175–176
Modigliani, Amedeo (1884–1920)
Life:
    appearance, 10–11, 15, 22, 38–39, 40–41, 61, 69, 101–102, 103, 222, 223, 224
    art studies, 12–13; Académie Colarossi, 35; Florence, 19–21; Pietrasanta, 21; Rome, 19, 22; southern Italy, 17–18; Venice, 22–23
    attitude to women, 110, 147, 185–186